IMAGES
of America

CLARK'S FORK VALLEY

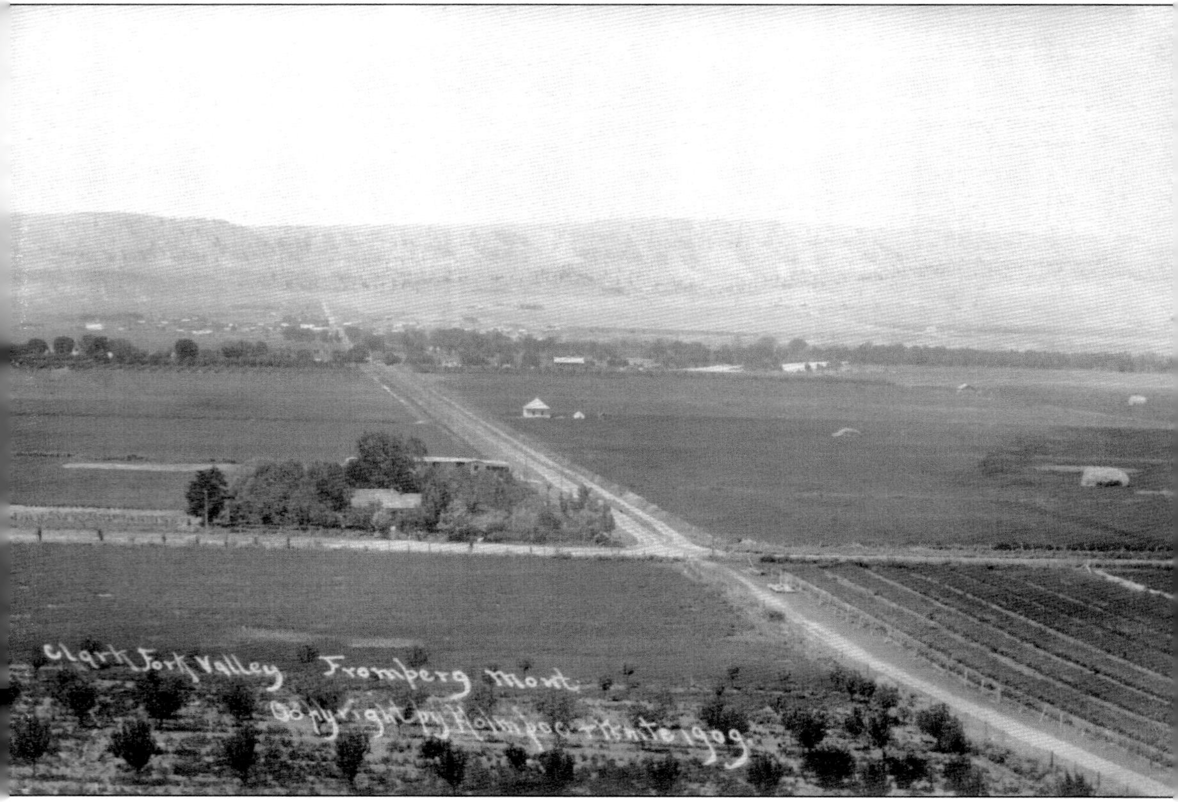

This Clark's Fork Valley photograph illustrates the scope of the fertile Clark's Fork River lowlands and the variety of crops it supports. These fertile lands, made viable by extensive irrigation projects, stretch from Laurel, Montana, in Yellowstone County, south to Carbon County's town of Belfry. Taken from the valley's eastern hills looking west towards Fromberg, this photograph shows orchards and vegetable crops dominating the foreground of the photograph, while sugar beet and grain crops appear in the middle. In the distance, the line of trees delineates the Clark's Fork River's path with even more farmland on the other side. The far sandstone bluffs once held the town of Gebo and the Clark's Fork Coal Company mine. (MOTB.)

ON THE COVER: A group of Bridger area youngsters from the early 1900s pose for a photograph before beginning the annual May Day celebration Maypole dance. The May Day celebration and maypole dance originated in pre-Christian Europe where it marked the end of the winter half of the year. Immigrants brought these customs with them to America. By the time of this photograph, both customs represented a worldwide celebration of labor rights and achievements known as International Worker's Day. With the growing popularity of May Day celebrations in the Soviet Union during the 1950s, the U.S. Congress designated May 1 as "Loyalty Day" in 1958. (CCHS.)

IMAGES
of America

CLARK'S FORK VALLEY

Jeff McNeish, Clark's Fork Valley Museum,
and Carbon County Historical Society

ARCADIA
PUBLISHING

ISBN 978-0-7385-8167-5

Published by Arcadia Publishing
Charleston, South Carolina

Printed in the United States of America

Library of Congress Control Number: 2010934147

For all general information, please contact Arcadia Publishing:
Telephone 843-853-2070
Fax 843-853-0044
E-mail sales@arcadiapublishing.com
For customer service and orders:
Toll-Free 1-888-313-2665

Visit us on the Internet at www.arcadiapublishing.com

To all who have lived in Clark's Fork Valley and the many who have worked to preserve its history

Contents

Acknowledgments		6
Introduction		7
1.	Silesia and Northern Carbon County	11
2.	Rockvale	21
3.	Edgar	31
4.	Gebo	37
5.	Fromberg	43
6.	Bridger and the Dry Creek Oil Camp	65
7	Belfry, Chance, and the Elk Basin Oil Camp	101
8.	Bowler, Warren, and Southeastern Carbon County	119

Acknowledgments

To my friend Steve Robbins, I owe you an immeasurable debt for again proofreading this book. To my family and friends, words cannot express the gratitude I have for your constant support.

I would like to thank my editor John Poultney for his invaluable assistance on this, our second book together. For preserving and sharing Carbon County's cultural heritage through photographs, I thank executive director Joan Andersen, Clark's Fork Valley Historical Society and Museum (CFVM), Fromberg, Montana; executive director Donna Madson, Carbon County Historical Society and Museum (CCHS), Red Lodge, Montana; executive director Debra Hronek, Joliet Public Library, Joliet, Montana; owner Shirley Smith, Little Cowboy Bar and Museum (LCB), Fromberg, Montana; executive director Penny Redli, Museum of the Beartooths (MOTB), Columbus, Montana; and executive director Krystal Zentner, Bridger Public Library, Bridger, Montana.

The photographs in this book collected from museums and libraries are thanks to the generosity of many donors. These include the following: from the CCHS, the Craig-Dilworth Collection, Ivan John "Toby" and Irma Hares, Bertha Forsman Hunter, Lee Lucas, Noel J. Montgomery, Walt and Addis Owens, Hazel Patek, Charles Wood, and Harold Hergenrider; from the CFVM, Clarence Johnson, Alfred Parker, and Fred Stark; from the JPL Joliet Centennial Collection, Bob Webber, Margie and Wally Blain, and Norm and Margaret Dewell; and from the MOTB, the Kem, Steele family collection.

For sharing their private collections with me, I thank Joan Andersen (Andersen), Ron and Peggy Ferster (Ferster), Karen M. Hergenrider (K. Hergenrider), John and Margaret Indreland collection courtesy of Trent and Colleen Indreland (Indreland), Nora Hogan Ogden collection courtesy of Bill and Deb Hogan (Hogan), Dick and Carolyn Thayer (Thayer), Joise Wolchesky (Wolchesky), and Bob and Jeanne Wakenshaw (Wakenshaw).

Special mention should be made of the early photographic work of Levi G. Webber. Many of this book's photographs illustrating the northern end of Clark's Fork Valley are thanks to Webber's pioneering photographic work.

To friends and local historians who provided invaluable historical research, I thank Annette Anderson, Nancy Asbury, Eva Belcher, Glenda Bell, Karen M. Hergenrider, fellow Arcadia author Patty Hooker, Phyllis Hoskin, Trent Indreland, Art Kidwell, Jack McNeish, Penny Redli, Betty McNeish Scott, Dick Thayer, Clarence and Dorothy Toogood, Bob Webber, and Joise Wolchesky.

INTRODUCTION

The Clark's Fork of the Yellowstone River, commonly referred to as the Clark's Fork River, is named after William Clark of the Lewis and Clark expedition, who recorded its existence on July 24, 1806, while camped at its confluence with the Yellowstone River southeast of Laurel, Montana. This 150-mile waterway begins in the mountains of Montana, east of Yellowstone National Park, and enters Wyoming. It travels through Wyoming, delineating the Beartooth and Apsáalooke mountain ranges with a 20-mile-long, 1,200-foot-deep canyon carved through the granite bedrock. On exiting the mountains, the Clark's Fork River reenters Montana, forming a fertile valley through the arid foothills of eastern Carbon County, before emptying into the Yellowstone River. The Clark's Fork River drainage includes portions of the Absaroka-Beartooth Mountains to its west and the Pryor Mountains, named for Sgt. Nathaniel Pryor of the Lewis and Clark expedition, to its east.

The richness in plants, wildlife, and water and the ease of travel through Clark's Fork Valley have attracted native and nonnative peoples for many centuries. Evidence that the valley is part of the Apsáalooke, or Crow, people's traditional land is easily found throughout the valley. Chief Plenty Coups State Park, on the Crow Reservation in neighboring Bighorn County, is a 19-mile drive from Edgar, Montana, in the Clark's Fork Valley and provides a top-of-the-line museum and interpretive center focused on the Crow people.

The known history of the Crow dates to at least 1000 A.D., when a group of their ancestors traveled west from Minnesota or Wisconsin to settle along the Missouri River in North Dakota. Here they became known as the Hidatsa and led a farming life for several centuries. Gradually, bands of the Hidatsa ventured farther west in pursuit of game on the open plains until some of them permanently settled and farmed the river bottoms of eastern Montana in the 1500s. By the 1700s, these Montana Hidatsa abandoned farming in favor of hunting the plains. They split into two main groups and took the new name Apsáalooke or Crow. One Crow band settled along the Yellowstone River and became known as the Mountain Crow, while another band settled farther north along the Missouri River and became known as the River Crow. Although separate, these two bands cooperated in defense of their territory against such adversaries as the Sioux, Shoshone, and Blackfeet.

Subsequent to the Lewis and Clark expedition's recording of this river valley in 1806, a steadily increasing stream of trappers, frontiersman, pioneers, miners, homesteaders, farmers, and cattlemen made their way into the valley. In 1807–1808, John Colter, noted frontiersman and Lewis and Clark expedition member, likely became the first nonnative to visit the southern end of the valley, see Sunlight Basin in the Absaroka-Beartooth Mountains, and gaze on the geothermal wonders of Yellowstone National Park. Other famous adventurers to visit the valley include Jedediah Smith, Joe Meek, and Thomas Fitzpatrick. The Rocky Mountain Fur Company first ventured into the Clark's Fork Valley in 1824 and 1825. In 1864, Jim Bridger blazed a wagon route through the Clark's Fork Valley to provide a safer alternative to the Bozeman Trail from Denver, Colorado, to the Helena, Montana, goldfields. This route, named the Bridger Trail, crossed the Clark's Fork River near the present-day town of Bridger, Montana, and followed the river north.

With this influx of eastern settlers came the inevitable conflict with the Crow. In 1825, the Crow signed the first treaty with the United States. Long Hair agreed to the treaty as leader for one band of Crow, but Sore Belly, leader of the second band, refused to sign. Major O'Fallon signed the treaty on behalf of the United States. Just 15 years later in 1840, the Crow suffered the first of three smallpox epidemics that reduced their numbers from 10,000 to 2,000 by 1850.

In 1851, the Crow signed the Fort Laramie Treaty. This treaty established the Crow Reservation and reduced Crow lands to 33 million acres in Montana and Wyoming. The reservation at this point contained all of present-day Carbon County, including Clark's Fork Valley. The treaty defined the reservation boundaries as Montana's Musselshell River on the north, the Rocky Mountains on the west, Wyoming's Rattlesnake Mountains on the south, and Montana's Powder River on the east. The Clark's Fork River Valley sat almost in the center of this land.

The second Fort Laramie Treaty of 1868 established the first Crow Agency, named Fort Parker, on Mission Creek east of Livingston, Montana. It also reduced the size of the Crow Reservation to 8 million acres but still included the Clark's Fork Valley. In 1875, the Crow Agency moved near Absarokee, Montana. The nearly continuous reduction in reservation size came as the Crow endured the devastation of plagues and defended themselves from constant attack by Lakota, Cheyenne, and Arapaho Indians. It also came despite the assistance Crow warriors provided the United States in protecting settlers along the Bozeman Trail and fighting for the U.S. Army at such famous battles as the Little Bighorn and Rosebud Creek.

In 1877, on their flight to safety in Canada, Idaho's Nez Perce led by Chief Joseph exited Yellowstone National Park at the Clark's Fork River Canyon and turned directly north, following the entire length of the valley to its confluence with the Yellowstone River near Laurel, Montana. Soon after crossing the Yellowstone River, they fought the last pitched battle with U.S. forces, near Canyon Creek, before their surrender at the Bear's Paw Battle in northern Montana. Today Chief Joseph's route through the Clark's Fork Valley is part of the National Nez Perce Historic Trail following Montana Highway 310.

The following year, 1878, a group of Bannock Indians from Idaho fled their reservation, following Chief Joseph's route through Yellowstone Park north into the Clark's Fork Valley. Col. Nelson Miles, with 70 soldiers and 35 Crow warriors, intercepted the Bannocks near Clark, Wyoming, and either captured or killed all 80 members of the group.

A succession of treaties and congressional acts in 1882, 1890, and 1892 steadily reduced the Crow Reservation eastward across Carbon County. The Congressional Act of 1882 moved Crow Agency from Absarokee, Montana, to its current location in Big Horn County, Montana. The Crow did not take this constant reduction in their land lightly, and in 1887, Wraps His Tail led an unsuccessful insurgency against the United States. In 1888, Two Leggings led a counterattack against a raiding party of Fort Peck Reservation Lakota near Clark's Fork Valley. This skirmish is believed to be the last intertribal battle on the northern plains. An act of congress in 1892 removed all remaining Crow-owned land from Carbon County, including the Clark's Fork Valley. This opened 2 million acres of Crow land to homesteading, and the influence of the Crow people in the early-20th-century Clark's Fork Valley vanished.

With Carbon County and the Clark's Fork River Valley completely open to nonnative settlement, the pace of industrial development escalated. As was the case with Carbon County's Bear Creek and Rock Creek Valleys, coal mining and railroads led to the development of towns along the railroad lines, and homesteaders eager to settle the recently available Crow land flocked to the area.

The Northern Pacific (NP); Burlington and Missouri River (B&MR); and Chicago, Burlington, and Quincy (CB&Q) railroad companies all crossed Clark's Fork Valley during its history. Originally, the B&MR and CB&Q operated as separate companies. However, when these two lines entered Clark's Fork Valley, the companies had merged but were still operating under separate names.

In 1890, the Rocky Fork and Cooke City Railroad (RF&CC) extended a branch from Laurel, Montana, along Clark's Fork Valley, then south along Rock Creek (or Rocky Fork) Valley, to the coal mines in Red Lodge. Within the year, the NP financed and finally owned the private RF&CC. Stops along the Rocky Fork line included Mason, Silesia, Hendey, Wilsey, Joliet, Boyd, Selmes,

Roberts, Fox, and Red Lodge. In 1895, Samuel Gebo found coal in the Clark's Fork Valley near present-day Fromberg, and by 1897, the NP extended a branch into the Clark's Fork River Valley as far as Fromberg. The town of Rockvale emerged at the point where the Clark's Fork Valley line split from the Rocky Fork line. Stops along this portion of the Clark's Fork Valley line included Rockvale, Blum, Edgar, Heiser, Overstreet, Fromberg, and Gebo. Copper King William A. Clark helped push the NP line farther into the Clark's Fork River Valley by financing an extension from Fromberg to his coal mines near Bridger in 1898.

Between 1899 and 1901, the B&MR constructed a line through the Clark's Fork Valley from Toluca in neighboring Big Horn County south to Cody, Wyoming. This line crossed the Pryor Mountains via a tunnel constructed in the Pryor Gap and skirted the eastern side of the Pryor Mountains through the Clark's Fork Valley. Stops along this line included Coburn, Morin, Keiser, Pryor, Chicopee, Oswald, Crockett, Bowler, and Scribner. Many Crow used this illegally built line crossing their land during its operation from 1901 to 1911. B&MR crews removed the entire line between a Saturday night and the next Monday morning in anticipation of the Crow filing an injunction to close the illegally built railroad. To mitigate this loss, the CB&Q opened a line in 1911 from Frannie, Wyoming, north through Warren, and on to the NP tracks at Fromberg. This line added stops of Duff, Tyndell, and Gupton.

Sensing further coal mining opportunity in Carbon County's Bear Creek Valley, just to the west of the Clark's Fork River Valley, a group of private investors began construction of a private railroad in 1905. Originally named the Yellowstone Park Railroad (YPRR), it ran from the NP's terminus in Bridger to the mouth of the Bear Creek Valley, necessitating the construction of the town of Belfry, and west into the Bear Creek Valley. Original plans to continue the line along the Clark's Fork River to gold mines near Cooke City, Montana, and into Yellowstone Park did not materialize. After the railroad went into receivership, its name changed to the Montana, Wyoming, and Southern Railroad (MW&S). Stops along the MW&S included Bridger, Jennings, Golden, Shupak, Belfry, Olivers, Foster, Bearcreek, International, Amalgamated (or Washoe), and Berwind.

The railroads' opening of Clark's Fork Valley to settlement and industry spawned the creation of post offices to serve both town and rural residents. Post offices were located at Silesia; Rockvale; Edgar; Gebo/Coalville; Fromberg; Bridger; Belfry; Riverview, south of Belfry; Dilworth, east of Chance; Musgrave, between Bridger and Warren; Scribner/Warren; and Bean. Post offices in the east Pryor Mountain included Shriver, Cummings, Hillsboro, and Ewing. Clark, Wyoming, post offices existed on the Sirrine Ranch, the Barber/Parker Ranch, the Lindquist General Store, Badger Basin, and the Lindquist Ranch.

Coal mining in the Clark's Fork River Valley could not match the production or quality of its neighbors in the Red Lodge and Bearcreek fields and ceased operations by the mid-1910s. This loss did not signal the end of the Clark's Fork River Valley communities as it had with so many other mining-based settlements in Montana. Other industries that developed during the valley's mining days helped it weather the loss. Homesteader-led agriculture and ranching throughout the valley; a brewery in Silesia; a brick factory in Fromberg; lumber mills in Bridger and Fromberg; the discovery and extraction of oil at Elk Basin, south of Belfry (1914), Moser Dome, east of Silesia (1929), and Dry Creek, west of Bridger (1929), mitigated the loss of the valley's coal mining industry and contributed to the valley's growth.

In the 1890s, farmers and ranchers began to take advantage of the fertile bottomland and abundant water of the Clark's Fork River with the cultivation and harvesting of hay to feed livestock. In 1906, sugar beets were introduced to the valley. Other crops grown in the valley included corn, potatoes, pinto beans, and various grains. Large-scale fruit orchards stretching from Silesia to Fromberg proved financially successful for several decades. Sugar beets remain a leading industry in the valley as does grain production and cattle ranching.

The shift to an agrarian economy in Clark's Fork Valley necessitated the creation of a number of rural schools to supplement those in the established towns of Silesia, Rockvale, Edgar, Fromberg, Gebo, Bridger, Belfry, Chance, Warren, and Clark, Wyoming. These schools included White Horse and Cole Creek Schools near Silesia; Paradise School in the Rockvale/Edgar area; Towne, Five Mile, Round Butte, and Bluewater Schools near Fromberg; Sand Creek, Cherry Springs, Bostic, New Prospect, Dry Creek, Sunnyside, Golden, and Tucker Schools near Bridger; Riverview and Tolman Schools between Belfry and Chance; Bowler, Wade, and Dry Head Schools near Warren; and Pioneer/Sirrine, Bennett Creek, Line Creek, Paint Creek, and Pat O'Hara Schools near Clark, Wyoming.

Ranching in the Clark's Fork River Valley produced top-notch herds of cattle, sheep, and horses. The ranching life produced world-champion cowboys and cowgirls. Of particular note is the Linderman family of Bridger and Belfry. During the 1940s and 1950s, brothers Bill, Bud, Lup, and Doug dominated the sport of rodeo. Walt Linderman, the next generation of Linderman champions, continued the family's winning ways. Deb Greenough, the latest rodeo champion in the storied Greenough family, hails from Fromberg.

Other celebrated figures from American Western history lived in or visited the Clark's Fork River Valley. Calamity Jane lived in Bridger for a time. Buffalo Bill Cody was a frequent visitor to the valley, traveling from nearby Cody, Wyoming, as was John "Liver-Eating" Johnston, sheriff of nearby Red Lodge and Scout during the Nez Perce campaign. Caroline Lockhart, noted author, journalist, and literary rival of Zane Grey, homesteaded in the Dry Head area of the Pryor Mountains.

For such a small county, Carbon County has an amazing number of sites, 56, listed on the National Register of Historic Places. Of these 56 sites, 37 reside in Clark's Fork Valley. Sites in and around Fromberg include the Baldwin Building; the Dr. Theodore J. Benson House; the Francis Rahrer House; the Fromberg Concrete Arch Bridge; the Fromberg High School; the Fromberg Methodist-Episcopal Church; the Fromberg Opera House; the Gebo Cemetery; the Hester E. Suydam Boarding House; the International Order of Odd Fellows Hall and Fromberg Co-operative Mercantile Building; the John Blewett House; the John Gibson House; the Fromberg Northern Pacific Railroad Depot, now housing the Clark's Fork Valley Museum; the Tracy McCall House; the Frank Brooder House; the Gebo Barn; and the Samuel Greenblatt House. Sites in and around Bridger include the Corey House, the Dr. Carl Marcus House, the Forsman House, the Glidden House, the Glidden Mercantile, the Heatherington Boarding House, the Henry Gebo House, the Methodist Episcopal Church and Parsonage, the Nutting Rental, the Wool Warehouse, the Bridger Coal Company House, the Bridger Opera House, and the Raymond Hough House. Sites in southeastern Carbon County include Bad Pass Trail, the Caroline Lockhart Ranch, Cedarvale, and the Ewing-Snell Ranch.

Today the Clark's Fork River Valley thrives on the agricultural and ranching base laid down over the past century. It continues to serve as one of Montana's key byways, being the primary route from Billings, Montana, to Cody, Wyoming, and Yellowstone Park, and it is heavily used by Montana and Wyoming residents and the many tourists to the region.

One

Silesia and Northern Carbon County

Silesia is the northernmost town in Clark's Fork Valley, located 15 miles south of Laurel, Montana, and 11 miles south of the Carbon County, Yellowstone County border. A Crow woman named Old Mary first held title to the land as part of a government allotment issued while it was still part of the Crow Reservation. In 1887, Congress granted the Rocky Fork and Cooke City Railroad Company (RF&CC) right-of-way across the Crow Reservation and Old Mary's land from Laurel to the Red Lodge coalfields. This railroad followed the Clark's Fork River to the mouth of Rock Creek, or Rocky Fork, one of the Clark's Fork River's tributaries, then continued along Rocky Fork to Red Lodge. The RF&CC sold this line to the Northern Pacific soon after its completion in 1890. In 1892, the boundaries of the Crow Reservation receded eastward and opened up 2 million acres to homesteading. Old Mary's second husband, U.S. Marshall J. L. Smith, purchased this land allotment when it became available for sale. Attracted by springwater and the nearby stagecoach stop of Hendry, Walter Lehrkind took ownership of this land from J. L. Smith in August 1899. Lehrkind platted 20 acres of the land for businesses and homes, installed wooden sidewalks, and established a brewery nearby around 1900. He named the town after the central-European region of Silesia, now located primarily in southwestern Poland, from which he emigrated. Soon a hotel, two general stores, and several saloons lined Silesia's main street. A cable swing bridge operated by the Webber family provided the only Clark's Fork River crossing at Silesia between 1899 and 1904. In 1904, the Security Bridge Company replaced it with a steel span. An influx of homesteaders around the early 1900s, many from Gentry County, Missouri, settled the area surrounding Silesia, giving it the nickname of "Little Missouri." These homesteaders raised sugar beets, grain, fruits, and vegetables in the fertile bottomlands of Clark's Fork Valley.

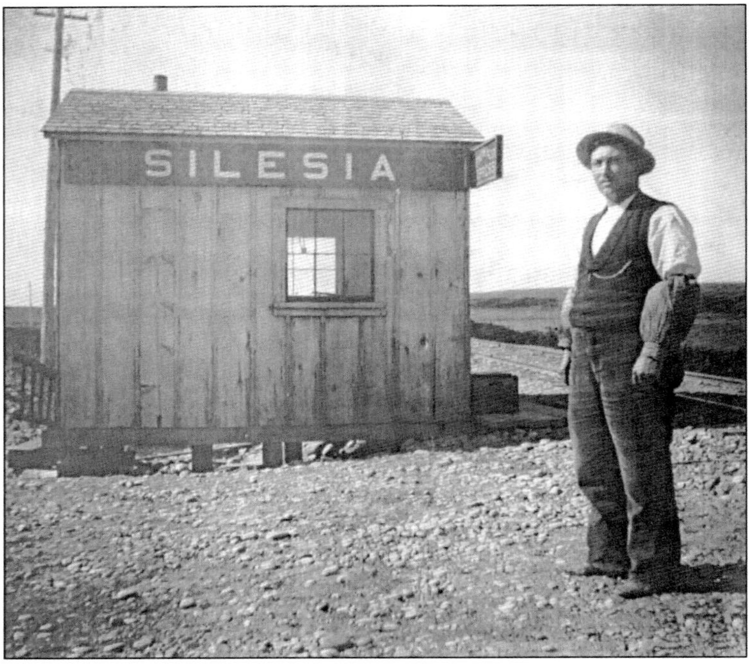

This photograph of Silesia's first train stop is thought to show Charles J. Buzzetti, Silesia's first railroad agent. After resigning as railroad agent, Buzzetti moved to Fromberg where he operated his own billiard hall and a mercantile store in partnership with Mac Emmett. Buzzetti later became president of the Clark's Fork Valley Bank in Fromberg. (CFVM.)

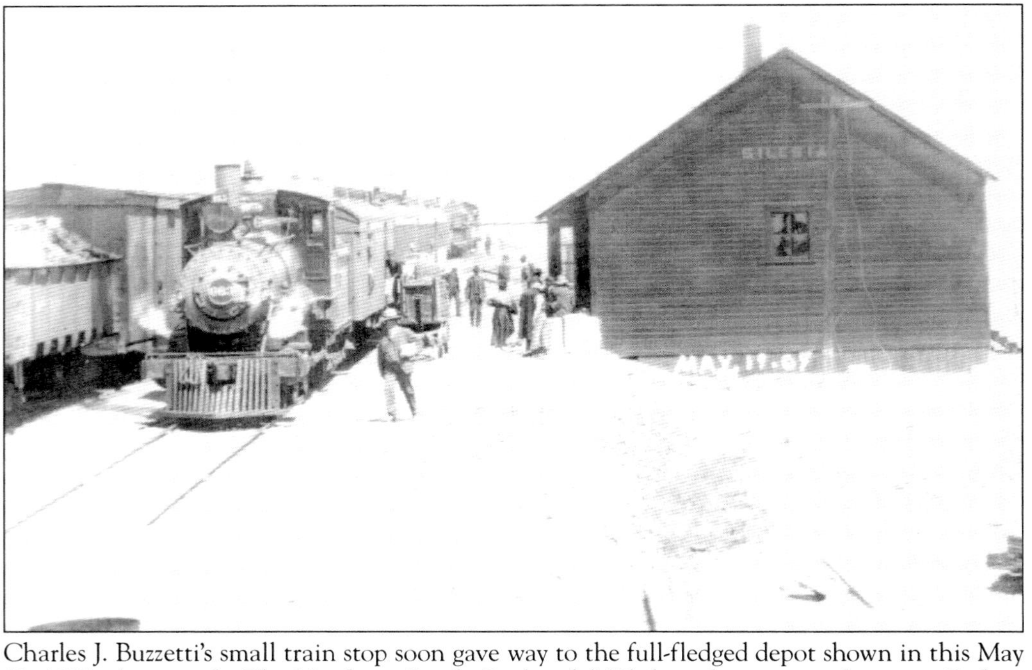

Charles J. Buzzetti's small train stop soon gave way to the full-fledged depot shown in this May 19, 1907, photograph. The Northern Pacific Railroad (NP) ferried passengers between Carbon County, southern Montana, and northern Wyoming and the larger towns of Billings, Montana, and Cody, Wyoming. The NP also freighted coal, sugar beets, and produce from the Clark's Fork Valley. (JPL.)

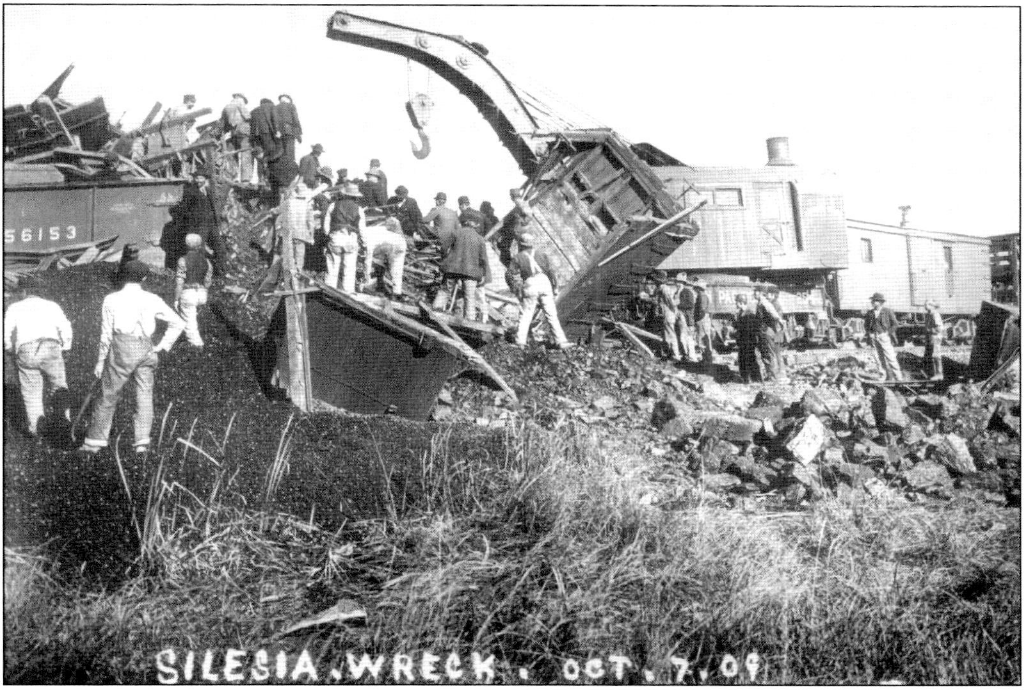

Railroad's provided the most efficient means of transportation in the valley, but not always the most reliable. This October 7, 1909, derailment photographed near Silesia by Levi G. Webber shows that these freight cars carried coal from either the Red Lodge, Gebo, Bridger, or the Bearcreek/Washoe mines, since all operated at the time of this photograph. (JPL.)

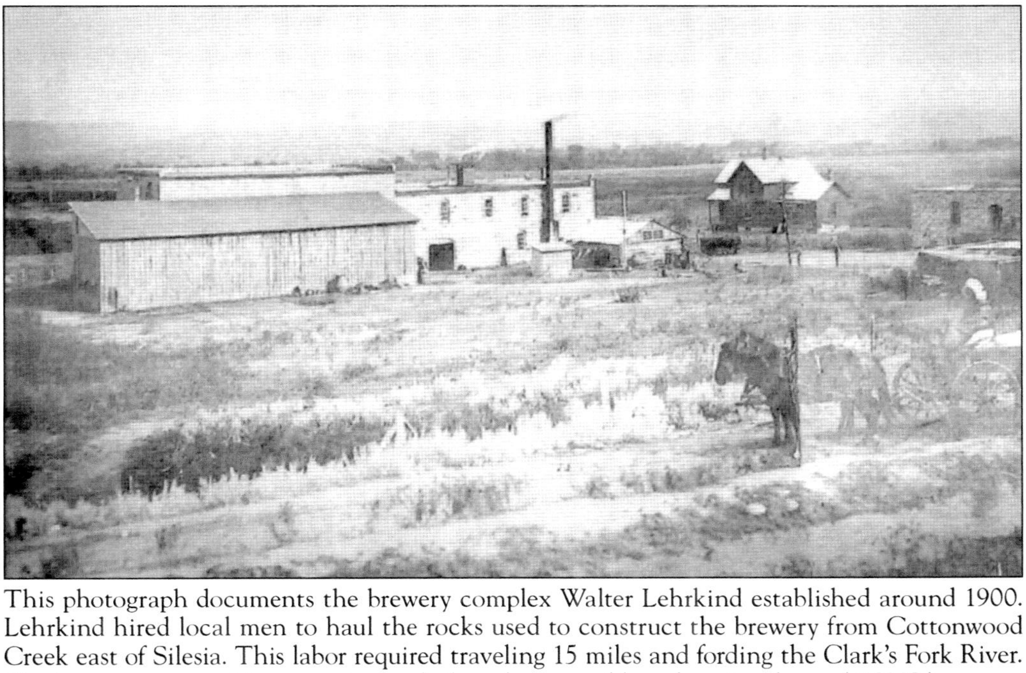

This photograph documents the brewery complex Walter Lehrkind established around 1900. Lehrkind hired local men to haul the rocks used to construct the brewery from Cottonwood Creek east of Silesia. This labor required traveling 15 miles and fording the Clark's Fork River. The brewery operated for several years before closing and later burning down. (CCHS.)

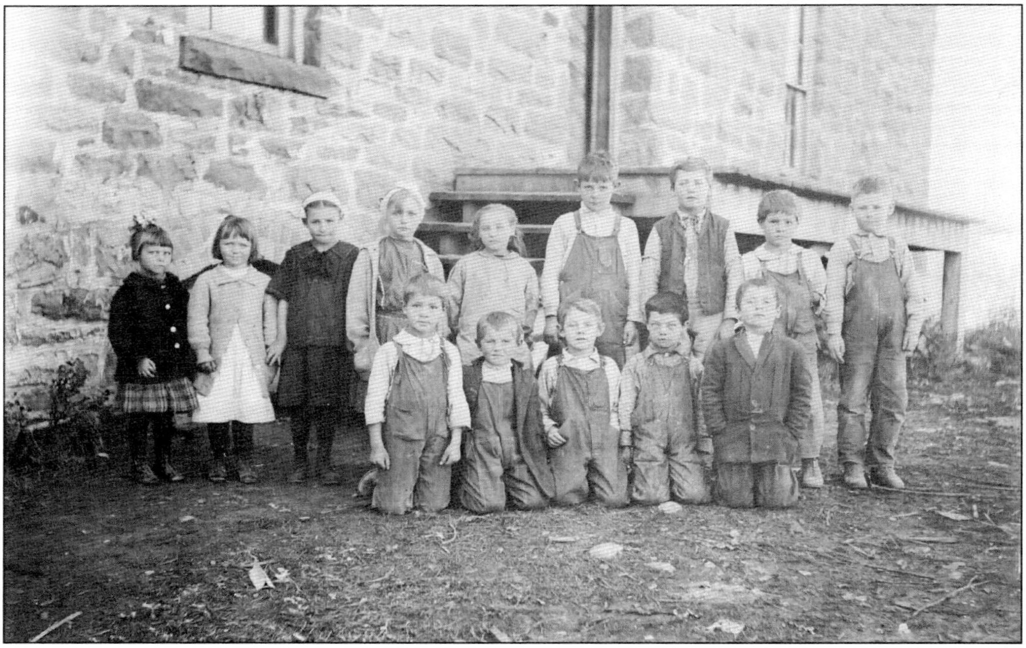

This group of children photographed in front of one of the Lehrkind Brewery's buildings is likely from the second Silesia school built nearby. The photograph serves to illustrate the Cottonwood Creek sandstone blocks used in construction of the brewery. It also illustrates typical attire for homesteading children during the early 1900s. (CCHS.)

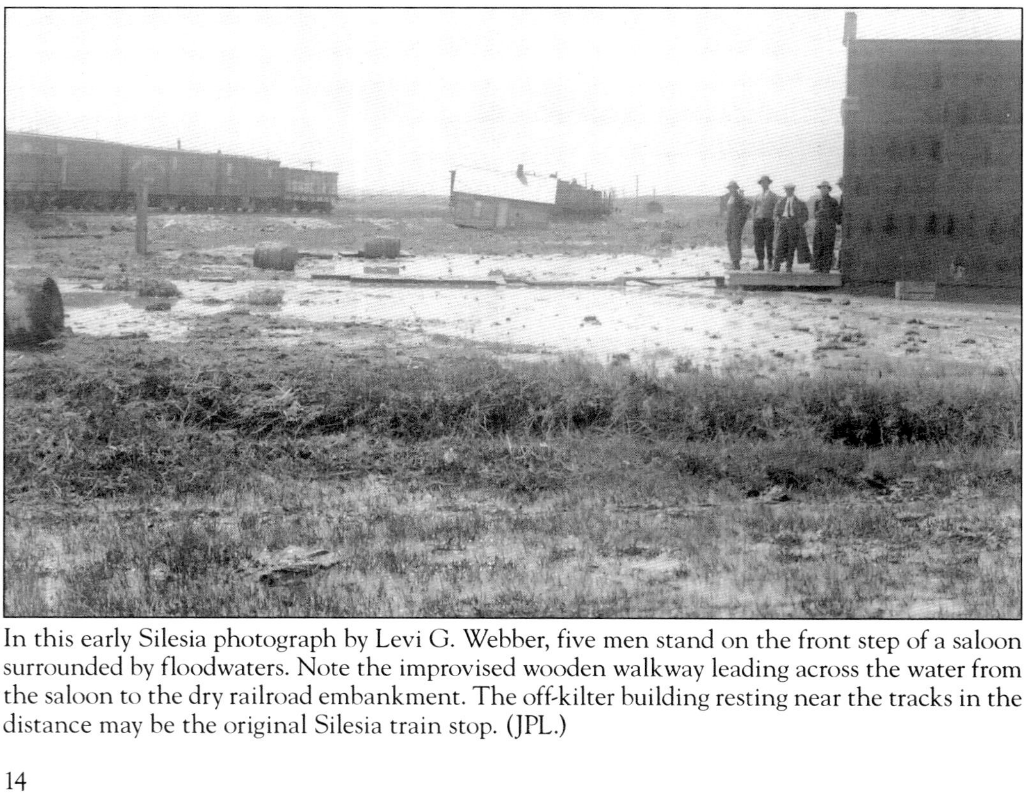

In this early Silesia photograph by Levi G. Webber, five men stand on the front step of a saloon surrounded by floodwaters. Note the improvised wooden walkway leading across the water from the saloon to the dry railroad embankment. The off-kilter building resting near the tracks in the distance may be the original Silesia train stop. (JPL.)

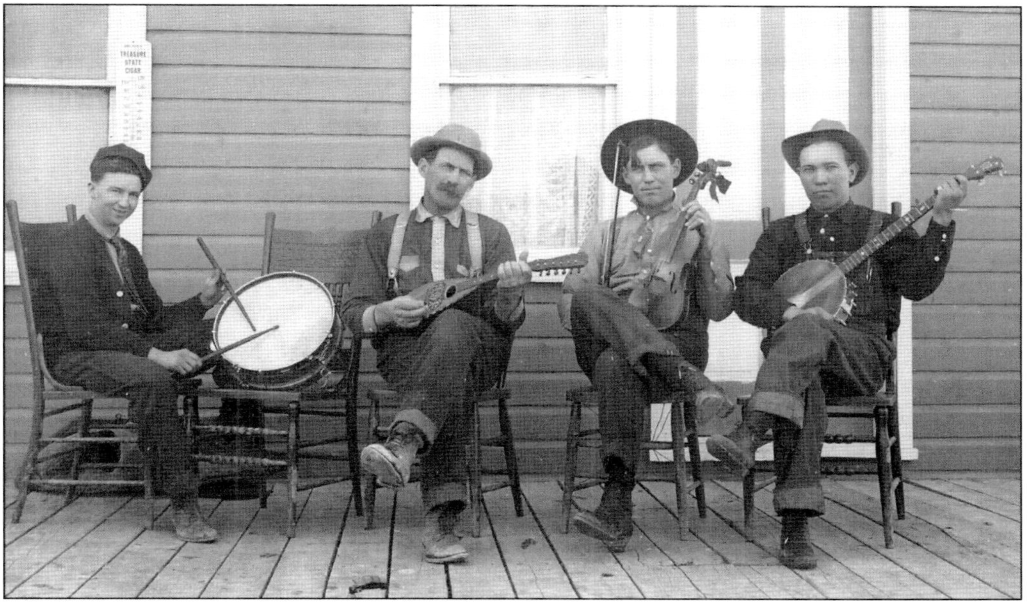

In another Levi G. Webber photograph, four musicians pose with their instruments on the porch of a Silesia saloon. The band members are, from left to right, Jim Conwey, Sam Webb, Kid Dauford, and Roy Pefley. Silesia housed at least three saloons at the time of this photograph. (JPL.)

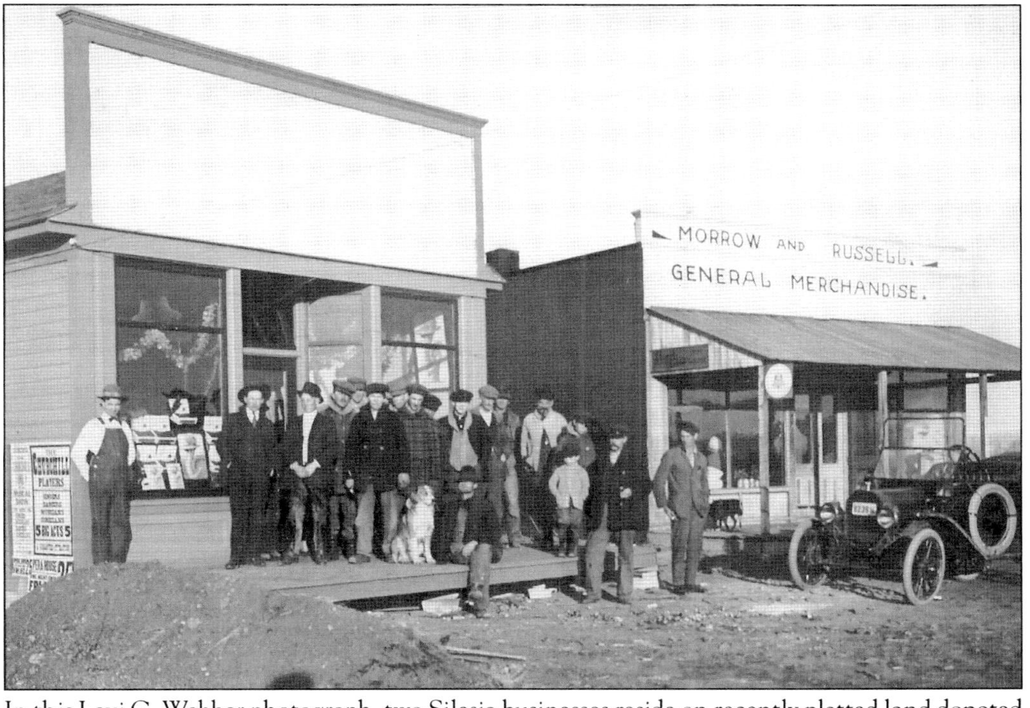

In this Levi G. Webber photograph, two Silesia businesses reside on recently platted land donated by brewer Walter Lehrkind. On the left is a clothing store, while the Morrow and Russell General Merchandise store stands next door. The circular white sign on the general merchandise store advertises the fact that it has telephone service. (JPL.)

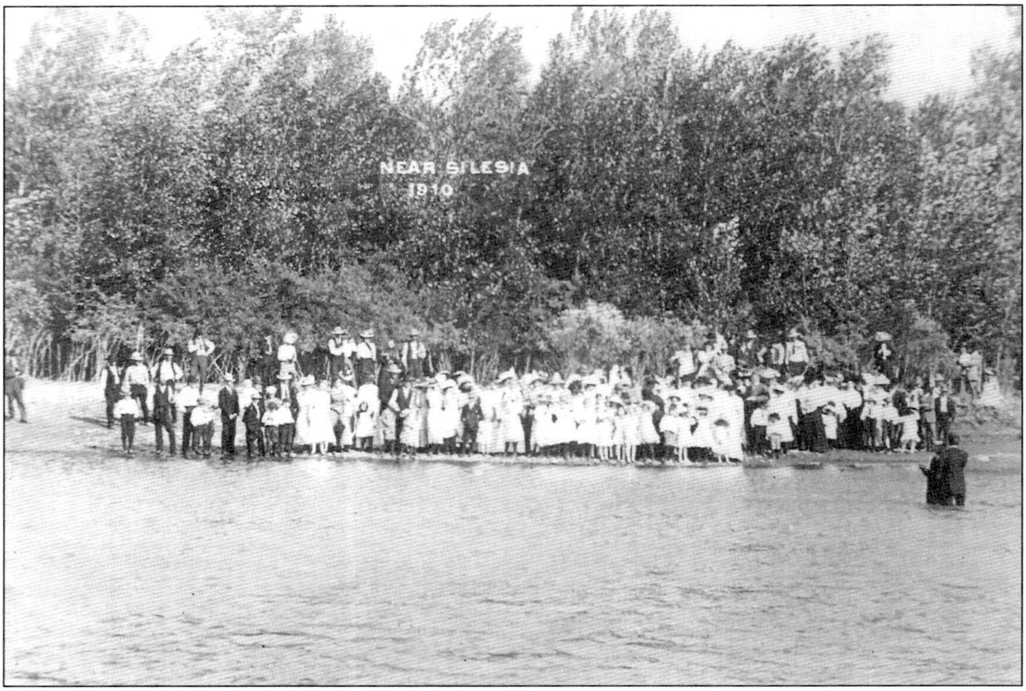

Although no permanent church is known to have existed in Silesia, citizens continued to worship in homes and out-of-doors. This 1910 Levi G. Webber photograph shows a baptism taking place in the Clark's Fork River near Silesia. Over 110 members of the congregation are counted in this photograph. (JPL.)

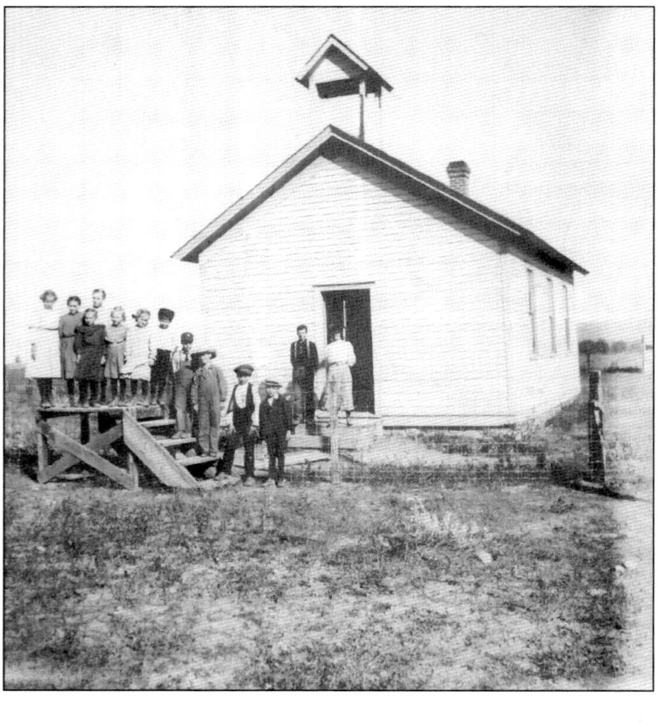

This 1908 Levi G. Webber photograph shows the second Silesia school built near the Lehrkind Brewery around 1900. A one-room log cabin built by the river in 1899 initially served area students. People shown in this photograph include teacher J. H. Lockridge, Jay Nail, Grace W., Mabel Dix, Bertha W., Elvah W., Ruby Dix, Jenny Bittick, Mel Dix, Pete Bittick, Arthur Moots, Elsie Bittick, and one unidentified. (JPL.)

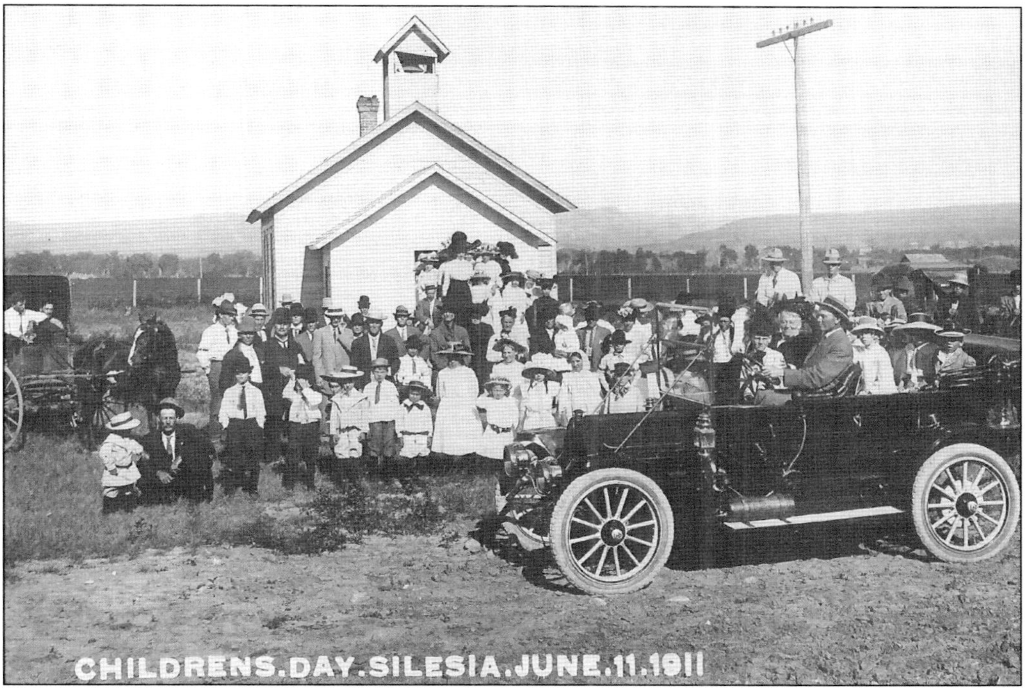

From the date on this Levi G. Webber photograph of Silesia's 1911 Children's Day celebration, the day likely marked the end of the school year. The second Silesia School serves as a backdrop for the celebrants. This school served students from 1900 to 1917, when residents completed the third and final Silesia school. (CCHS.)

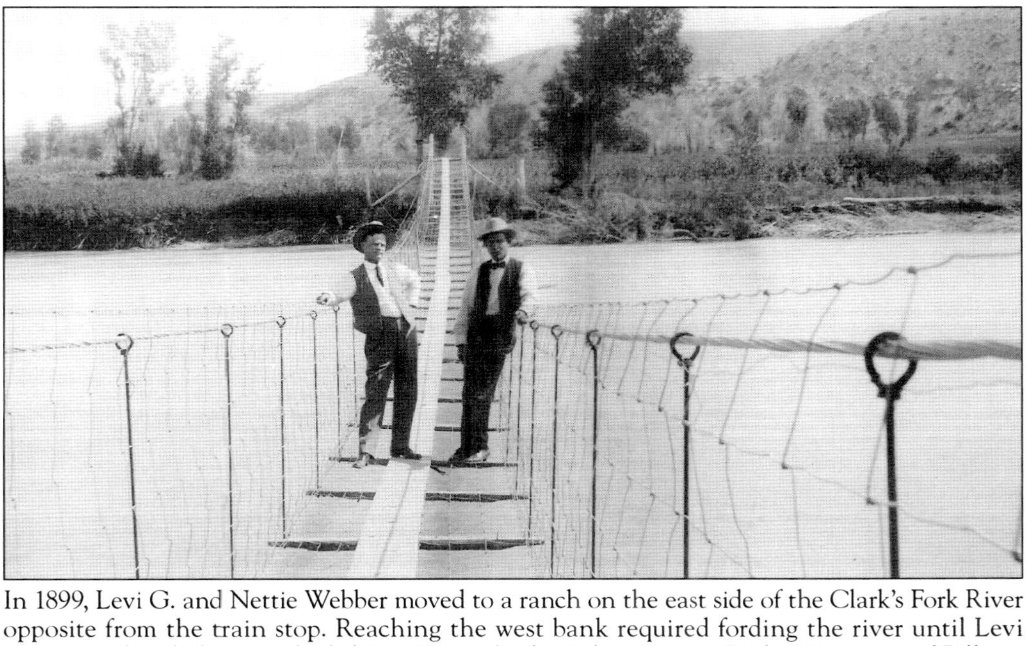

In 1899, Levi G. and Nettie Webber moved to a ranch on the east side of the Clark's Fork River opposite from the train stop. Reaching the west bank required fording the river until Levi constructed and photographed this swinging bridge. The Security Bridge Company of Billings built a 200-foot, single-span steel bridge near this one in 1904. (JPL.)

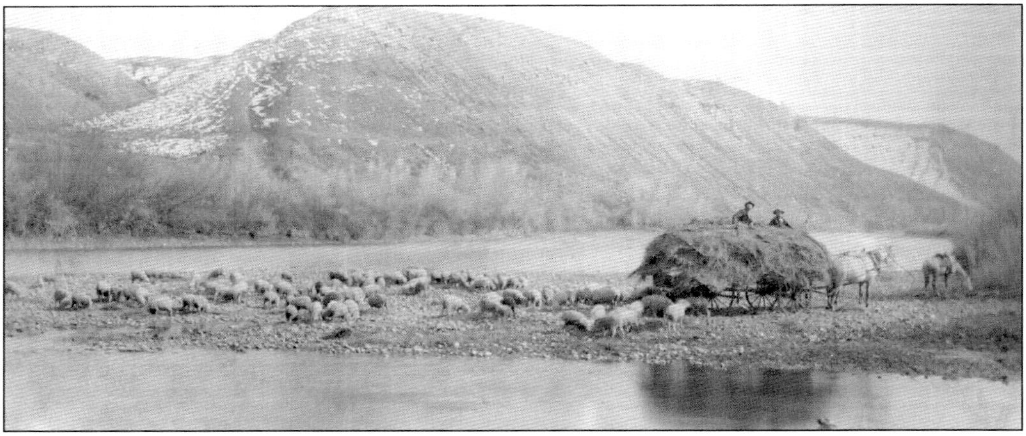

A herd of sheep gathers for their daily feeding at the confluence of the Rock Creek, or Rocky Fork, and Clark's Fork Rivers between Silesia and Rockvale. Railroad lines and highways mirror this junction with the railroad junction just south of Silesia and the highway junction at nearby Rockvale. (CCHS.)

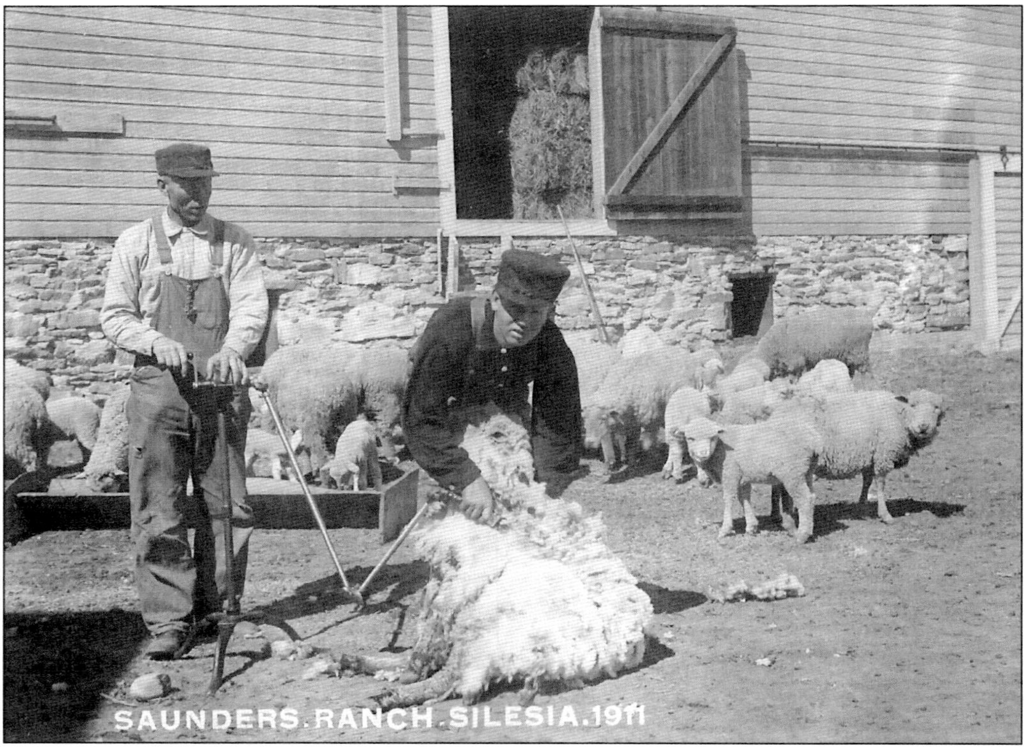

This 1911 Levi G. Webber photograph shows early homesteaders Bill Saunders (left) and Hallie Saunders (right) sheering sheep on their ranch near Silesia. The east and west benches of the Clark's Fork Valley provided fertile grazing land for livestock. Of particular interest in this photograph is the use of hand-cranked sheers powered by Bill Saunders. (CCHS.)

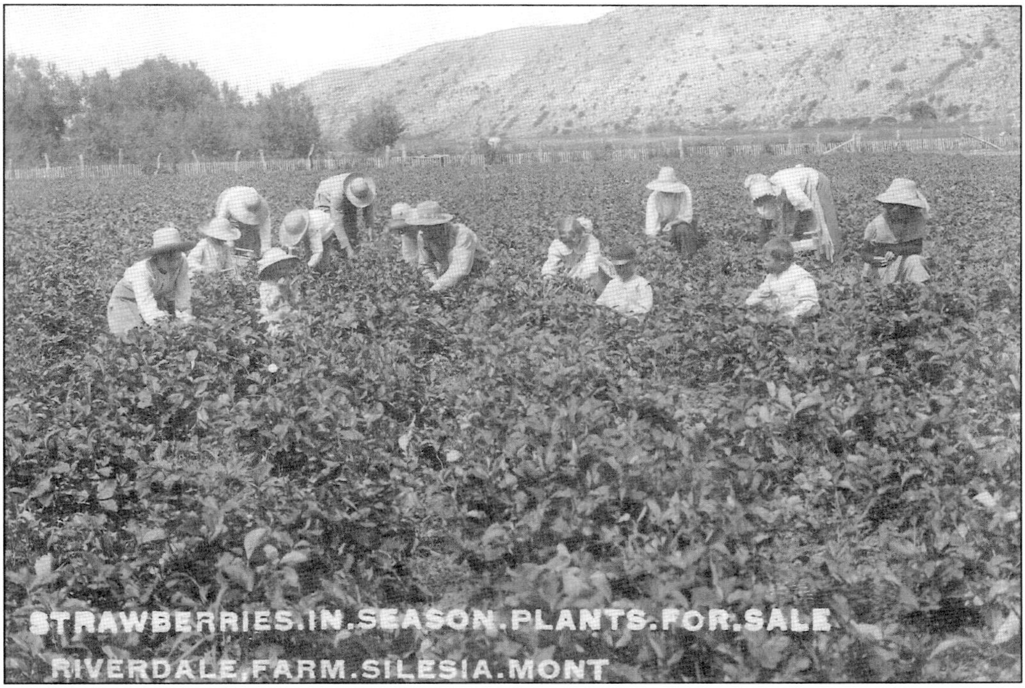

Irrigation ditches allowed sugar beets, vegetables, fruit trees, and strawberry bushes to flourish in the valley's lowlands. This agricultural productivity was evident when Levi G. Webber photographed pickers on his Riverdale Farm (above). The Smith Ditch, built by U.S. Marshal John L. Smith, served the lowlands while the 1907 White Horse Ditch served the west bench. (JPL.)

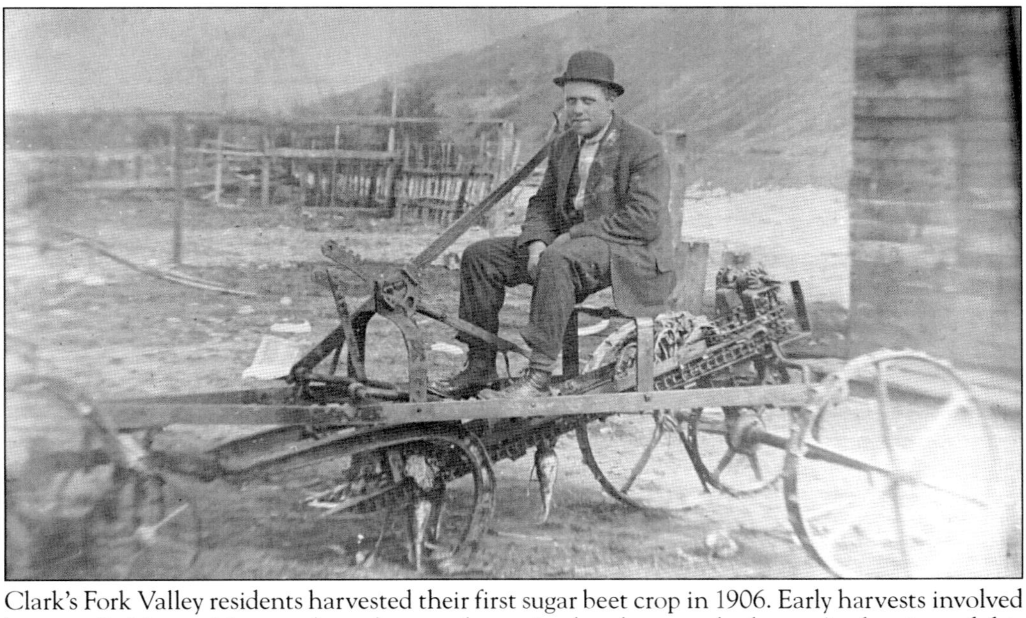

Clark's Fork Valley residents harvested their first sugar beet crop in 1906. Early harvests involved horse-pulled beet pickers such as the one shown in the photograph above. At the time of this photograph, this harvesting machine had recently come in from the fields and still had beets hanging underneath it. (CCHS.)

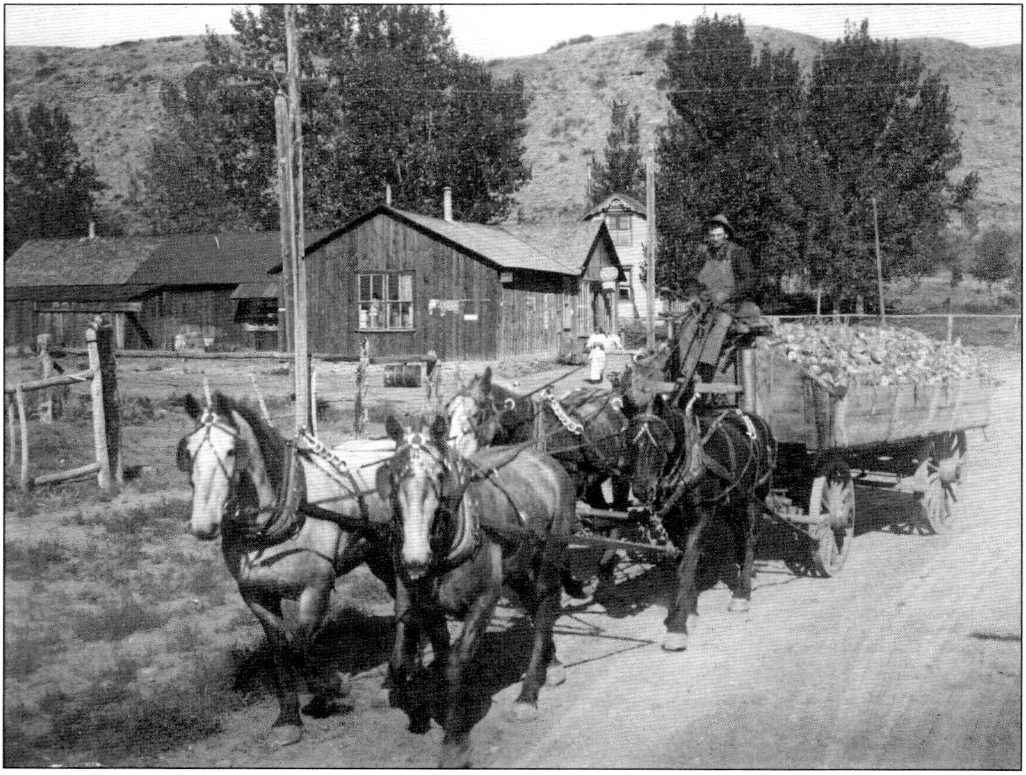

This Levi G. Webber photograph shows Roy James and one of his four-horse teams hauling harvested sugar beets to Silesia's beet dump. Beet dumps existed at almost every train stop and town in the Clark's Fork Valley. They provided a place for farmers to sell their beets and for the sugar companies to gather the product for shipping. (MOTB.)

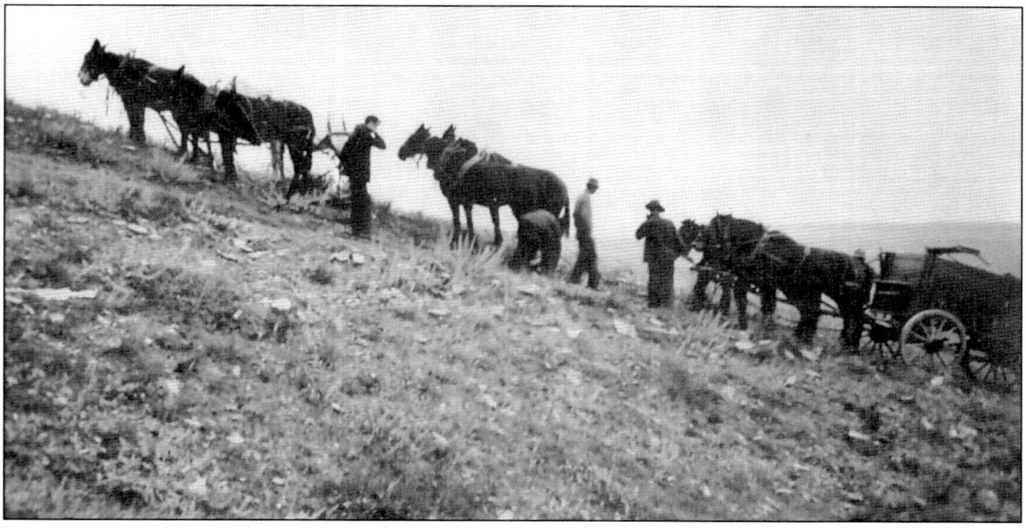

The James family and their teams of horses hauled a wagon loaded with supplies up the east bench of Clark's Fork Valley near Silesia in this 1915 photograph. This photograph captures them adding one additional team of two horses to the middle of the train. (Thayer.)

Two

ROCKVALE

Two highways provide access to Clark's Fork Valley, paralleling the Clark's Fork River and nearby railroad tracks. U.S. Highway 310 stretches from Laurel, Montana, to Bridger, Montana, where it departs from following the Clark's Fork River and continues into northeastern Wyoming. Along the Laurel to Bridger portion of U.S. Highway 310 are the Carbon County towns of Silesia, Rockvale, Edgar, Fromberg/Gebo, and Bridger. Important Carbon County intersections occur at Rockvale and Bridger. At Rockvale, U.S. Highway 212 branches southwesterly from U.S. Highway 310 to follow Rock Creek to Red Lodge, then over the Beartooth Pass and on to Yellowstone National Park. Montana Highway 72 departs U.S. Highway 310 at Bridger as it continues following the path of the Clark's Fork River southwest into northern Wyoming where it eventually reaches Cody, Wyoming. Rockvale lies just 3 miles south of Silesia near the convergence of Rock Creek, or Rocky Fork, and the Clark's Fork River. It is debatable as to whether Rockvale should be considered part of Clark's Fork Valley or Rock Creek Valley. In truth, it likely belongs to both valleys given its geographic position and the key highway intersection of U.S. Highway 310 and U.S. Highway 212. Given the proximity to Silesia and the location at this important Carbon County intersection, Rockvale has been included in this book. Early pioneer Orren Clawson and his family arrived in the Rockvale area from Park City, Montana, in 1893. Clawson immediately established a store and a post office to serve other pioneer families gathering in the area. He named the fledgling town Rockvale after nearby Rock Creek. With convenient access to neighboring Silesia, Edgar, and Joliet, Rockvale remained a supply and schooling point for rural families in the area, although some families did live in Rockvale itself. These families established one of the earliest Carbon County schools, likely before 1895. The post office closed in 1914. A succession of stores, supper clubs, and fueling stations has served Rockvale from its inception to today.

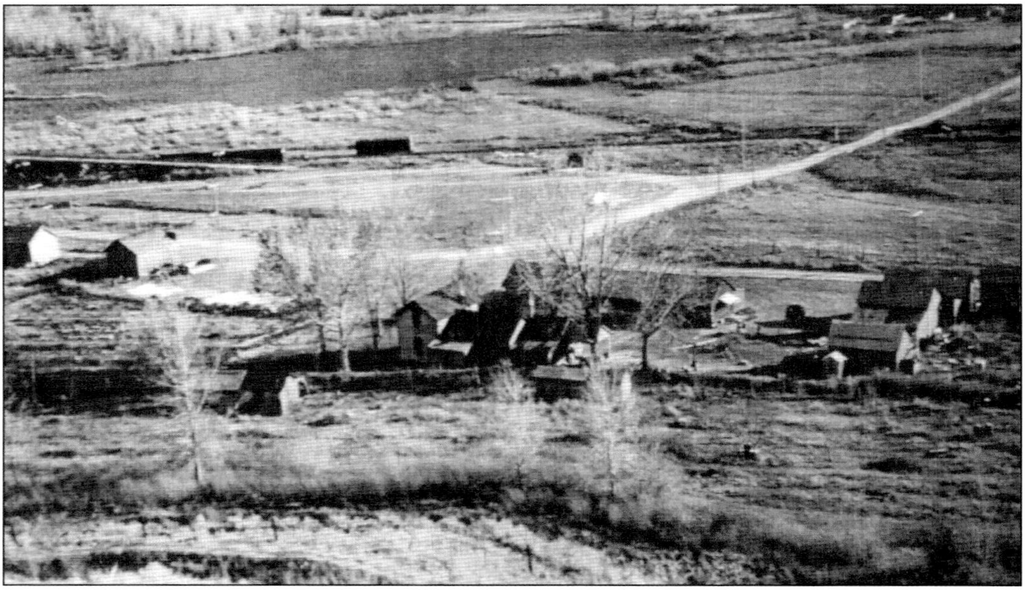

The 1917 photographs on this page show that, despite its 1893 birth, Rockvale did not grow beyond a small supplies and education outpost for area homesteaders. The photograph above, taken from the western hills of Clark's Fork Valley, shows Rockvale's small size. The photograph below focuses on the original Rockvale School. Built in 1899, the first Rockvale School, second from the right, sits next to the home built for the schoolteacher on its right. In 1913, schoolteacher Homer Worth and his family lived in this house for nine months. The building on the far left of this photograph is the Rockvale blacksmith shop. (Above, JPL; below, CCHS.)

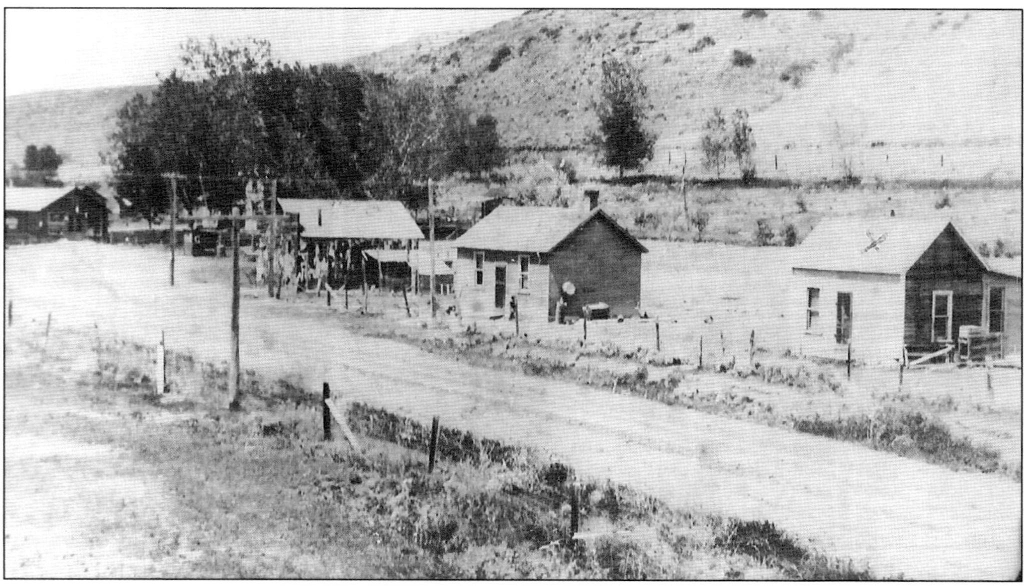

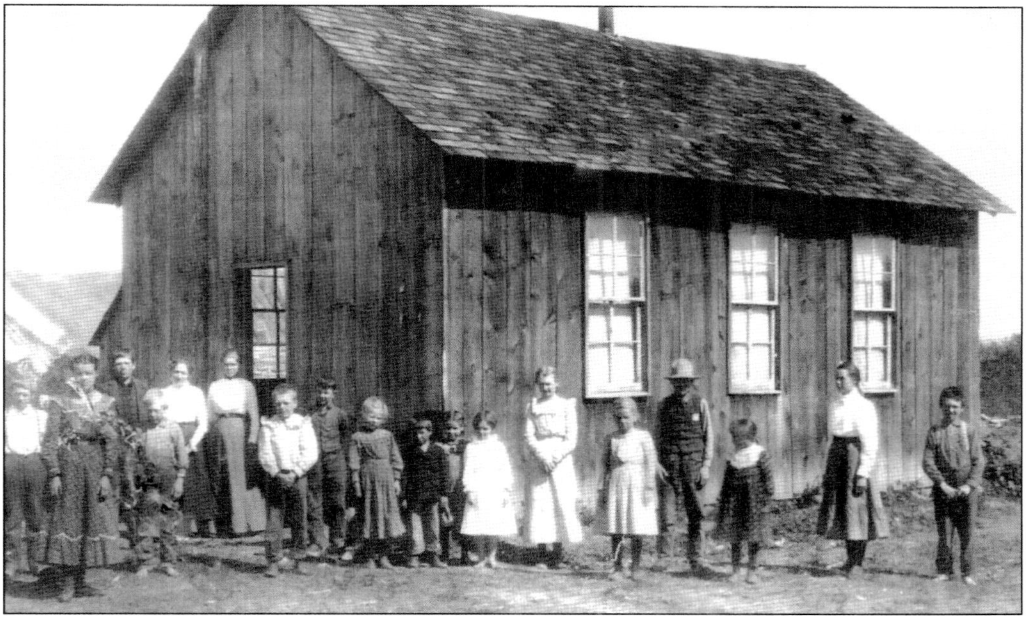

A closer look at the first Rockvale School in 1901 (above) shows a class of 17 students with the first teacher to serve Rockvale, Amelia Holland. Posing for the photograph are, from left to right, Harry Luke, Pearl Simpson, Willie Henry, Jim James, Ethel Luke, Amelia Holland (teacher), unidentified, Earl Clawson, Mary McClintock, Carl Henry, Bertha Nelson, Becca James, Dallis James, Druzilla Craig, Ray James, Minnie Craig, Laura Craig, and Clarence Balden. The second Rockvale School (below) stood just south of town and eventually burned down. (Above, JPL; below, CCHS.)

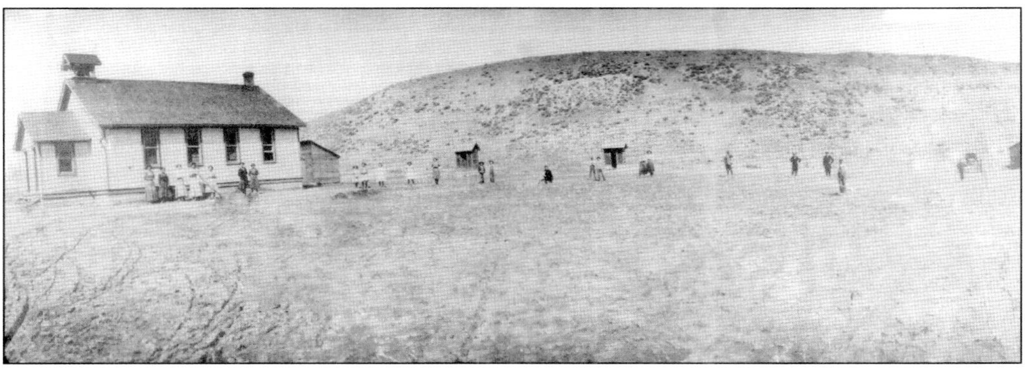

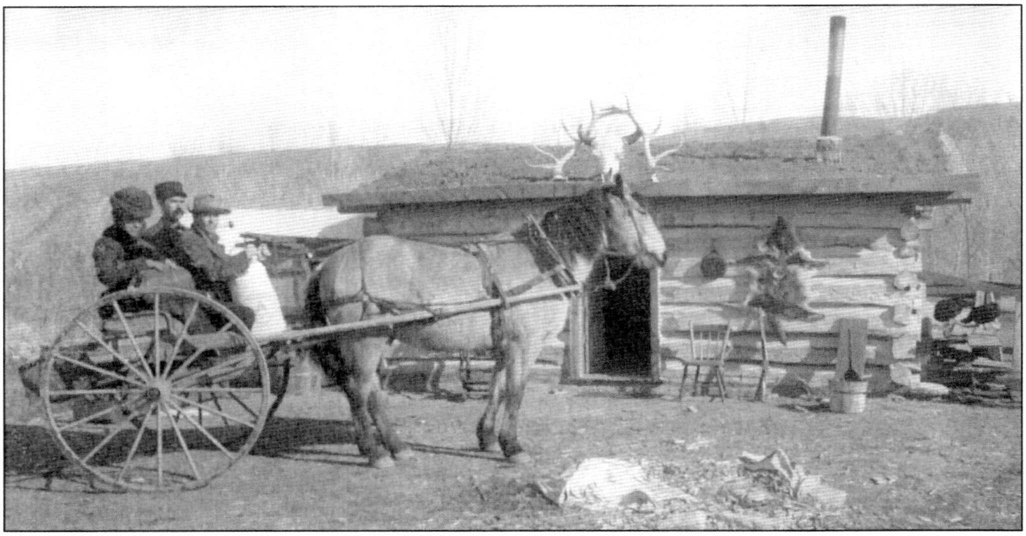

Many homesteaders in the Rockvale area built small rudimentary homes and immediately began raising livestock and preparing the land for cultivation of hay, grains, vegetables, and fruit. The Taylor and Adeline Craig home (above) had dirt floors, no running water, and a ceiling just high enough to stand upright. The Craigs eventually moved their home half a mile south of this location, added a floor, and raised the roof. The photograph below documents the Craigs feeding hay to their cattle and horses during the winter. Pictured in this photograph are, from left to right, Adeline Craig, Adeline and Taylor's granddaughter Druzilla Craig, and Taylor Craig. (Both, CCHS.)

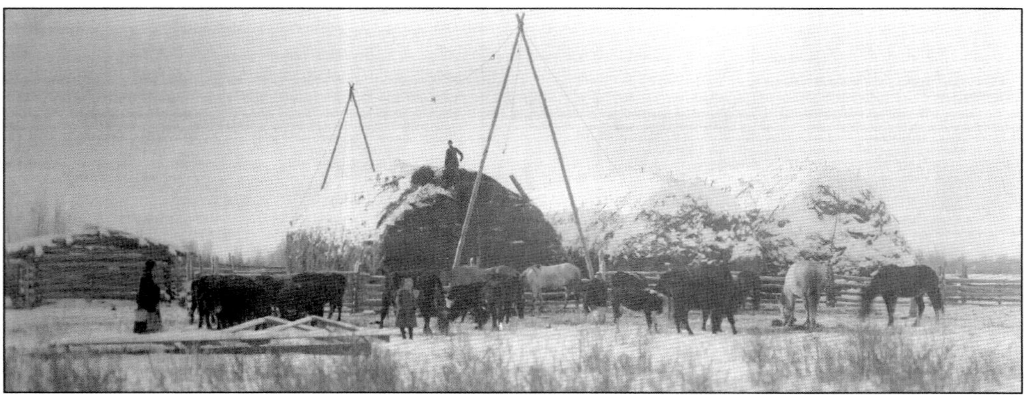

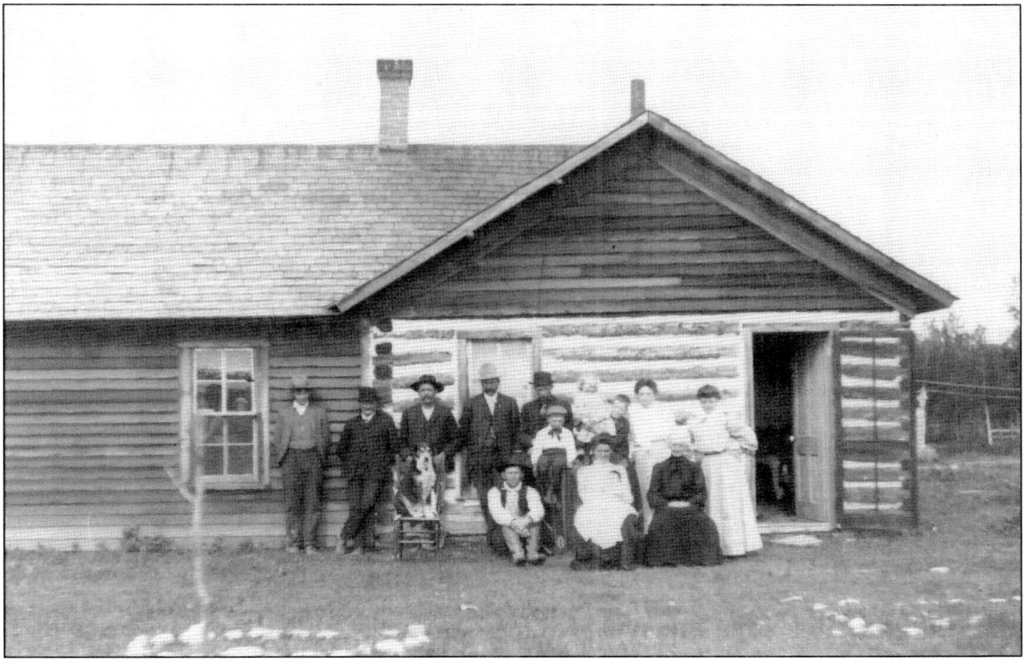

The homesteads of two early Rockvale area families are shown in these photographs. The Gibson family homestead is shown in the photograph above, and the Orren Clawson family home in Rockvale is shown in the 1890s photograph below. Orren Clawson moved his family to the Rockvale area in 1893 from Park City, Montana. Orren's sons John, Earl, and Archie also settled in this area. In addition to the Clawsons, Craigs, and Gibsons, other early settlers included the Barker, Boulder, Burger, Caley, Chilcott, Dix, Edgell, Hughes, McClintock, Nelson, Simpson, and Sutton families. (Both, CCHS.)

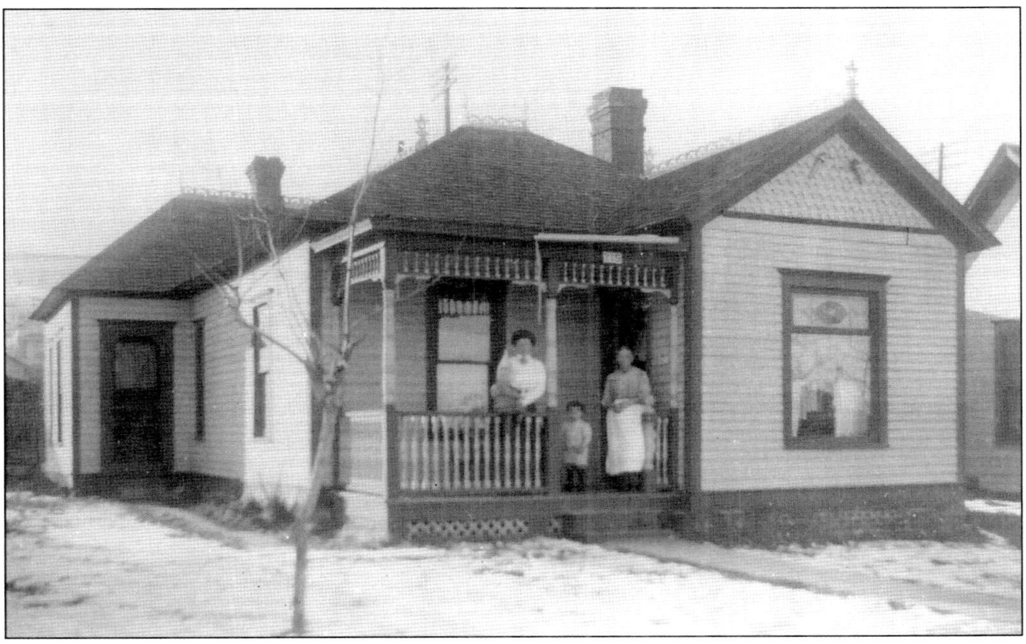

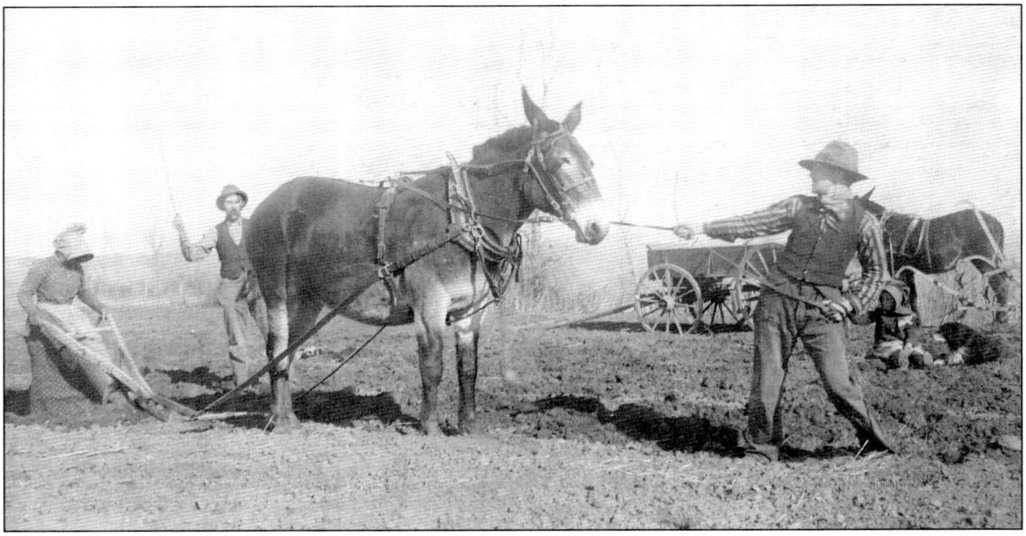

Without good land and water, no homesteader could successfully live on his land long enough to claim title to it. Preparing the land for planting (above) and implementing irrigation projects (below) became the top priorities for early settlers. The photograph above shows Mr. and Mrs. Pierce using a mule to plow a field while Homer Craig and his daughter Druzilla watch in the background. The Levi G. Webber photograph below shows Jim Dix's waterwheel moving Clark's Fork River water into an irrigation ditch near Rockvale. Levi G. Webber and Schuyler C. "Guy" Webber of Silesia built this wheel. The men in this photograph are unidentified. (Above, CCHS; below, JPL.)

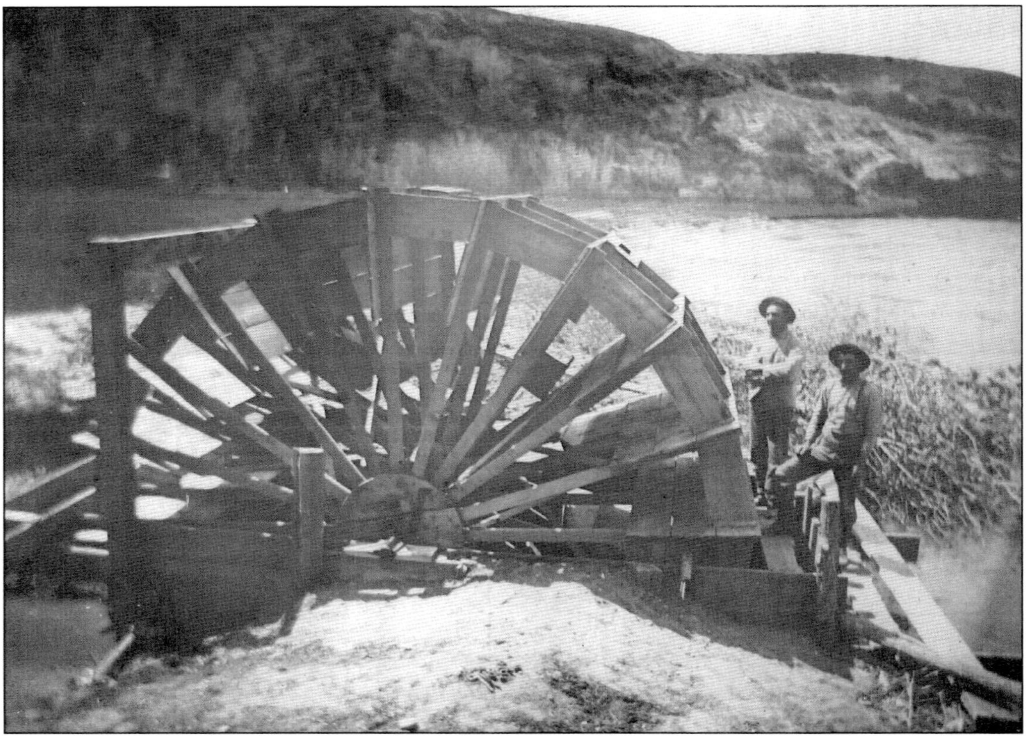

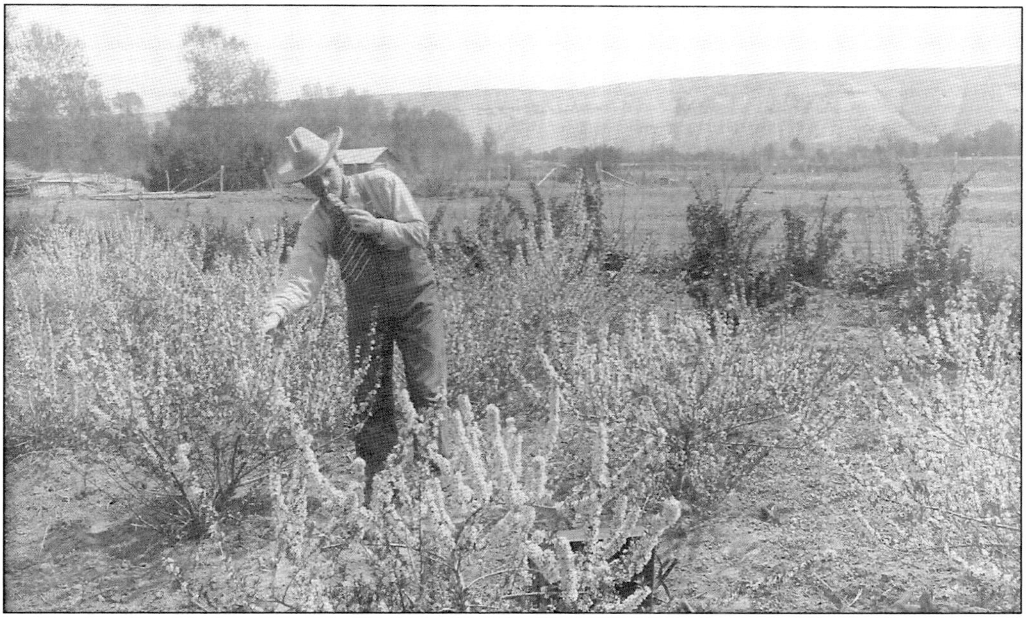

The most successful agricultural ventures in the early days of Rockvale and Silesia involved fruits and vegetables. Sugar beets, grains, and pinto beans later supplanted these crops in the area. The Nutting Bush Farm proved to be a leader in fruit and vegetable production. The Nutting Bush Farm occupied land north of Rockvale towards Silesia and produced cherries, apples, and potatoes. The photograph above shows Arthur Pierce in the Nutting Bush Farm cherry patch, and the photograph below shows Dan and Mrs. Pierce in a potato field. Dan Pierce and Arthur Pierce were brothers. (Both, CCHS.)

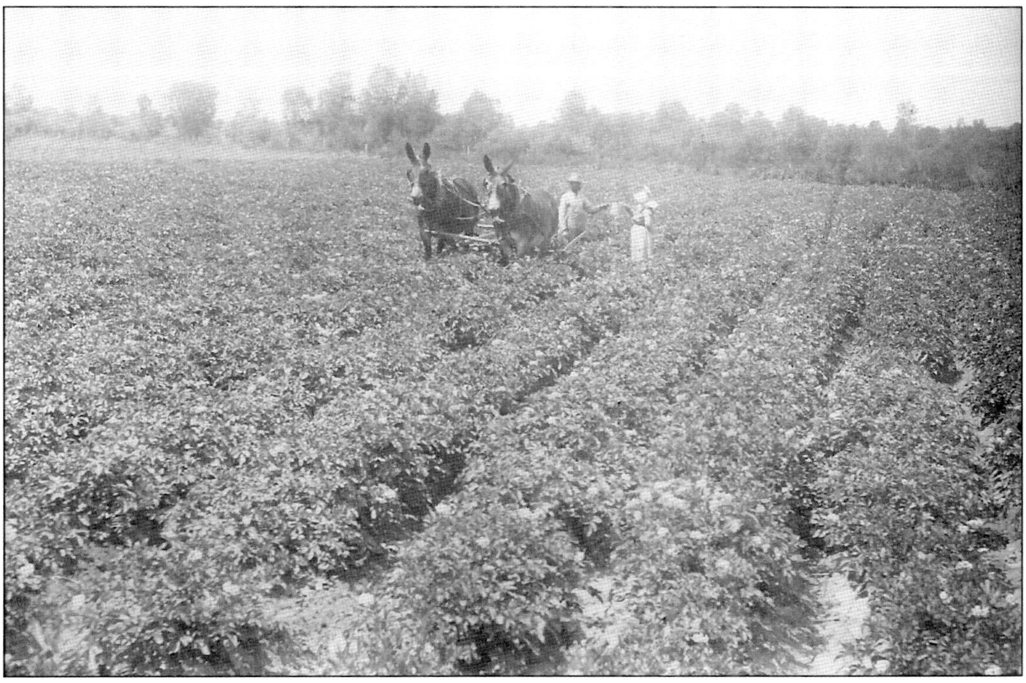

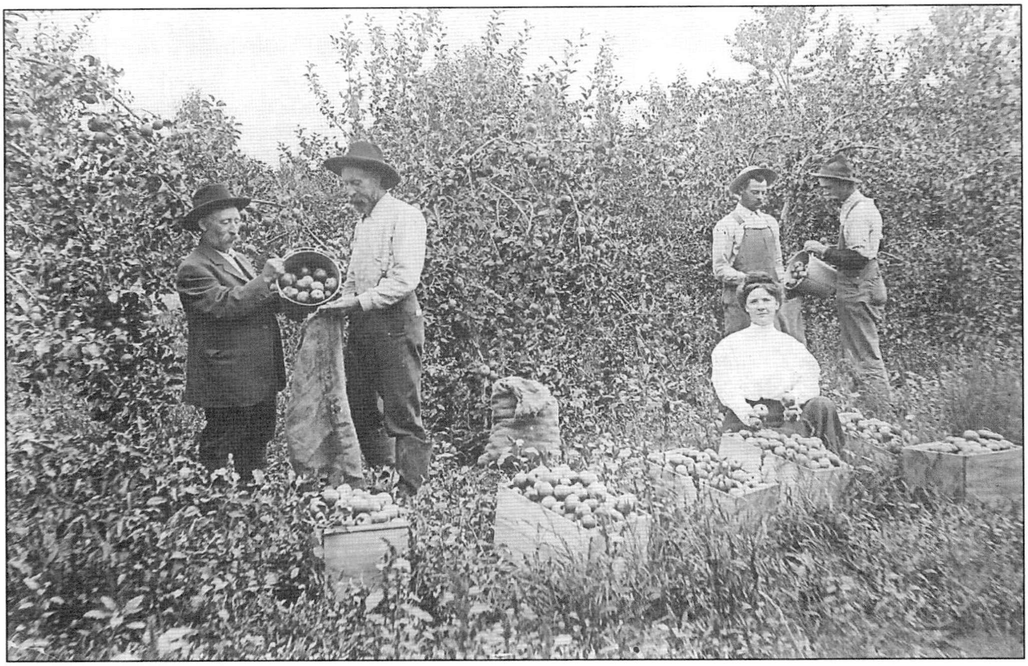

The Chilcott Nursery, another successful Rockvale agricultural venture and competitor of the Nutting Bush Farm, took advantage of the irrigated fertile soil near Rockvale to raise apple, cherry, plum, and pear trees, as well as currant and strawberry bushes. The photograph above shows, from left to right, Dave Mann, Taylor Craig, Ada Enochs, Gary Webber, and Ed Enochs harvesting apples from the Nutting Bush Farm. The photograph below shows workers tending young plants in one of the Chilcott Nursery fields. (Both, CCHS.)

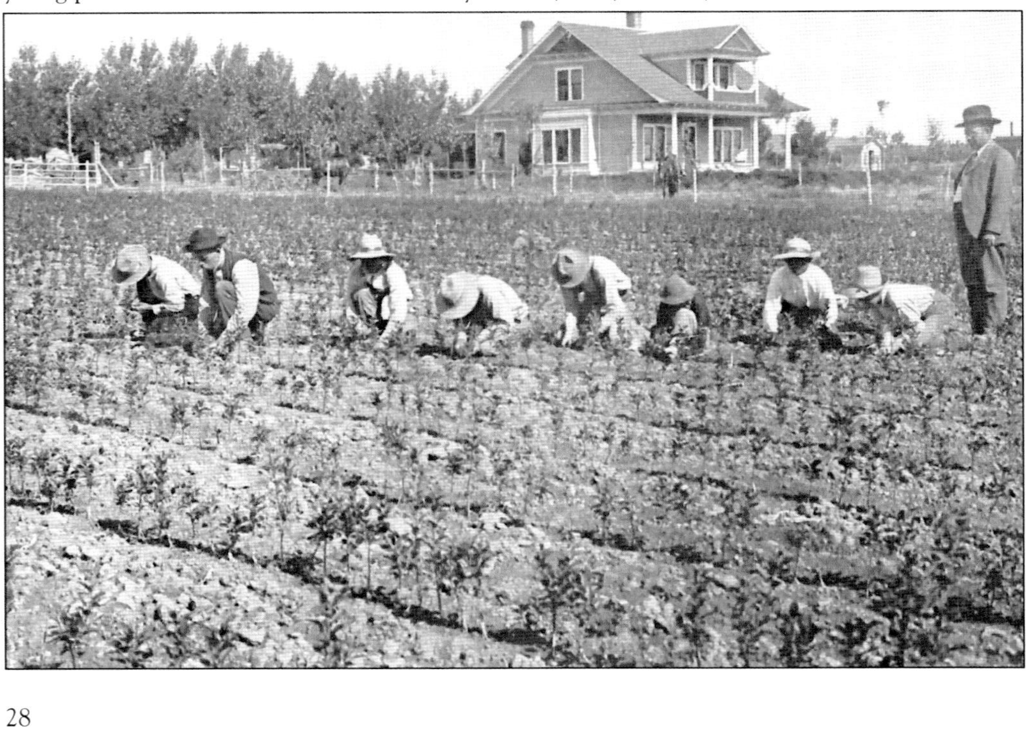

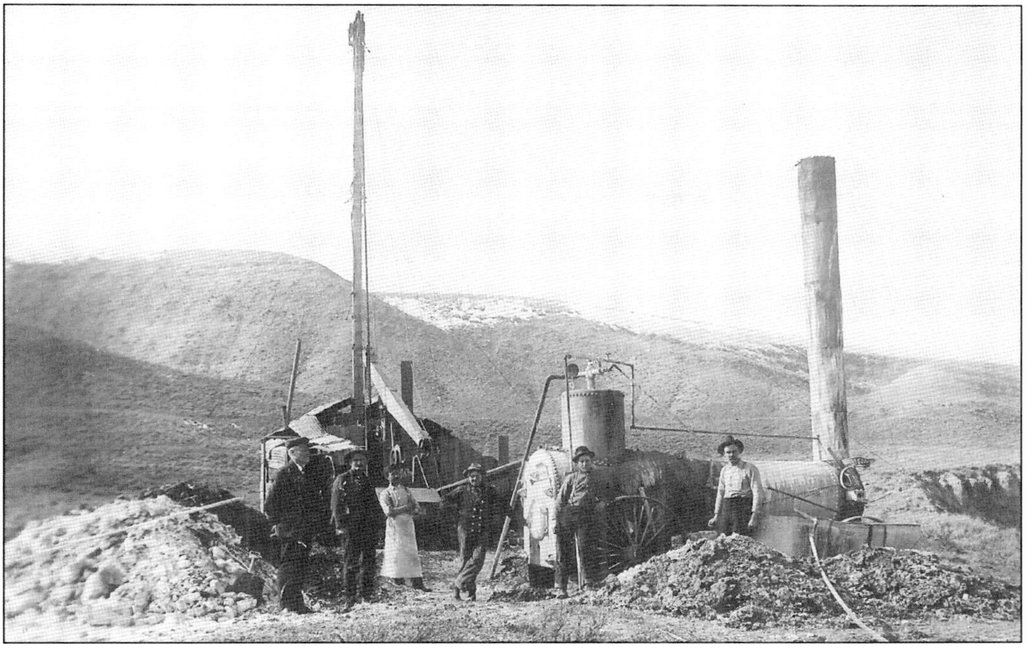

This photograph illustrates an early oil-prospecting attempt on Cottonwood Creek east of Rockvale and Silesia. Note on the right of this photograph the mobile coal-fired boiler used to power the operation. Oil prospectors eventually found and developed a successful oil field named the Moser Dome Field not far from the location of this photograph. (CCHS.)

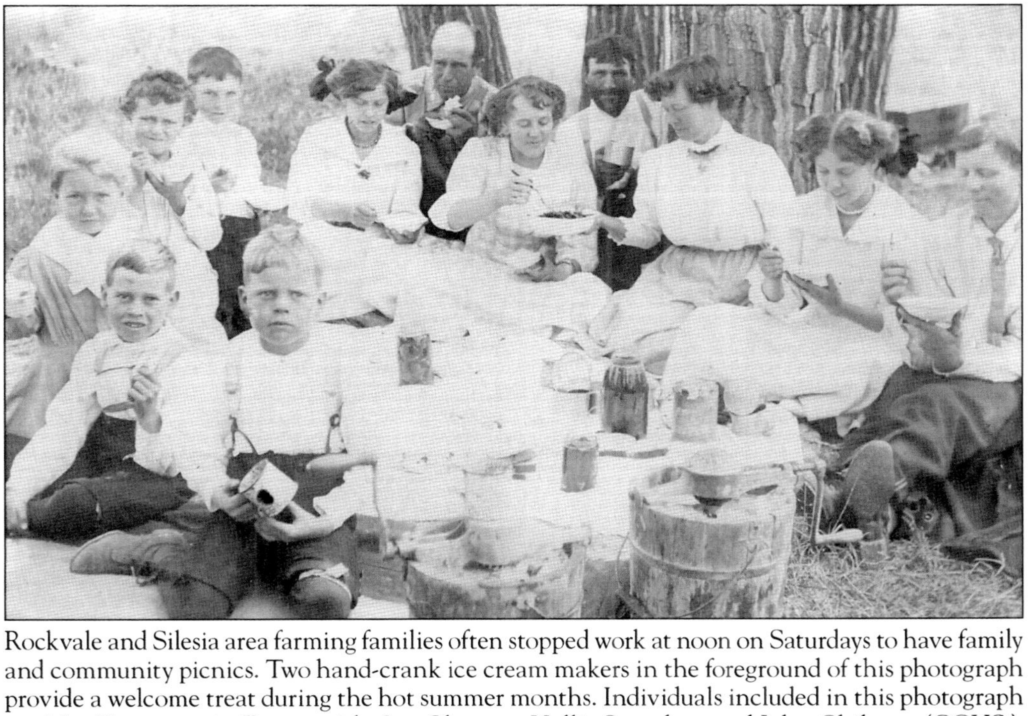

Rockvale and Silesia area farming families often stopped work at noon on Saturdays to have family and community picnics. Two hand-crank ice cream makers in the foreground of this photograph provide a welcome treat during the hot summer months. Individuals included in this photograph are Mrs. Farmer, twin Farmer girls, Ina Clawson, Hallie Saunders, and John Chilcott. (CCHS.)

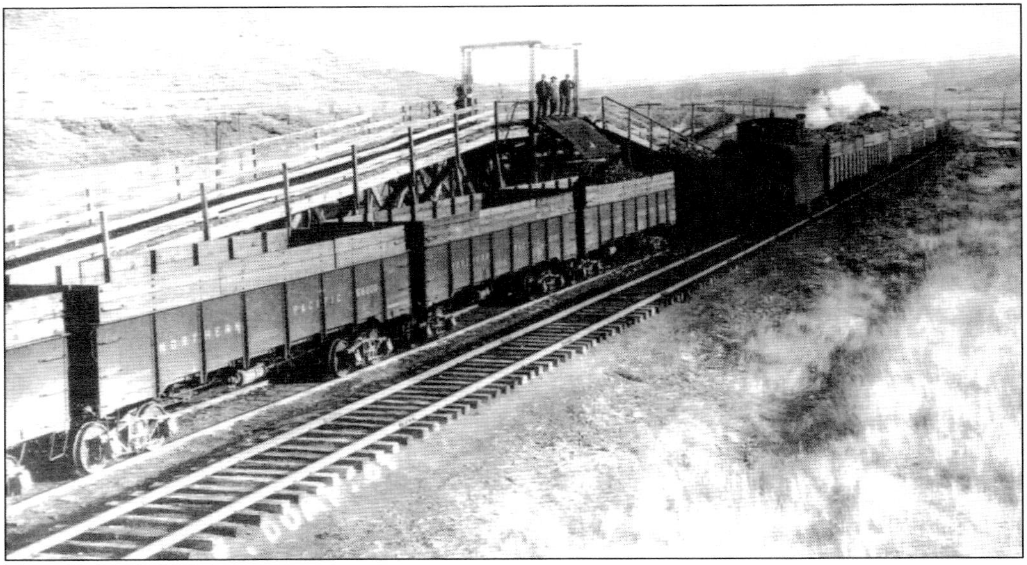

These c. 1910 photographs illustrate the operation of the Rockvale sugar beet dump. At the beet dump, the railroad constructed a short length of track parallel to the main line to hold empty boxcars. Next to this loading line sat a platform raised above the boxcars with approach and exit ramps for beet-laden wagons (above) and a loading ramp aimed toward the boxcars (below). The Levi G. Webber photograph below illustrates a farmer unloading his sugar beets by removing one side of the wagon and shoveling his beets down the ramp and into the boxcars. (Above, JPL; below, K. Hergenrider.)

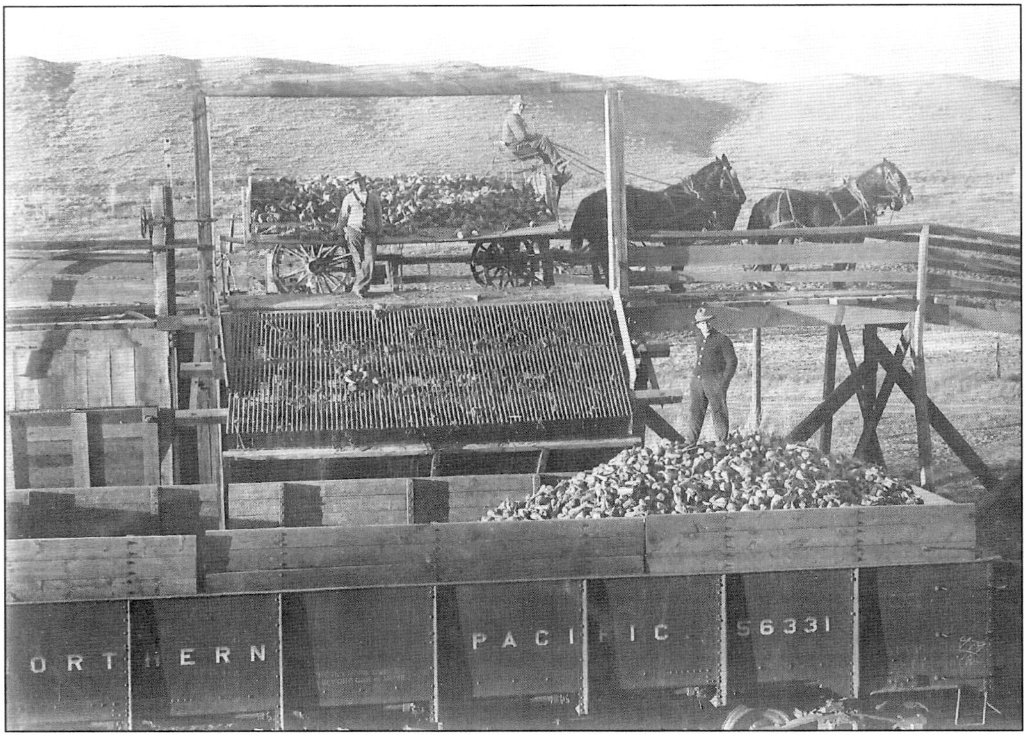

Three

EDGAR

J. J. Thornton conceived of and established Edgar with his purchase and subsequent donation of land from the Pendergast homestead in 1907. Thornton stipulated, in addition to a self-imposed prohibition of alcohol, that a park be installed near the Northern Pacific line running near town. There are two explanations for Edgar's name. The first claims it was named after Henry Edgar, one of the discoverers of the Alder Gulch goldfield. The other claims J. J. Thornton named the town after his brother. Located halfway between Rockvale and Fromberg, Edgar's location provided a more convenient point of commerce for residents of the Crow Reservation town of Pryor, 19 miles to the east, and nearby Poverty Flats to the west, where the Paradise Valley Elementary School was located. Poverty Flats took its name from the dire situation homesteaders in that area faced as they attempted to grow dryland crops while waiting for irrigation ditches to deliver Clark's Fork River water to them. In its heyday, downtown Edgar sported such commercial establishments as the Edgar State Bank, a livery stable, a meat market, lumber yards, blacksmith shops, theaters, cafés, pool halls, a drugstore, a garage, and feed stores. Economic opportunities came to Edgar when the Great Western Sugar Company contracted area residents to raise sugar beets in 1910, the construction of a railroad depot in 1913, and the building of a grain elevator not long after. Not far upstream from the current Edgar bridge across the Clark's Fork River stood the original steel bridge built in 1906. Citizens built a Methodist church in 1912 and three area schools between 1899 and 1919. Students attended the first school in 1899, southwest of town, and the final school was erected in city limits in 1919. High school classes began in 1921.

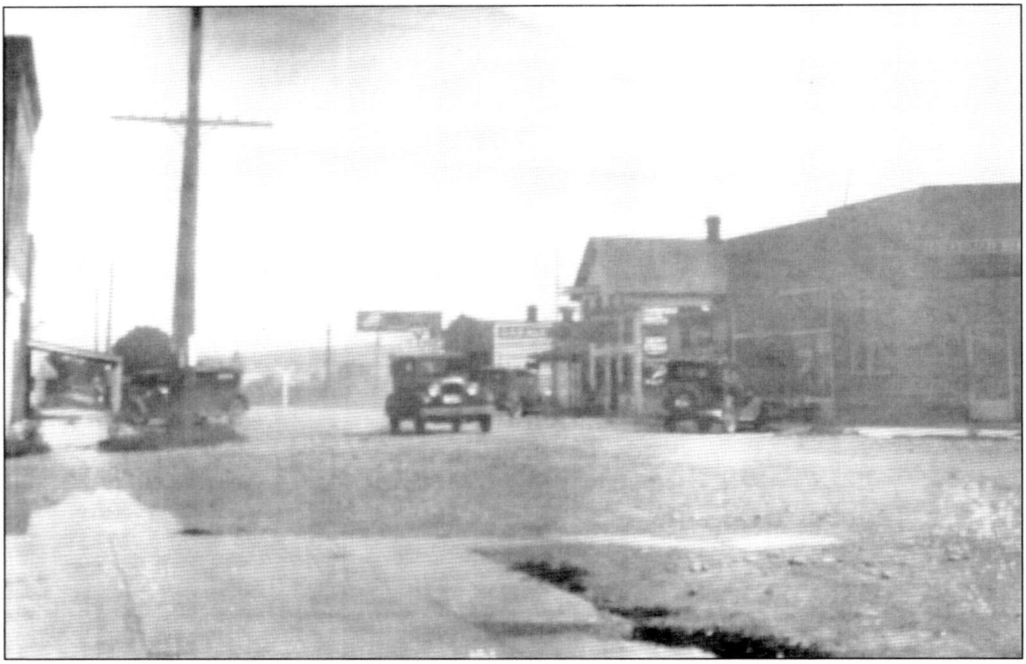

These c. 1920 photographs of Edgar illustrate the large number of businesses that once lined its main street. Like Silesia, Fromberg, and Belfry, Edgar's main street ran perpendicular to the neighboring Northern Pacific Railroad tracks rather than parallel to them, as was the case with Rockvale and Bridger. Businesses along this street included grocery stores, a post office, a livery stable, a meat market, a hotel, a blacksmith shop, a lumberyard, an auto body shop, and a gas and bulk oil station. The photograph above shows the Edgar State Bank building on the far right, and the photograph below shows the Edgar Cash Trading Company store. (Both, CCHS.)

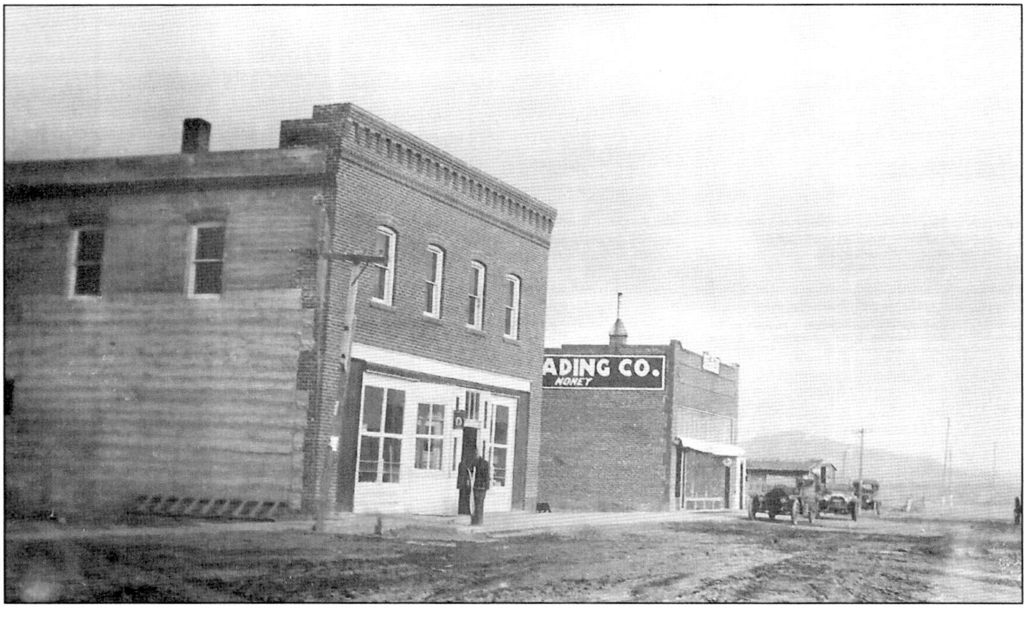

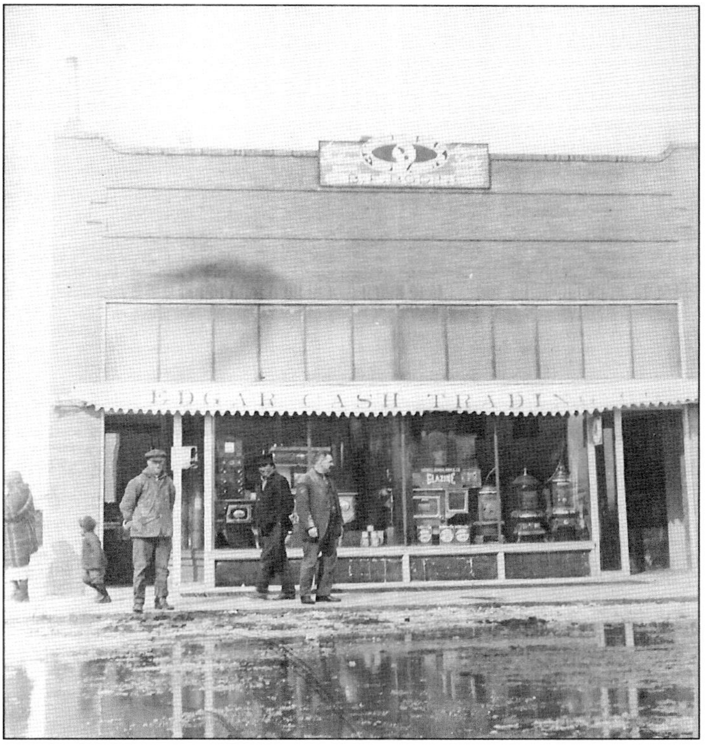

This photograph provides a detailed view of the Edgar Cash Trading Company. Items displayed in the store's front window include coal heating stoves on the right and coal cooking stoves and furniture on the left. A barely visible sign under the store's awning advertises the availability of telephone service inside. (CCHS.)

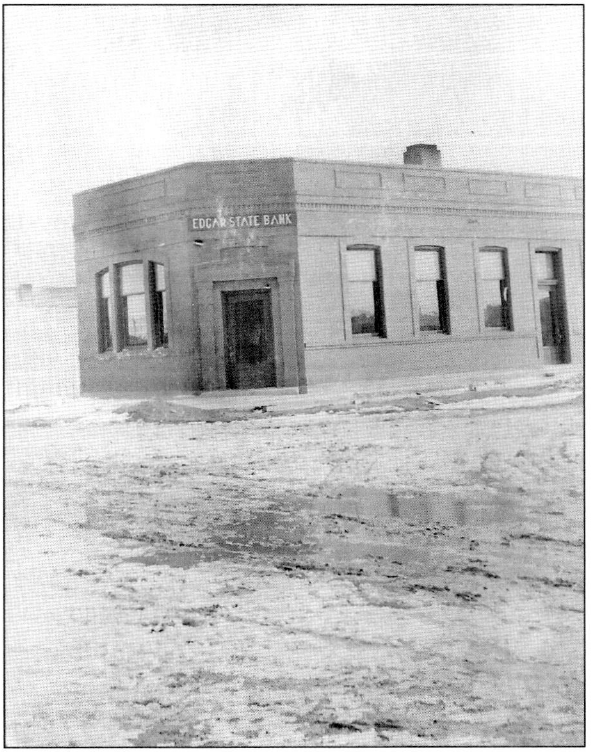

The Edgar State Bank in the photograph at left began operation in 1913. It operated for a decade before closing in 1923. Early directors of the bank included S. J. McPherson, L. F. Thornton, L. C. Jensen, J. M. Colvin, and J. W. Stansbury. (CCHS.)

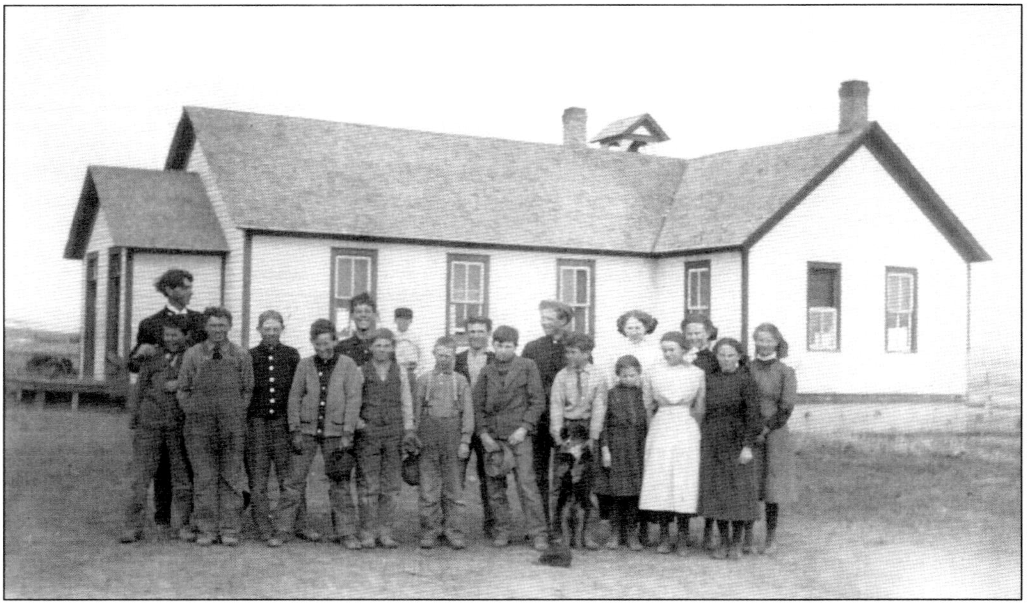

This photograph shows students posing in front of the Paradise Valley School southwest of Edgar on Poverty Flats. Built in 1899, this school educated children from the area before the town of Edgar existed. In 1915, Edgar residents built a school in town. This school burned in 1917 and was replaced with the second Edgar School. (CFVM.)

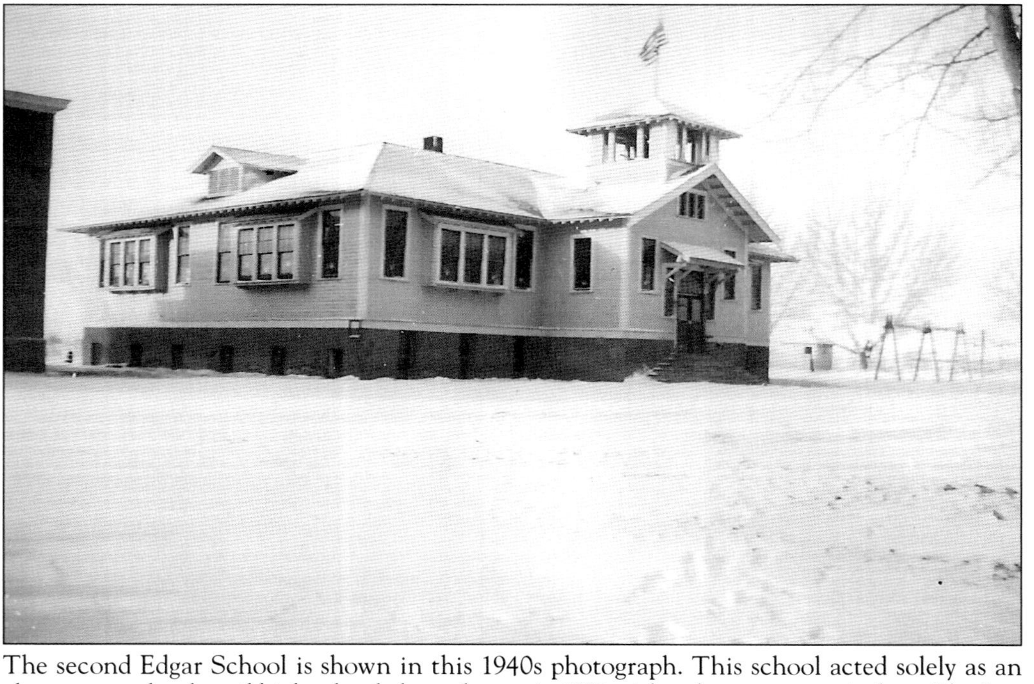

The second Edgar School is shown in this 1940s photograph. This school acted solely as an elementary school until high school classes began in 1921 with a three-year curriculum. The first high school class graduated in 1924. (CCHS.)

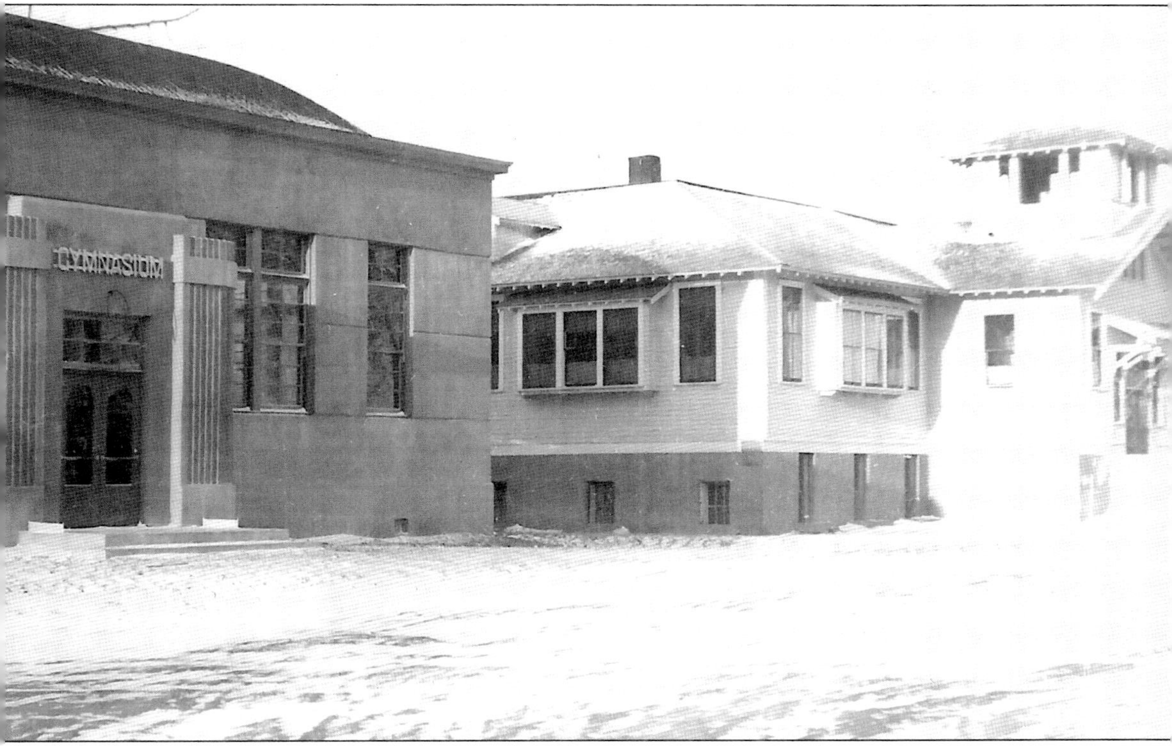

During the late 1930s, the Work Projects Administration (WPA) built the gymnasium shown in this photograph next to the Edgar High School. The WPA constructed government buildings, sidewalks, and other public buildings from 1935 to 1943. Enrollment in Edgar High School varied from a low of 25 students, with four to six graduates, to a high of 100 students. The influx of students came when students from nearby Pryor, Montana, in Big Horn County, began attending school in Edgar. These Pryor students endured a daily 38-mile round-trip bus ride over rough backcountry roads. During these years, the Edgar High School flourished. The boy's high school basketball teams were a perennial powerhouse and won the Montana State Class C Championship in 1966 with a 59-44 win over Stanford. (CCHS.)

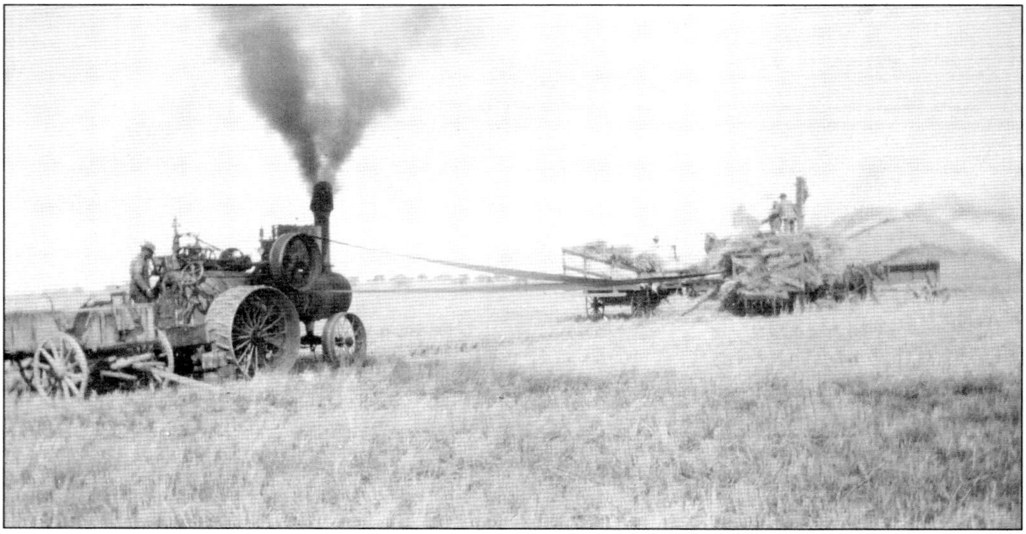

Threshing grain using steam-powered tractors vastly improved farming efficiency but required a steam operator's license to be done safely. This photograph, taken on the Ralph Oliver and Mabel Steele farm, shows a steam-powered tractor (left) providing power to the threshing machine (right) via an external belt drive. Ralph Steele possessed a steam operator's license. (MOTB.)

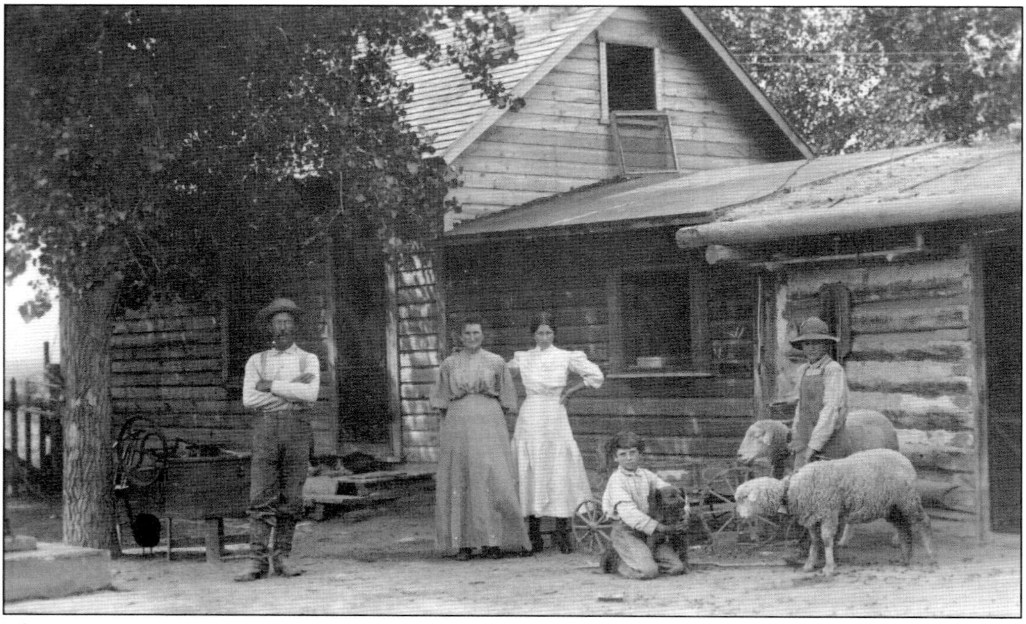

The George and Victoria Schumm family pictured above came to the Edgar area from Minnesota in 1906. The Schumm family purchased land on the Clark's Fork River adjacent to the construction site of the first Edgar bridge. Victoria and daughter Lenora cooked meals for the bridge construction crew to earn extra money. (MOTB.)

Four

GEBO

The first settlement in the Fromberg area was the now-extinct coal camp named Gebo. It was located a mile west of present-day Fromberg. Samuel Gebo discovered coal in this part of Carbon County in 1894 and secured funding to start his Clark's Fork Coal Company mine and open a coal mining camp named Gebo in 1897. Gebo started as a tent city and did not begin to acquire permanent structures until Fredrick H. Davis platted the town in April 1898. Gebo housed a peak population of 1,000, providing such amenities as a post office, a school, a newspaper, a drugstore, boardinghouses, and bars. The one necessity of life that Gebo could not provide was water. Residents hauled water from the Clark's Fork River or paid local contractors for the service. Looking after the education and spirituality of the town, Gebo citizens erected an elementary school and began Catholic and Methodist church services in tents almost immediately. In 1906, Rev. Charles Trueper organized construction of a small Catholic church near Gebo. Eight years later, Rev. Francis Shevlin arranged for the building of the larger St. Joseph's Church at its present location in Fromberg. Similarly, Rev. John G. Clark oversaw construction of a United Methodist church in Fromberg in 1908. With the opening of the Clark's Fork Coal Company mine, the Northern Pacific Railroad (NP) advanced a line up the Clark's Fork Valley from Rockvale to Gebo in 1897 and installed a train stop nearby named after NP stockholder Conrad Fromberg. Competitive pressure from the recently opened Bear Creek Valley mines to the southwest led Gebo to sell his coal company and town in 1907. The coal company was renamed the Bituminous Coal Company, and the town was renamed Coalville. In 1912, the Coalville mines closed under that competitive pressure, the nearby settlement of Fromberg incorporated as a town, and Gebo's abandonment began. In 1987, all remnants of Gebo, with the exception of its cemetery, were removed in the name of public safety. The Gebo Cemetery is now listed on the National Register of Historic Places.

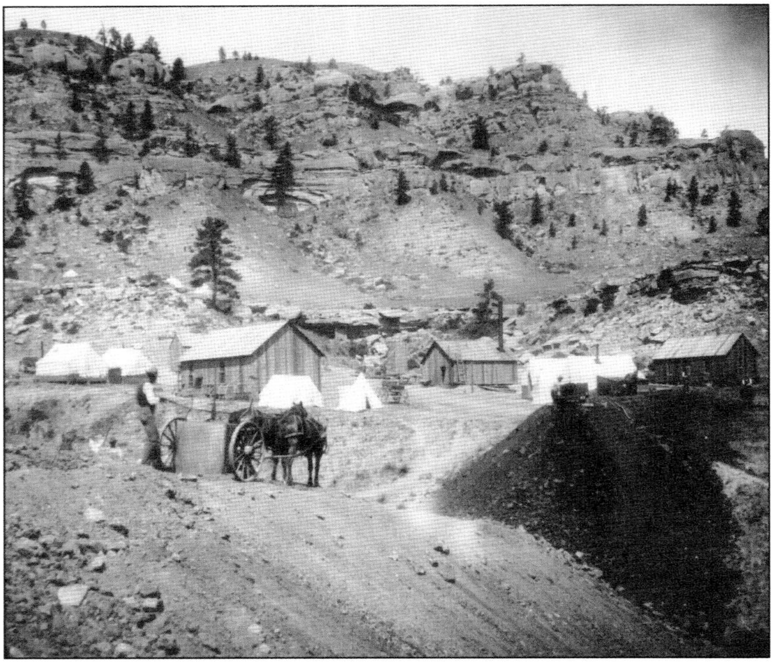

Development of the Clark's Fork Coal Company mine began so rapidly that miners flocking to the area often found themselves without any form of permanent housing to rent or buy. Consequently, Gebo, shown in this pre-1900 photograph, temporarily became a tent town composed of everything from simple teepee-like structures (center) to canvas wall tents (right). (CCHS.)

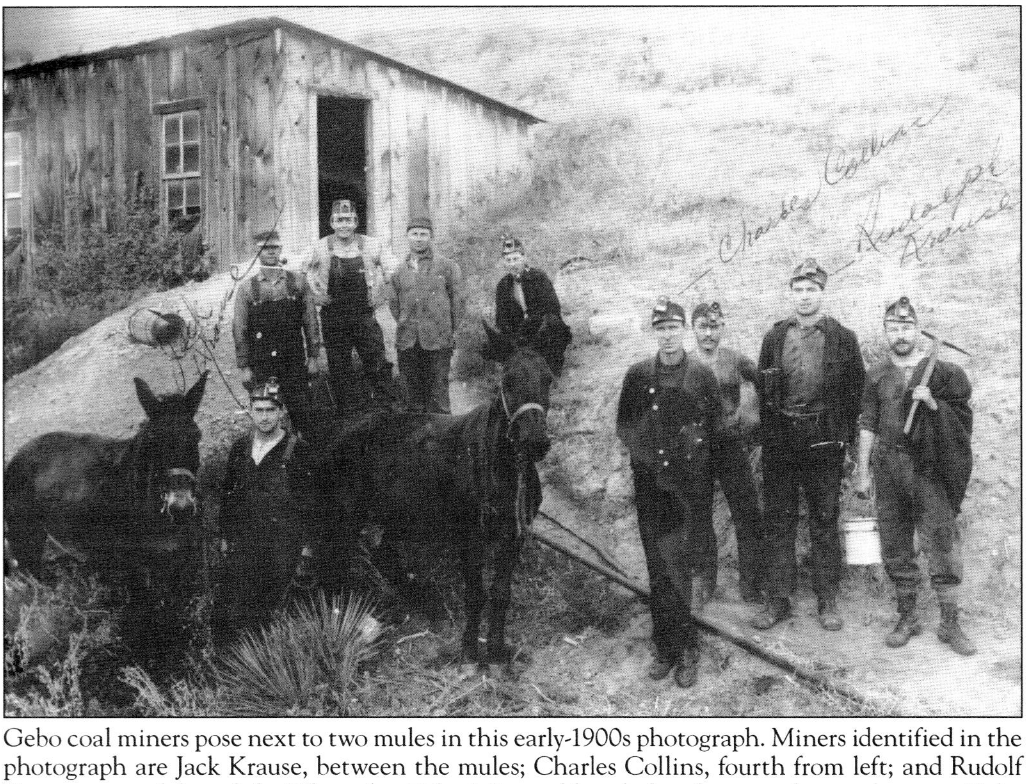

Gebo coal miners pose next to two mules in this early-1900s photograph. Miners identified in the photograph are Jack Krause, between the mules; Charles Collins, fourth from left; and Rudolf Krause, second from left. When the Gebo Mine sold and closed, soon afterwards many Gebo miners found work in the Bear Creek Valley and Red Lodge coal mines. (CCHS.)

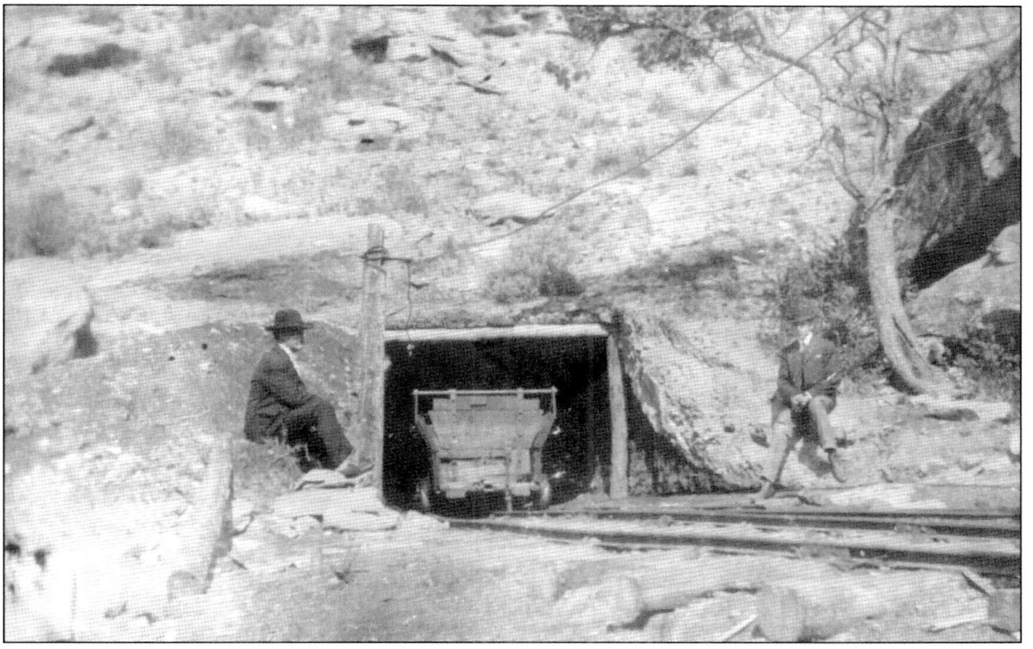

Samuel Gebo sits to the left of one entrance to the Clark's Fork Coal Company mine in this photograph. Gebo went on to develop a coal mine at Frank, Alberta, Canada; the Spring Creek Mine near Lewiston, Montana; and the Owl Creek Coal Mine in Gebo, Wyoming. He also provided early financial backing for several power and electric companies. (CCHS.)

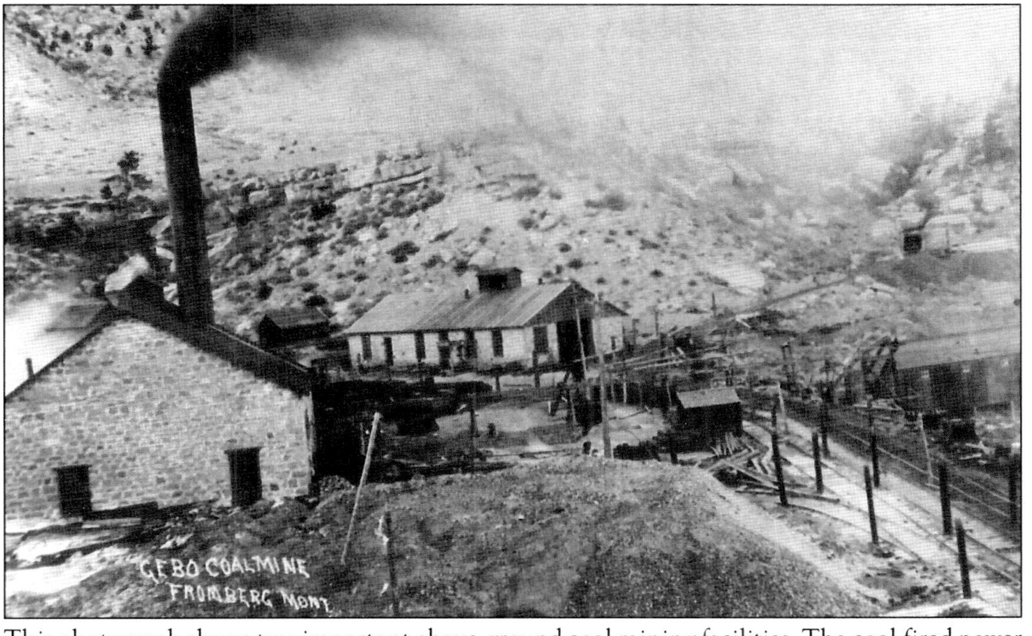

This photograph shows two important above-ground coal mining facilities. The coal-fired power plant (left) generated electricity for use in the mine and mine camp. The machine shop (middle) affected the necessary repairs to coal cars and mine equipment. Note that a mine entrance appears as a black square in the far right of this photograph. (CCHS.)

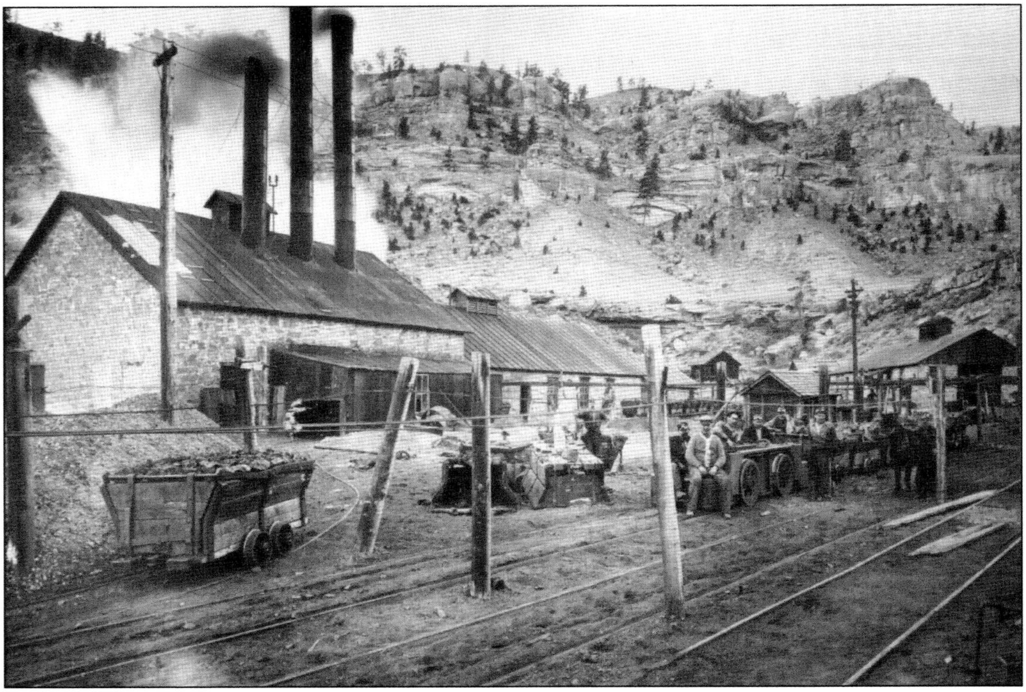

In this early-1910s photograph of the Clark's Fork Coal Company power plant, a group of miners sits on an electric-powered motor. These motors eventually replaced horses and mules for hauling coal cars out of the mine. The presence of horses in the photograph indicates that this was a transitional time before horses were fully phased out. (CCHS.)

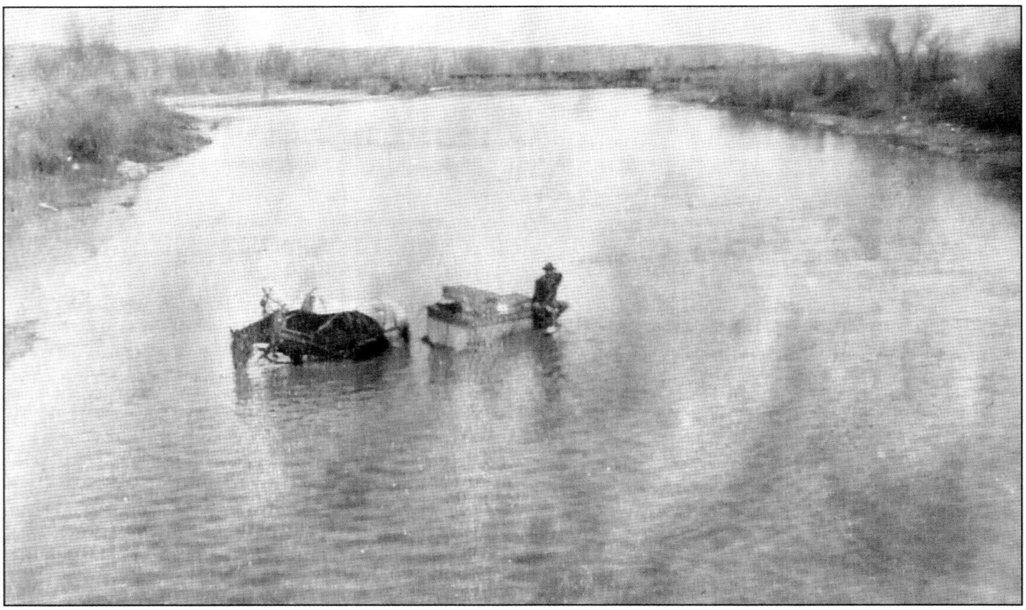

This photograph shows Ed Lester filling barrels with Clark's Fork River water for delivery to customers in Gebo. Without its own water source, Gebo residents purchased water from Lester at 25¢ per barrel rather than collecting it themselves. (CFVM.)

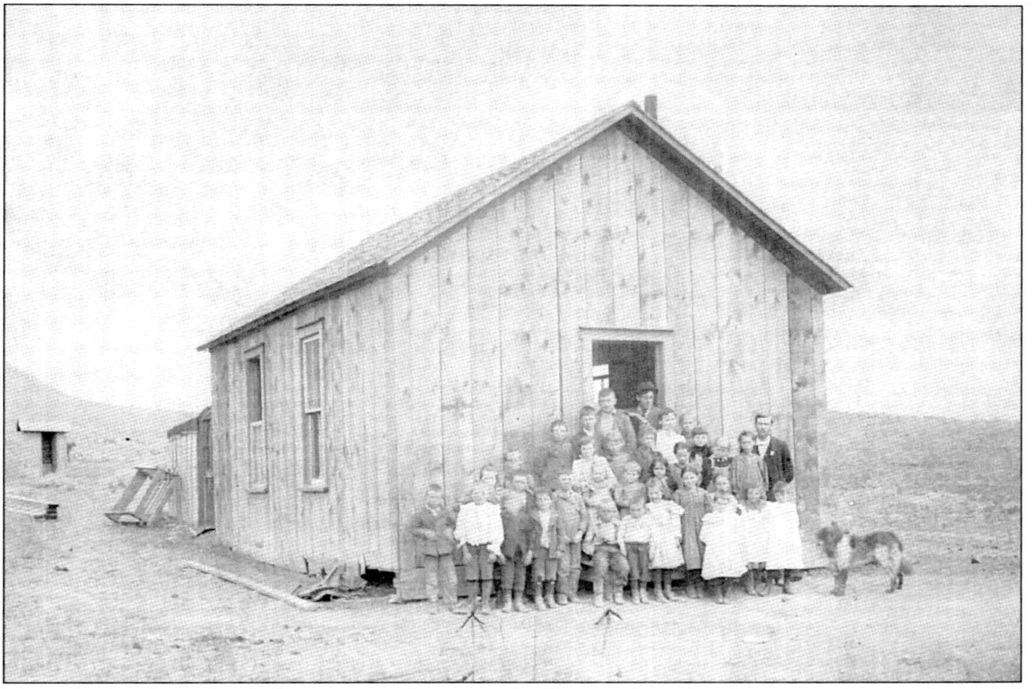

These December 18, 1902, photographs show the first Gebo schoolhouse and its students. Ed N. Logan taught school in Gebo at this time. The Gebo School provided instruction for grades one through eight. A closer inspection of the class photograph below reveals that very few boys over the age of 10 appear in the photograph, because boys of this era often began work in the mines as young as the age of nine. Prior to the building of this school, classes met in the back of a barbershop. In 1903, a two-room brick building replaced this schoolhouse. (Both, CFVM.)

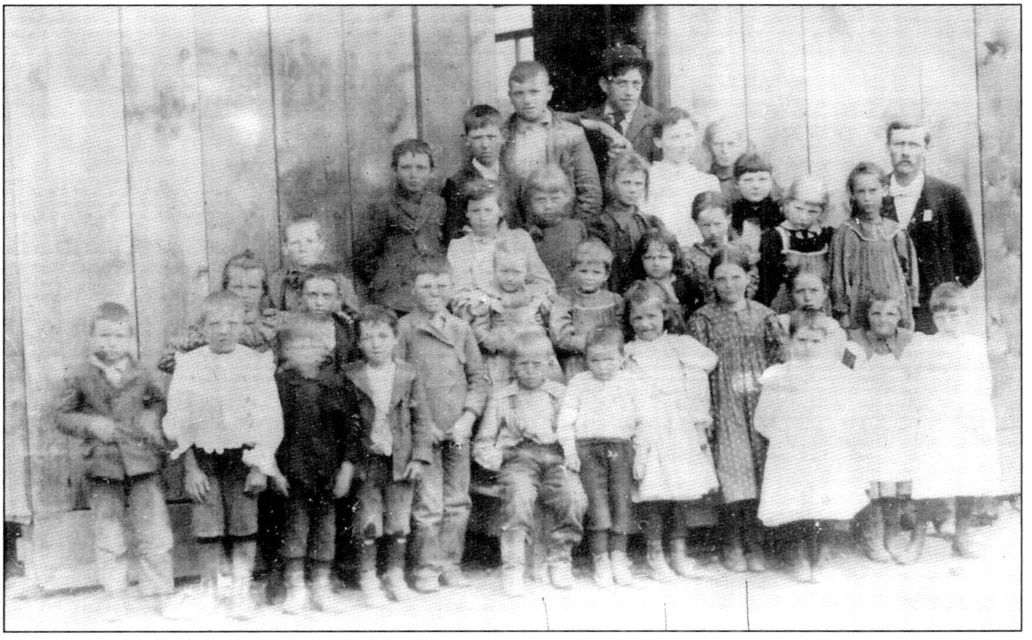

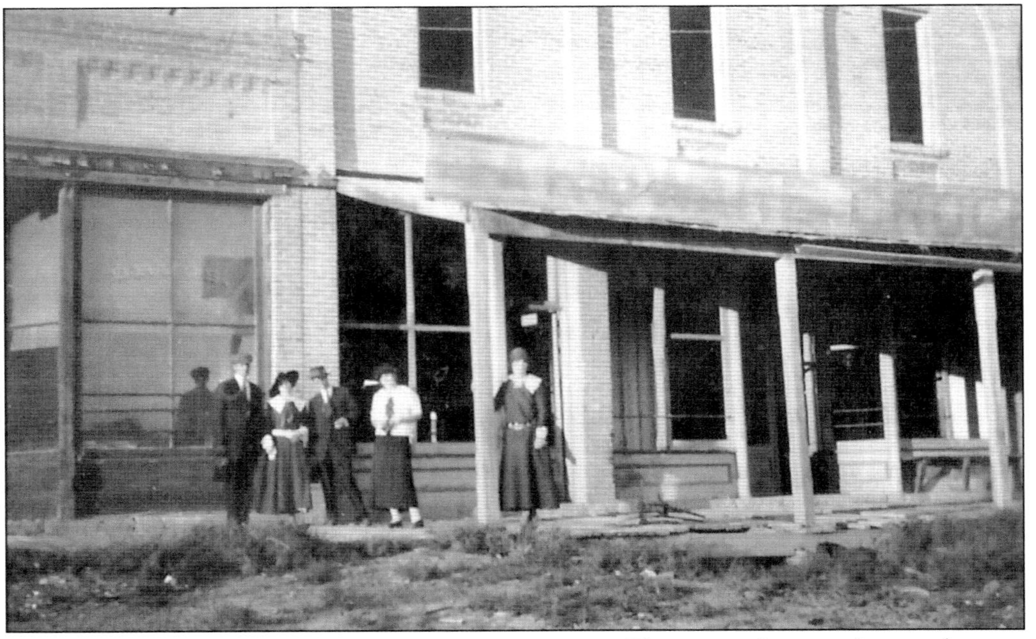

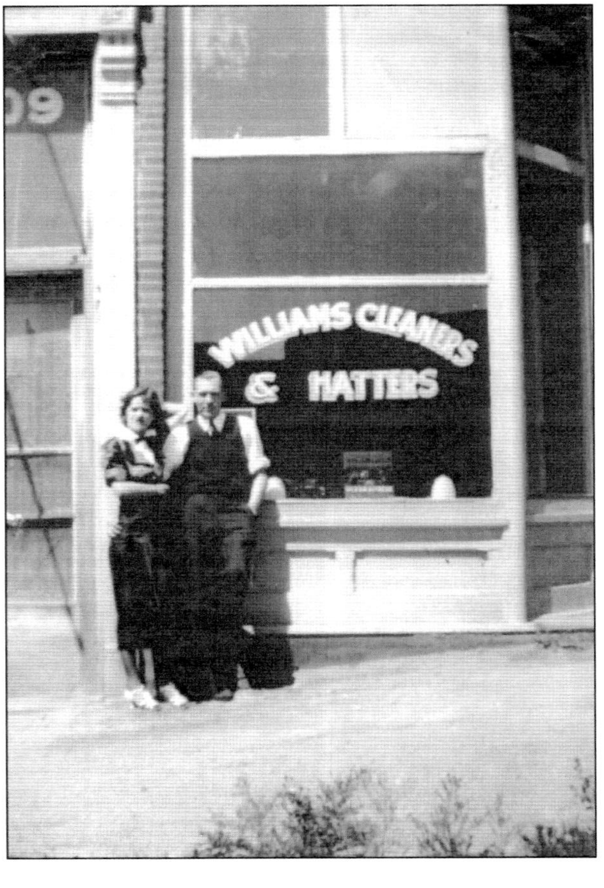

These rare photographs reveal some of the many businesses that once lined Gebo's Main Street. The condition of the street and buildings indicated that these photographs were taken long after Gebo became a ghost town, probably in the 1930s. The photograph above shows, from left to right, a drugstore, a hardware store, and a grocery store. The Gebo Dance Hall occupied the second floor of the hardware and grocery building. The photograph at left shows the Williams Cleaners and Hatters store. Other professional services found in Gebo during its heyday included a post office, newspaper office, Mr. Woodward's law office, and Dr. Boyle's medical practice. (Both, CFVM.)

Five

FROMBERG

Fromberg owes its origins to the now-extinct coal camp of Gebo, located a mile west of the town against sandstone bluffs. With the arrival of the Northern Pacific's (NP) Fromberg depot, William Swallow realized that his land adjoining the depot provided a more attractive town site than Gebo. Swallow platted six blocks of his land and laid the foundation for the town of Fromberg. A post office was opened in 1903, and Fromberg was incorporated in 1912. Fromberg drew an ever increasing citizenry and buildings from the rapidly abandoned Gebo. Businesses sprang up to serve this influx of miners as well as immigrant homesteaders farming the fertile valley floor. The 1911 arrival of the Chicago, Burlington, and Quincy Railroad (CB&Q) from the south, merging with the NP tracks from the north, spurred on this business development. The Clark's Fork National Bank, Fromberg Pressed Brick and Tile Company, Gibson Culvert Company, Martin Pickling Company, and Baldwin Lumber Company are just a few of the Fromberg manufacturers who took advantage of the ease with which they could now transport their goods. Physician Dr. T. J. Benson, Buzzetti and Emmett's Mercantile, a number of saloons, and a billiard hall provided for the day-to-day needs of Fromberg's citizens. The United Methodist and St. Joseph's Churches continued to thrive in Fromberg. In 1908, a newly constructed school in Fromberg augmented Gebo's elementary school in educating area students. The Fromberg School added grades 9 and 10 in 1913 and grades 11 and 12 in 1914 to complete the pre-college education of its students. Many of the early settlers planted fruit orchards in the fertile bottomlands along the Clark's Fork River. United Methodist minister Rev. John G. Clark quickly became one of the more prominent and successful orchard owners in the valley. The overwhelming success of these orchards led Fromberg to be nicknamed "The Fruit Basket of Carbon County." Today the orchards are gone, replaced over the years by sugar beet, grain, and pinto bean farming and cattle ranching.

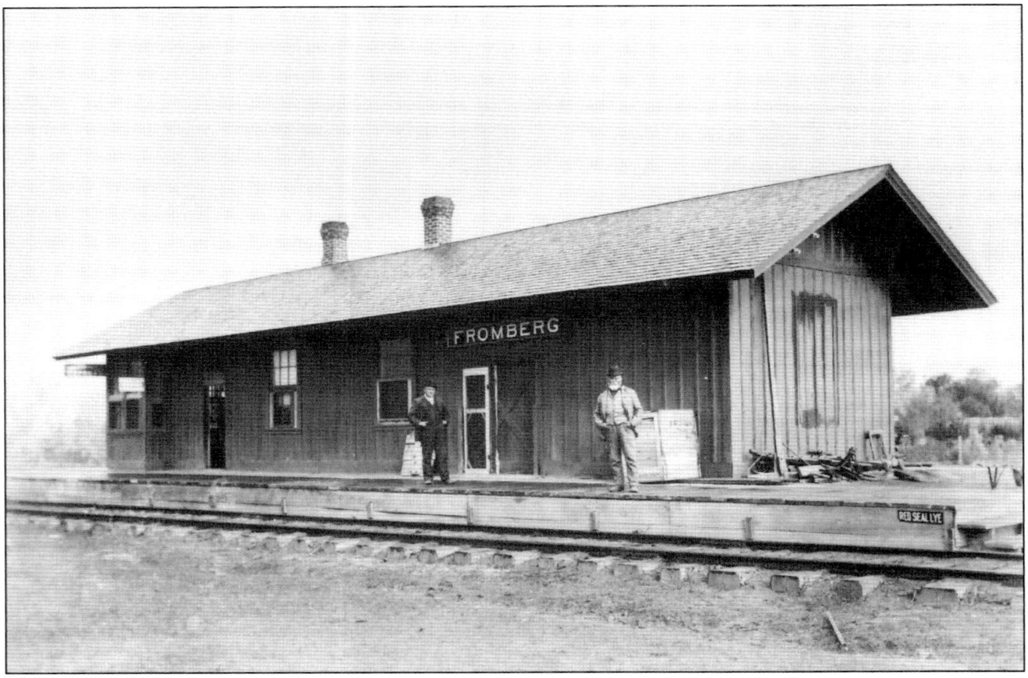

These vintage images of the Fromberg train depot show an early version of the depot (above) and a later version with local motoring enthusiasts gathered for the start of a race (below). The joining of the Northern Pacific Railroad line from the north and the Chicago, Burlington, and Quincy Railroad from the south occurred within yards of the Fromberg depot. On a late February day in 1911, John Blewett, president of Fromberg's Commercial Club, drove home a golden spike to officially join the two railroads. The Fromberg Train Depot currently houses the Clark's Fork Valley Museum. (Above, CFVM; below, CFVM via the Haynes Foundation Collection.)

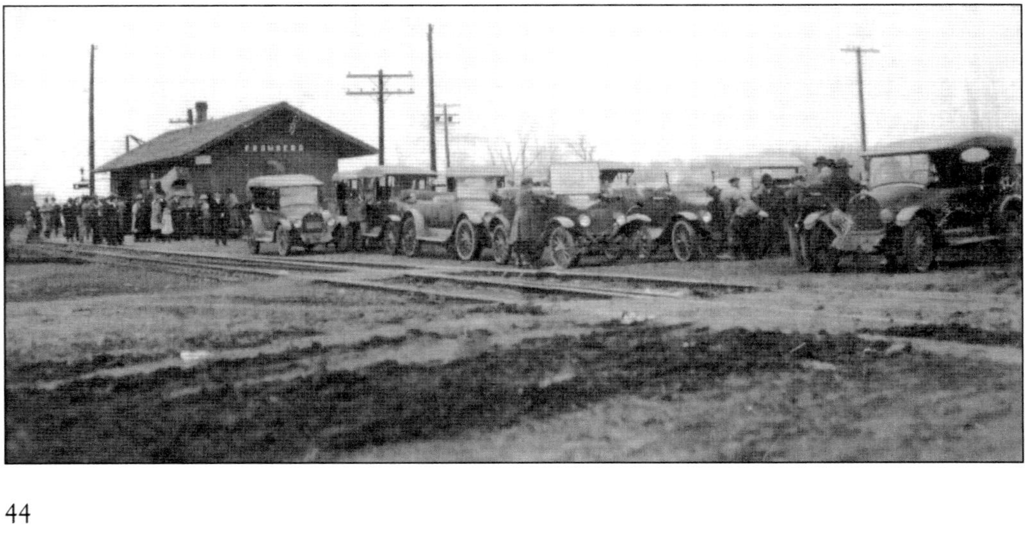

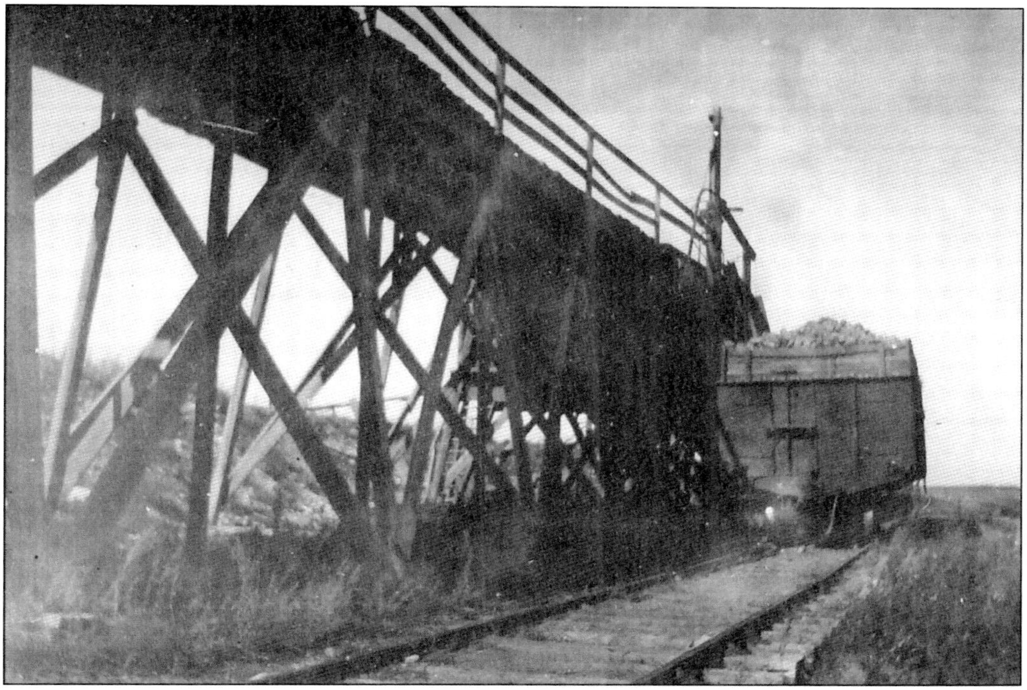

The Fromberg sugar beet dump, with a fully loaded Northern Pacific boxcar, highlights the importance railroads played in the Clark's Fork Valley's development. Extremely fertile land and extensive irrigation systems yielded bountiful crops throughout the valley, but only the railroads made delivery of these crops to market commercially viable. (CFVM.)

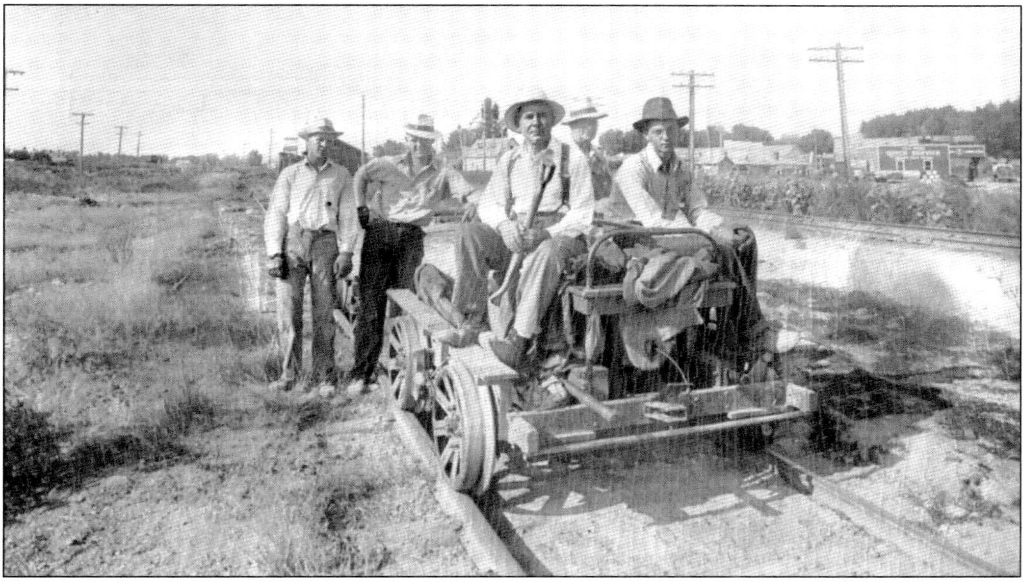

Heavily loaded boxcars of coal punished Clark's Fork Valley's rail lines daily. This wear and tear made track maintenance a priority. In this photograph, a Northern Pacific section crew from Fromberg poses with its handcar. The crewmen in this photograph are, from left to right, Dave Johnson, Paul Reichert, Tiefel Buechler, Paul Stark, and Clarence Johnson. (CFVM.)

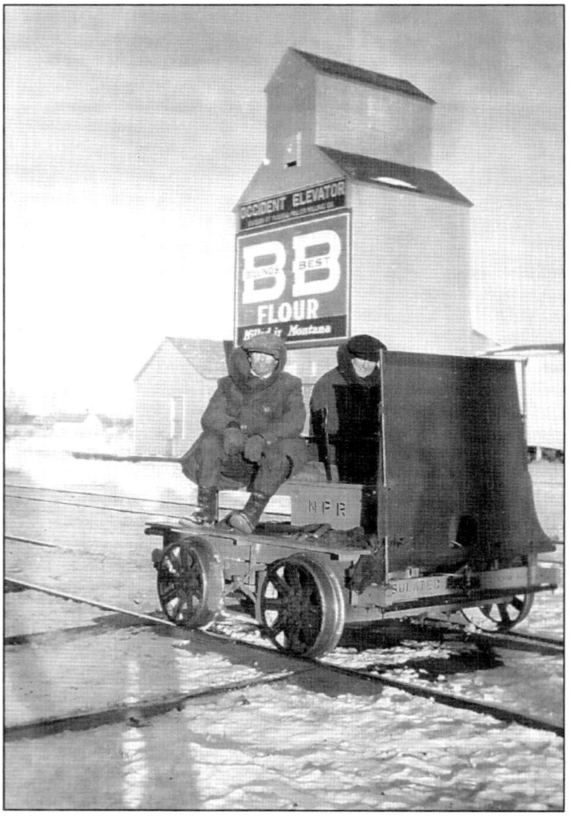

The Fromberg grain elevator provides a backdrop to Northern Pacific trackmen Dave Johnson (left) and Paul Reichert (right). Owned and operated by Billings Best Flour, the elevator acted as a grain collection and storage point. Analogous to sugar beet dumps, grain elevators provided a place to load the product onto boxcars for delivery to market. (CFVM.)

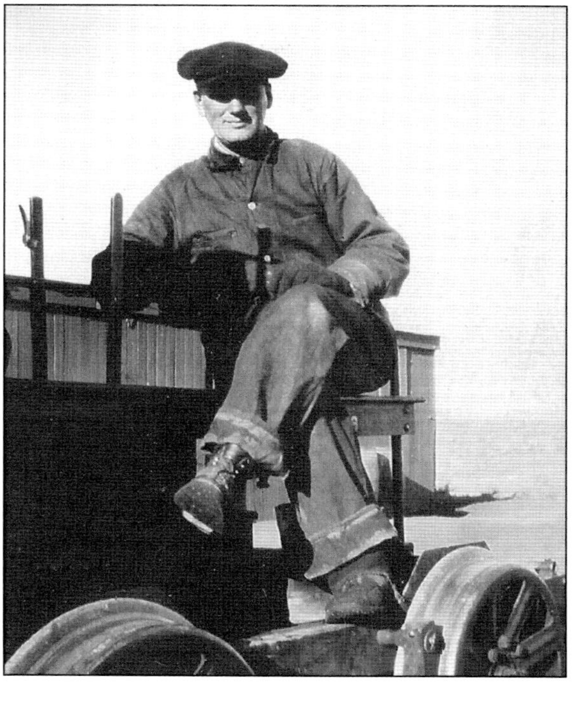

Northern Pacific trackman Dave Johnson poses with his section crew's handcar. Maintenance and repair of railroad lines required strength and stamina. A track man's duties included replacing worn ties, repairing rail beds, and using levers to manually force tracks displaced by the heavily loaded trains back into place. (CFVM.)

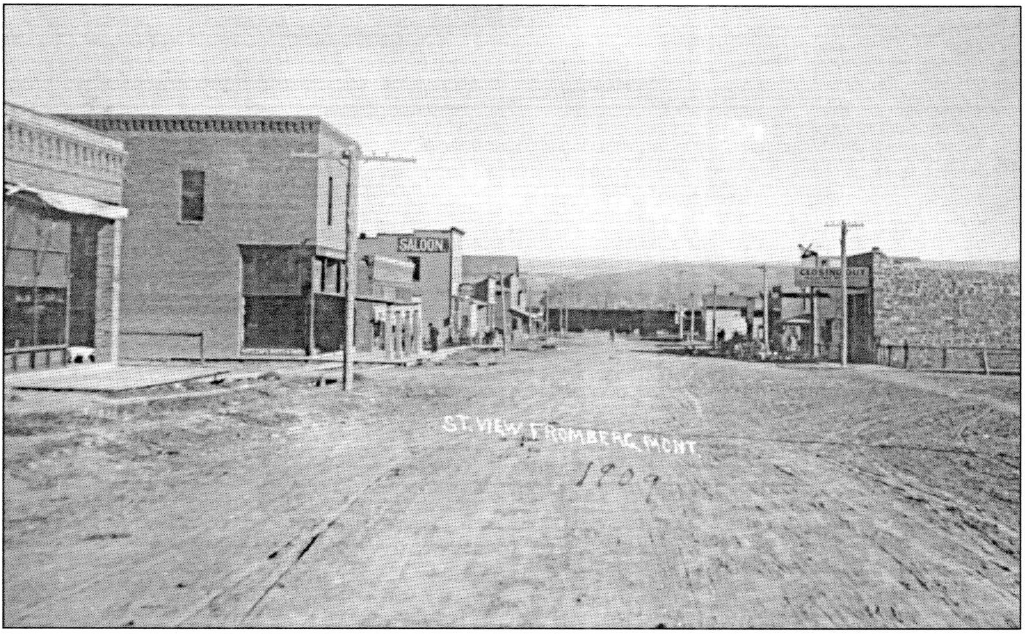

This 1909 photograph of Fromberg's River Street looks east toward a passing train on the railroad tracks. The electric power poles in this photograph provided the necessary infrastructure for the addition of telephone service in 1910 and streetlights in 1912. (CFVM.)

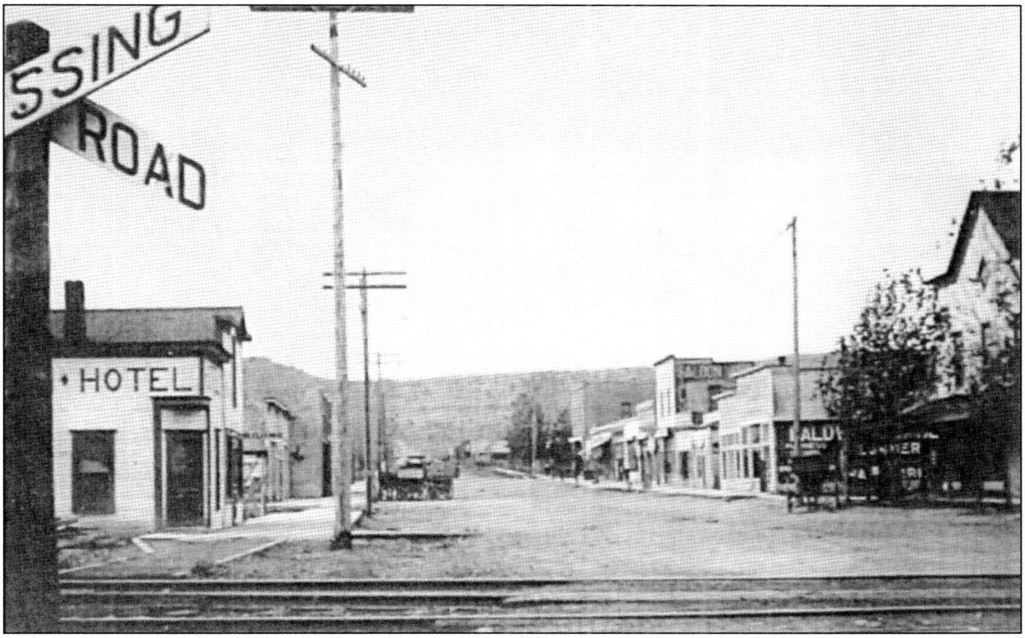

A west-looking view of Fromberg's River Street shows a trackside hotel on the left and the Baldwin Lumber and Hardware Store diagonally across River Street. The hotel pictured in this *c.* 1915 photograph is the Wall Hotel, previously known as the Hotel Osborne and the Valley Hotel. Today the Little Cowboy Bar and Museum occupies the western portion of Baldwin's Lumber and Hardware Store. (LCB.)

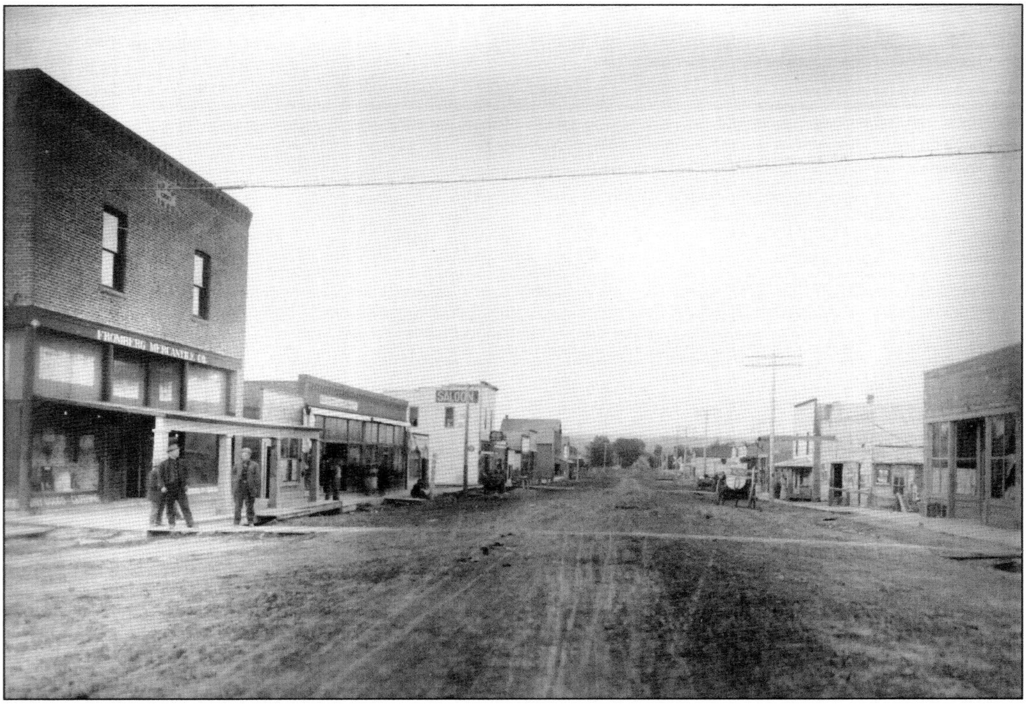

This 1910s photograph provides a detailed view of the growing business district operating along River Street. On the left, from foreground to background, are the Fromberg Mercantile Company, the Buzzetti and Emmett Store, a drugstore, and the Silver Dollar Saloon. On the right, the second building from the foreground is probably the blacksmith shop. (CFVM.)

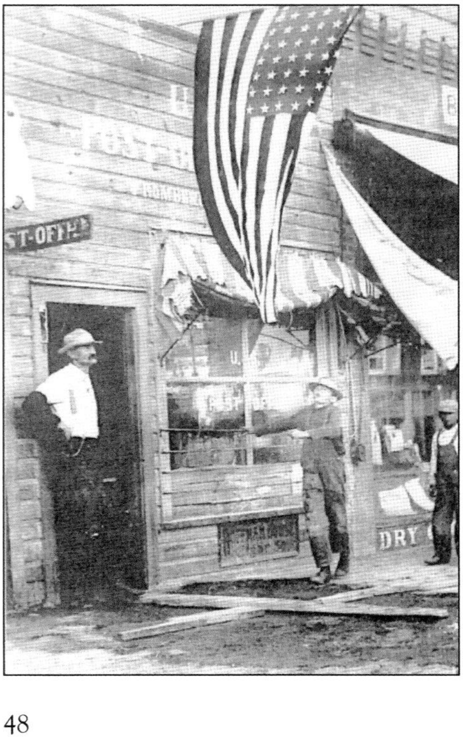

This very early Fromberg photograph reveals that the Fromberg Post Office once resided in a wooden building next to the Buzzetti and Emmett Store on the southern side of River Street. In other River Street photographs, the site of this building is empty. It is unknown when the building was demolished. (LCB.)

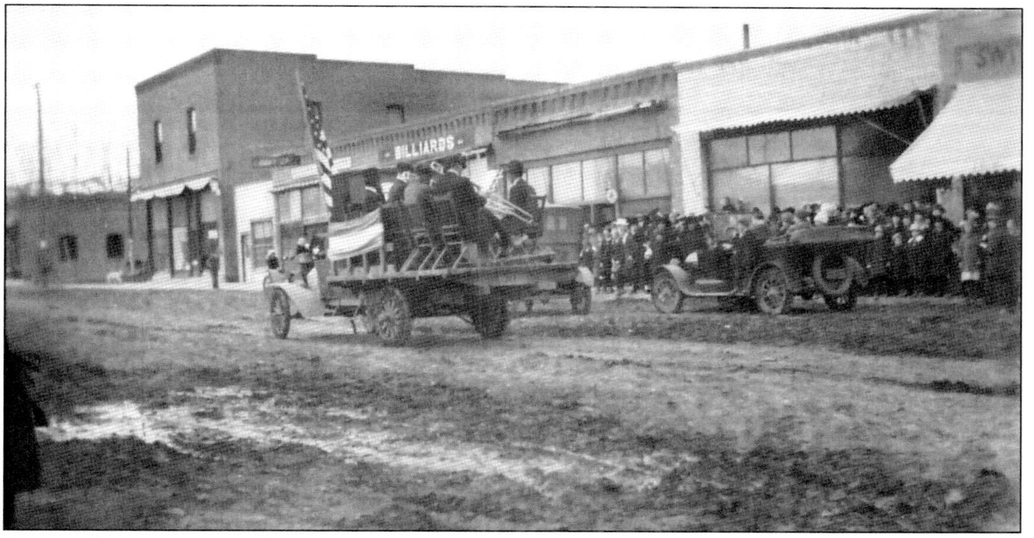

Pete Madsen, owner of a local auto, livery, and dray service, drives a community band along River Street during a 1913 parade. Madsen's business is out of frame on the left side of River Street. Identifiable instruments in use by the band included two trombones, a drum, and a piano loaded against the cab of the truck. (CFVM.)

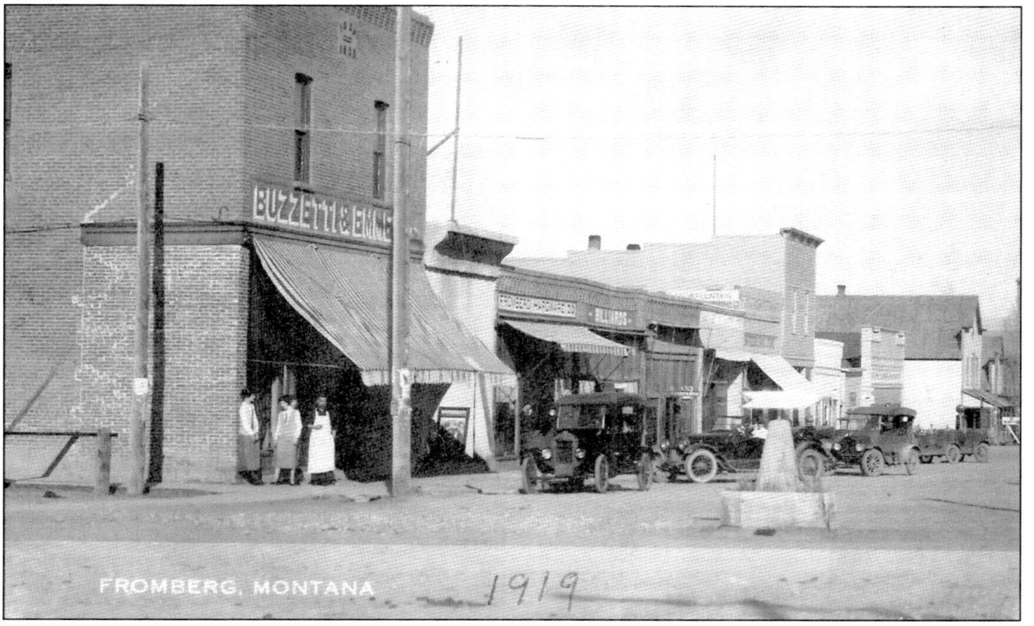

By 1919, businesses on the north side of River Street included, from foreground to background, the Buzzetti and Emmett Store, the Fromberg Hardware Company, the Buzzetti Billiards Hall, two unidentified stores, a drugstore with soda fountain, two more unidentified, and the Baldwin Lumber and Hardware Store. (Thayer.)

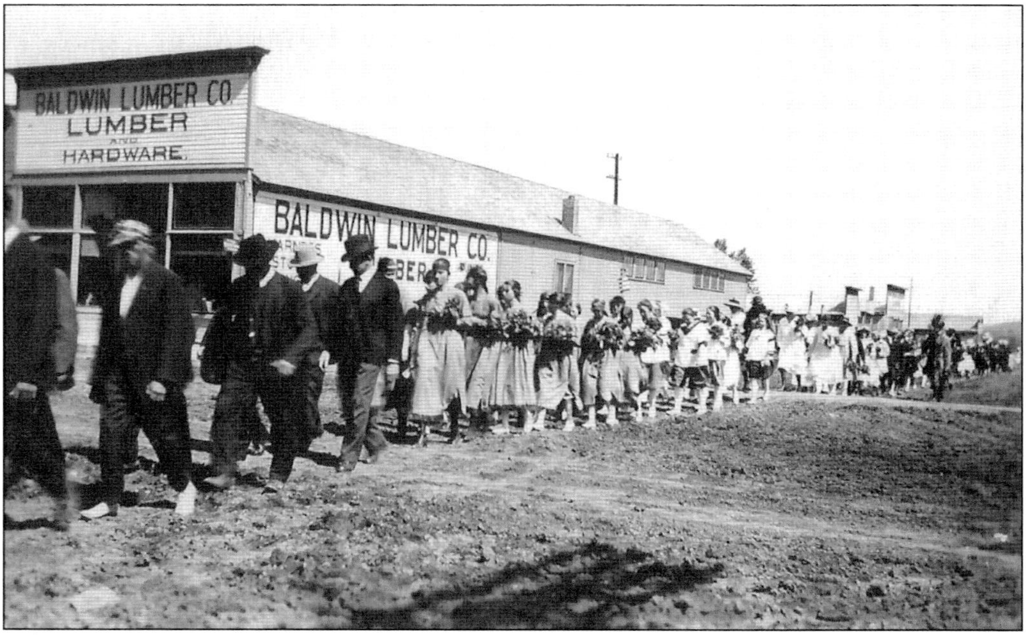

Either a May Day or Memorial Day parade marches across River Street past the Baldwin Lumber Company's lumber and hardware store. Note the muddy unpaved streets. Fromberg's streets remained unpaved until 1966 when the community funded, without bond issue or federal assistance, the paving of 30 blocks. Volunteers helped complete the project in only two weeks. (CFVM.)

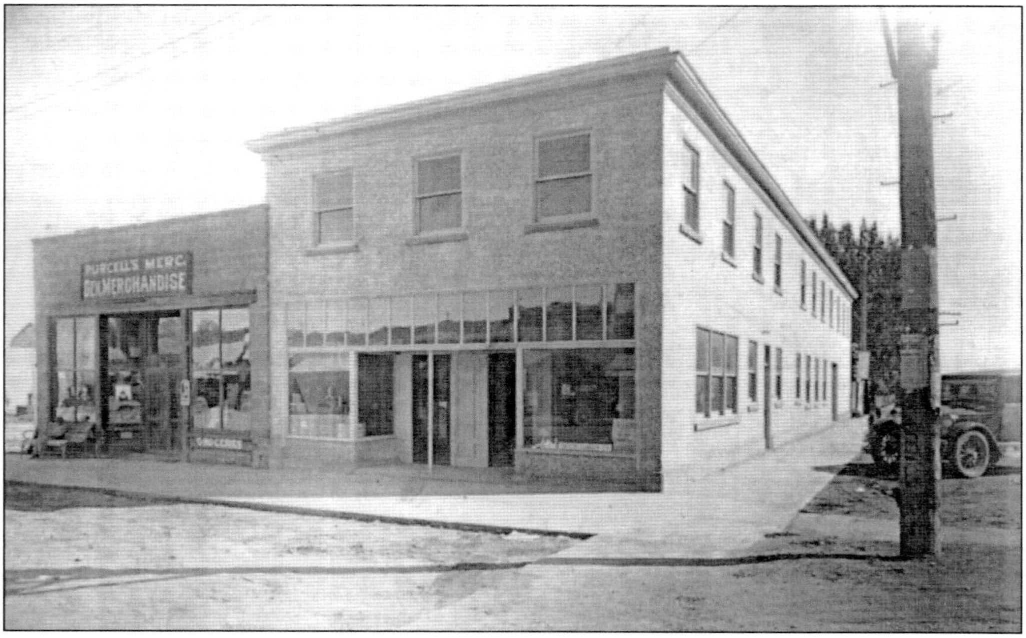

Businesses in this photograph are, from left to right, Purcell's Mercantile and the Gibson Lumber Company offices. Purcell's Mercantile primarily sold groceries. The Gibson Lumber Company competed with the Baldwin Lumber Company in Fromberg as well as several lumber companies in nearby Bridger and Belfry. (CFVM.)

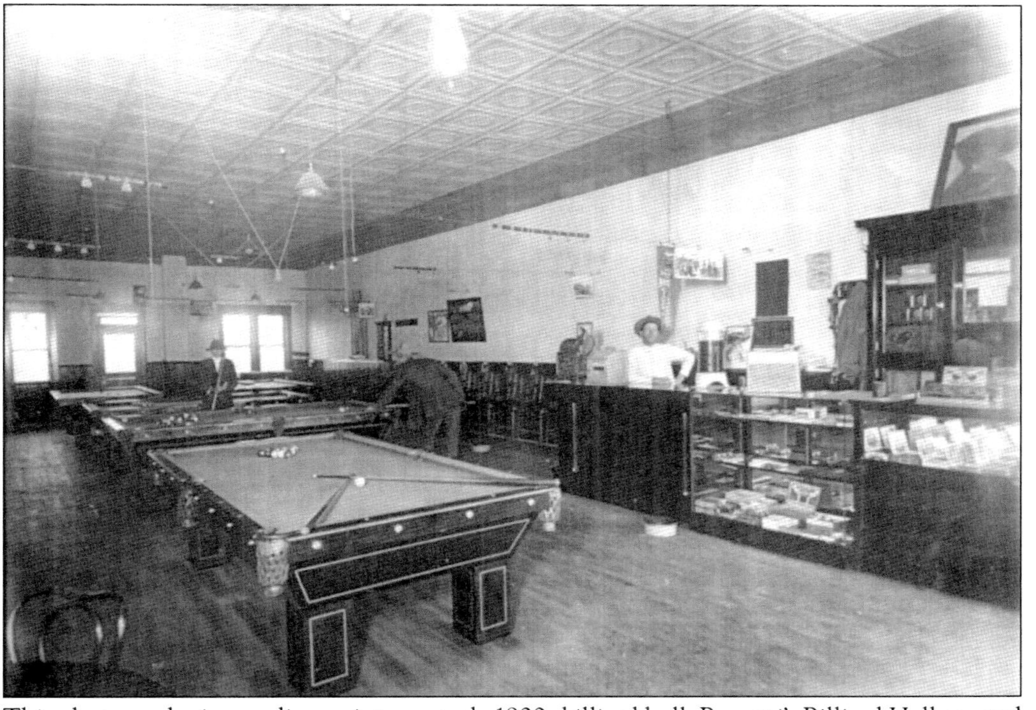

This photograph gives a glimpse into an early-1900s billiard hall. Buzzetti's Billiard Hall sported at least five billiard tables. The counter display includes a wide assortment of pipes, cigars, and chewing tobacco—notice the white spittoons on the floor. The men in this photograph are, from left to right, Mr. Massin, Joe Pokarney, and Frank Buzzetti. (CFVM.)

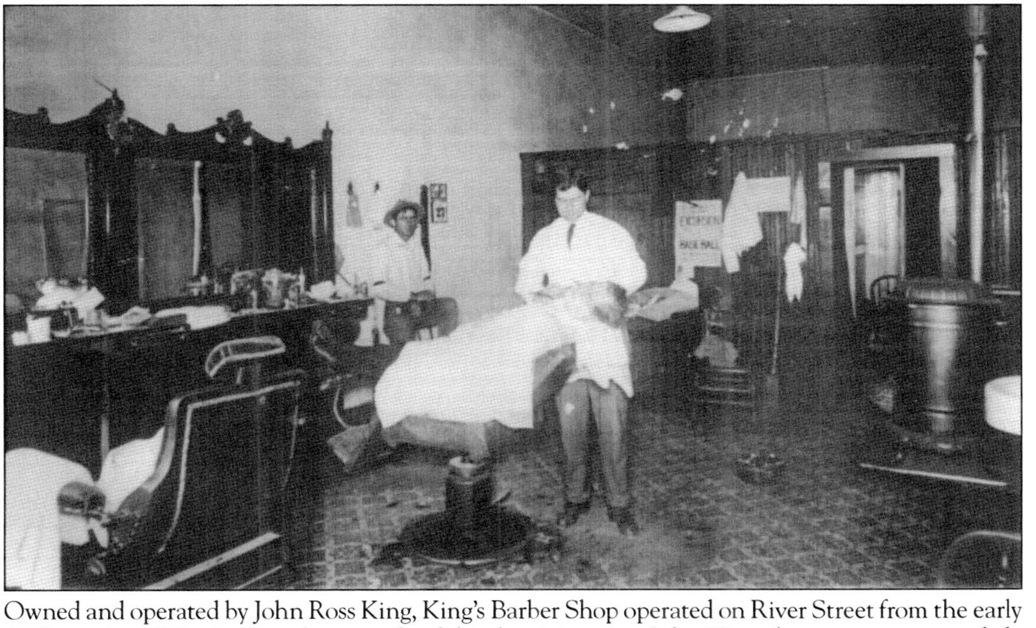

Owned and operated by John Ross King, King's Barber Shop operated on River Street from the early 1910s to the 1950s. In this photograph of the shop's interior, John King shaves a customer while another customer waits for his turn next to the razor strop hanging on the wall. (CFVM.)

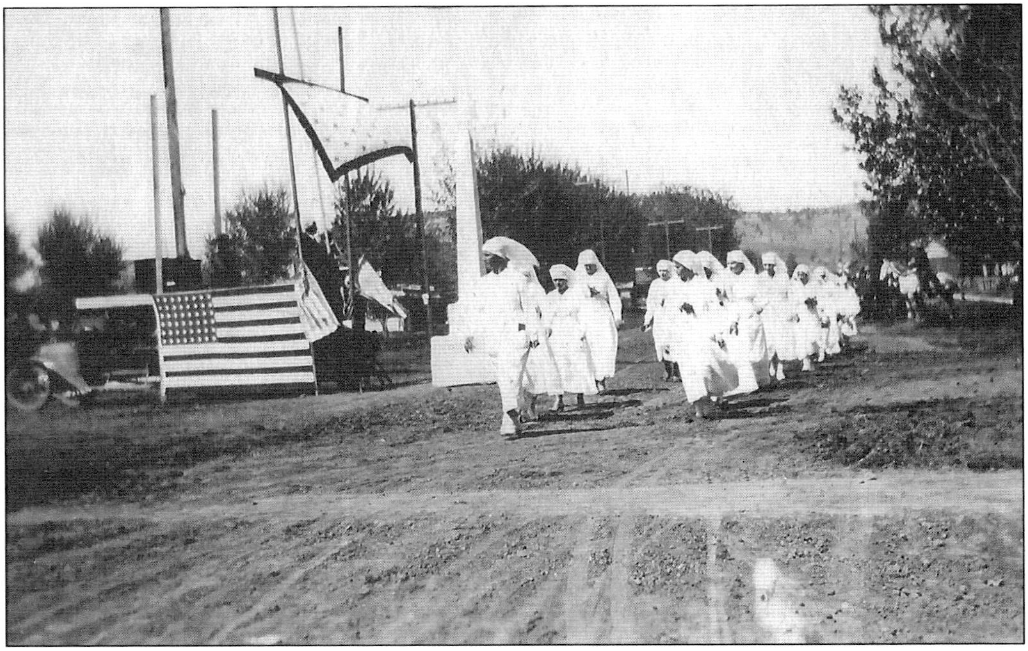

The fervent patriotism brought on by World War I made its way into the Fromberg High School when school superintendent Lambert added a boy's military drill team and girl's sewing circle to the curriculum. The girl's sewing circle knitted many blankets and sent them overseas to American soldiers. In these photographs, the Fromberg High School boys and girls show off their talents and patriotism during the 1918 Labor Day parade. The girls (above) dressed as nurses for the parade, while the boys performed a military drill with wooden rifles (below). The drill sergeant in this photograph is Donald McCall. (Both, CFVM.)

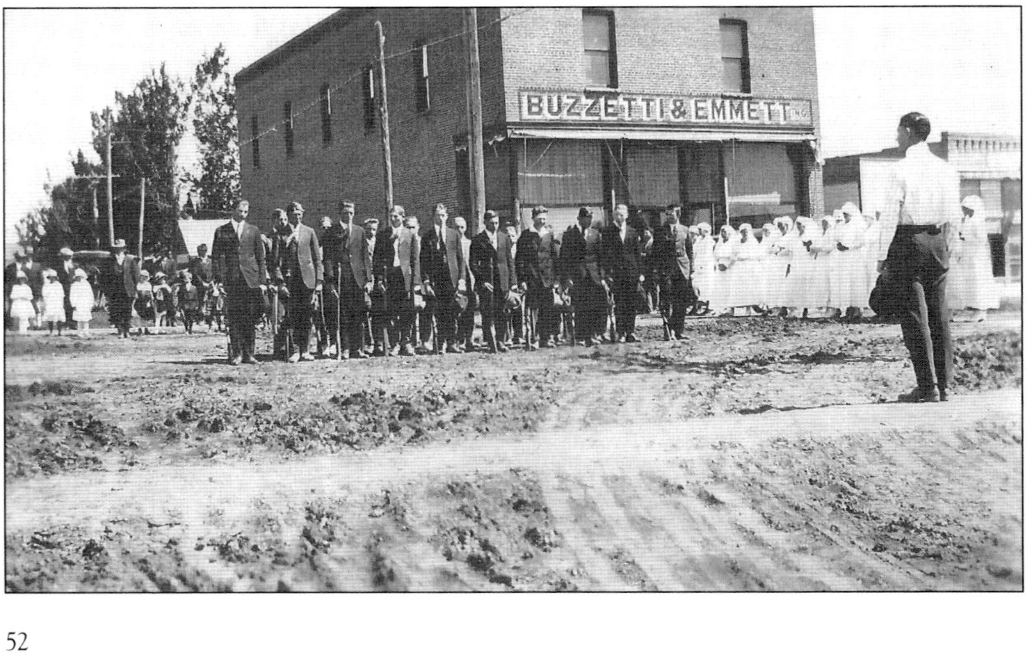

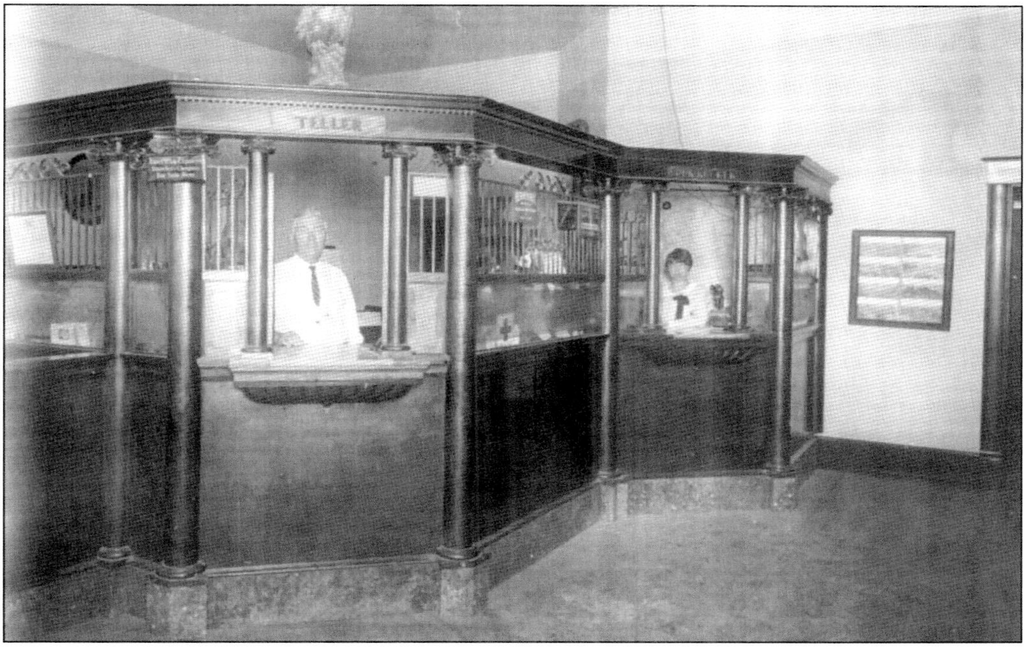

The Clark's Fork Valley Bank received its Montana State Charter in 1908. Unlike so many Carbon County banks, the Clark's Fork Valley Bank survived the Great Depression and continued on as a State bank until 1963 when it transferred to a national charter. This photograph shows a 1920s view of the interior of the bank. (CFVM.)

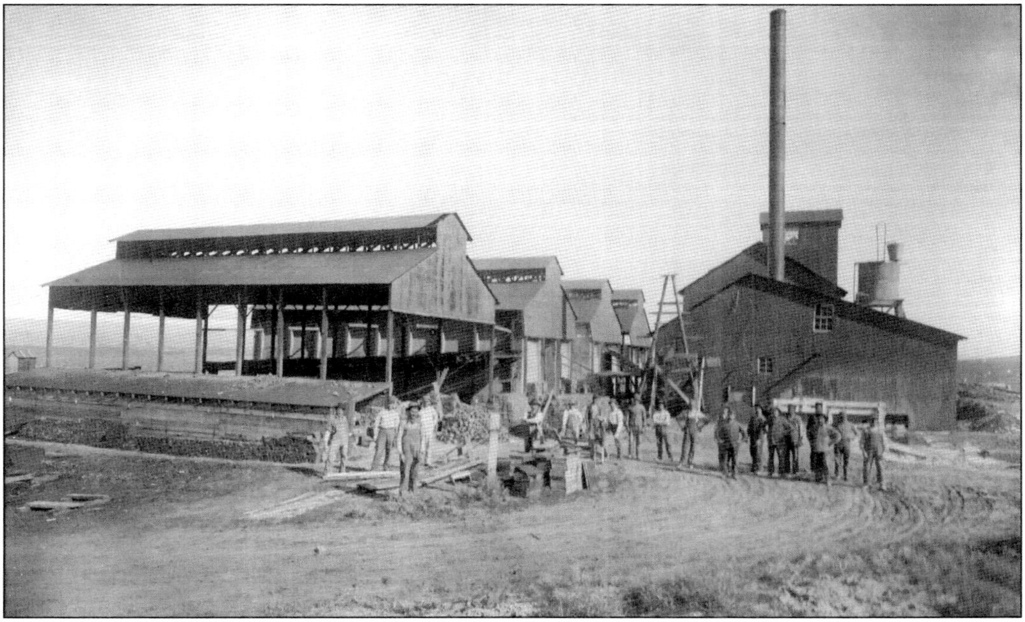

In addition to his many coal interests, Samuel Gebo founded the Fromberg Pressed Brick and Tile Company. At peak production, the factory produced 20,000 bricks a day using four kilns. No remnants of the factory remain, but its legacy lives on in the many buildings constructed of Fromberg bricks and still in use a century later. (CFVM.)

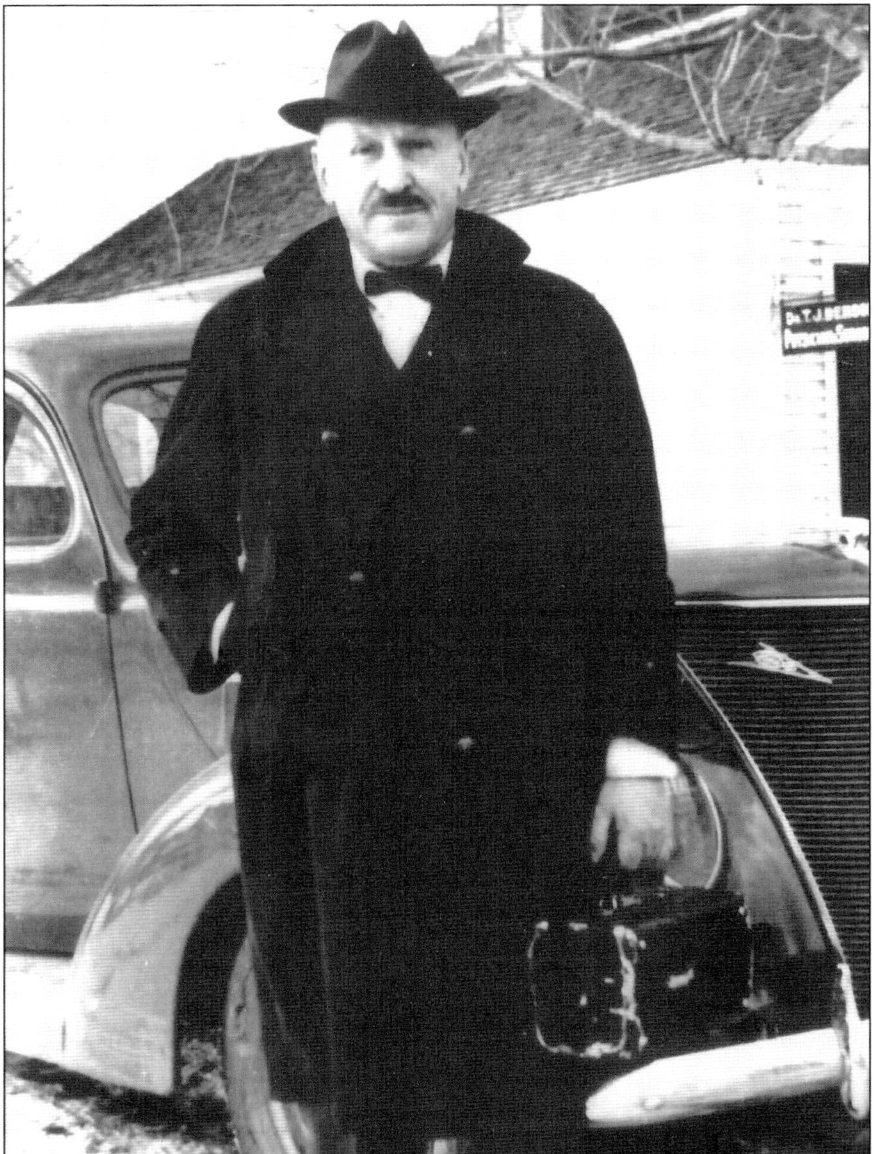

Only three years old at the time, Dr. Theodore J. Benson likely did not remember the 1876 undoing of the James-Younger gang in his hometown of Northfield, Minnesota. However, he did learn the strong sense of community cooperation the citizens of that small Minnesota town exhibited that day. A University of Minnesota graduate, Dr. Benson came to Bridger in 1906 to practice with classmate and eventual Billings Clinic founder, Dr. Arthur J. Movius Sr. Benson soon relocated to Fromberg, which had no practicing doctor at that time, to become the Clark's Fork Coal Company's physician. Dr. Benson's 45 years of service to Fromberg and the surrounding areas included delivering nearly 3,000 babies, serving as mayor, serving on the school board, and supporting many civic projects throughout the area. Dr. Benson's generosity included financial assistance to friends and neighbors for things such as home and land purchases and college tuition for their children. (CFVM.)

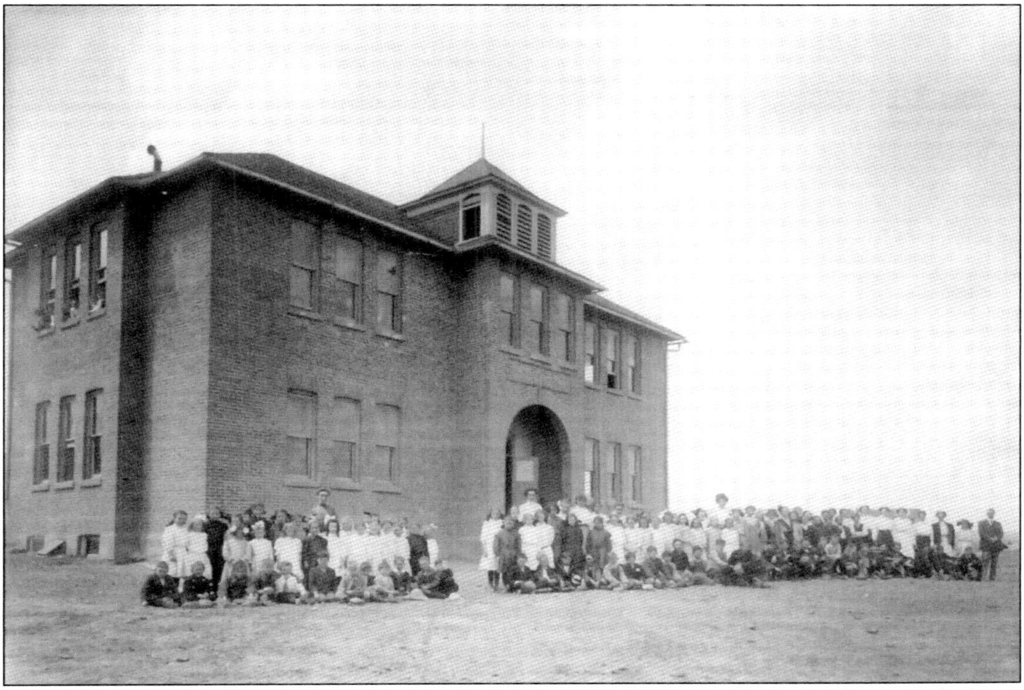

These photographs show Fromberg's first brick schoolhouse built in 1908. The photograph above shows 110 students and four instructors posed in front of the school. The photograph below shows the interior of a classroom with 42 students. Although fire destroyed this school in 1915, a replacement brick building welcomed students the very next year. (Both, CFVM.)

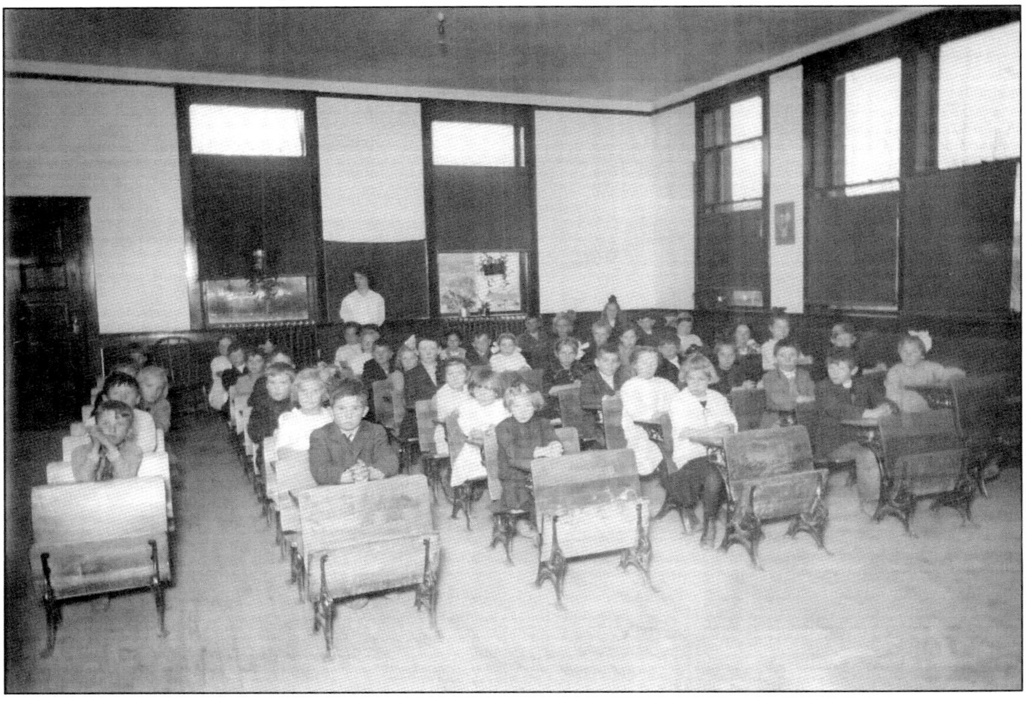

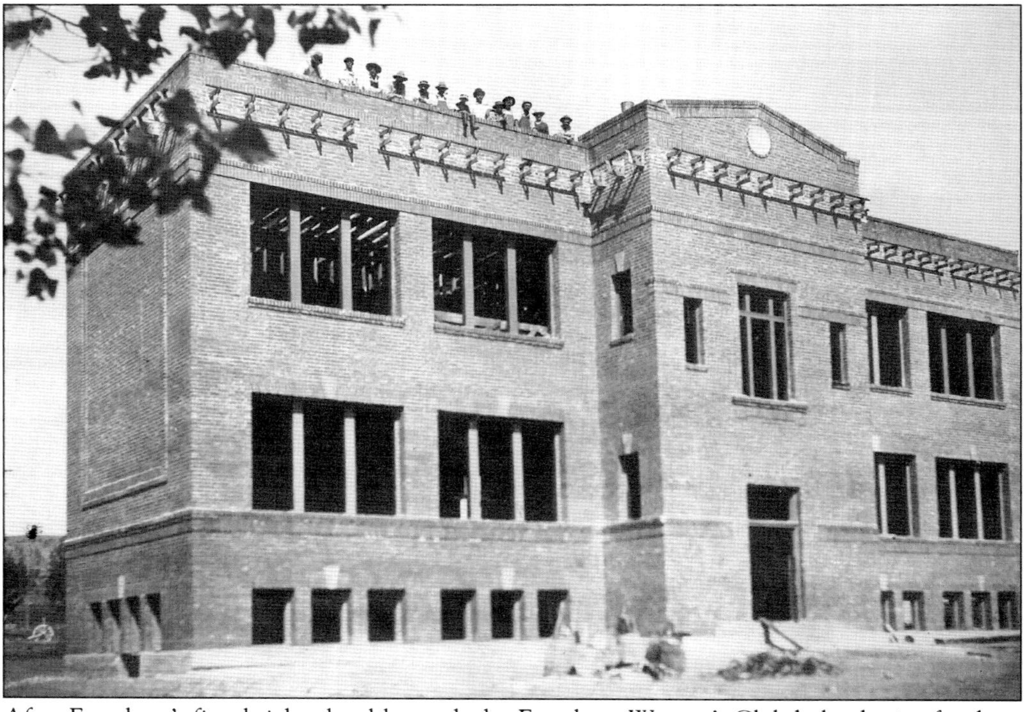

After Fromberg's first brick school burned, the Fromberg Women's Club helped raise funds to build a new brick structure by selling brick-shaped pages out of booklets at 10¢ each. The new school opened in 1916 under Principal Bill Ross. The Fromberg School District added the first and second years of high school in 1913 and the third and fourth years of high school in 1914. These photographs show the new school building during its construction (above) and some years later (below). Over the years, this structure saw several remodels and the addition of a gymnasium to keep up with increasing student populations. (Both, CFVM.)

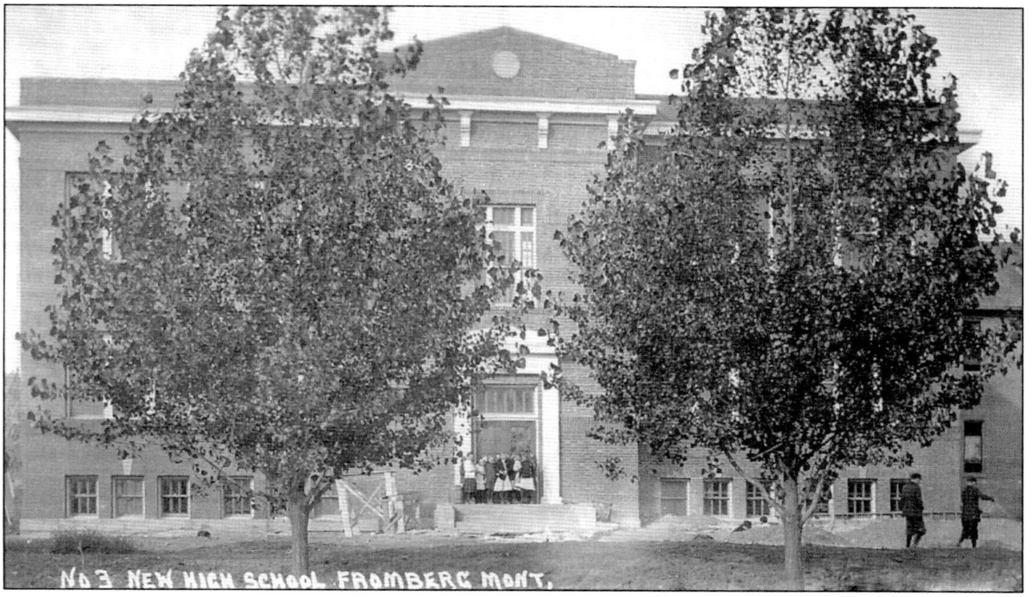

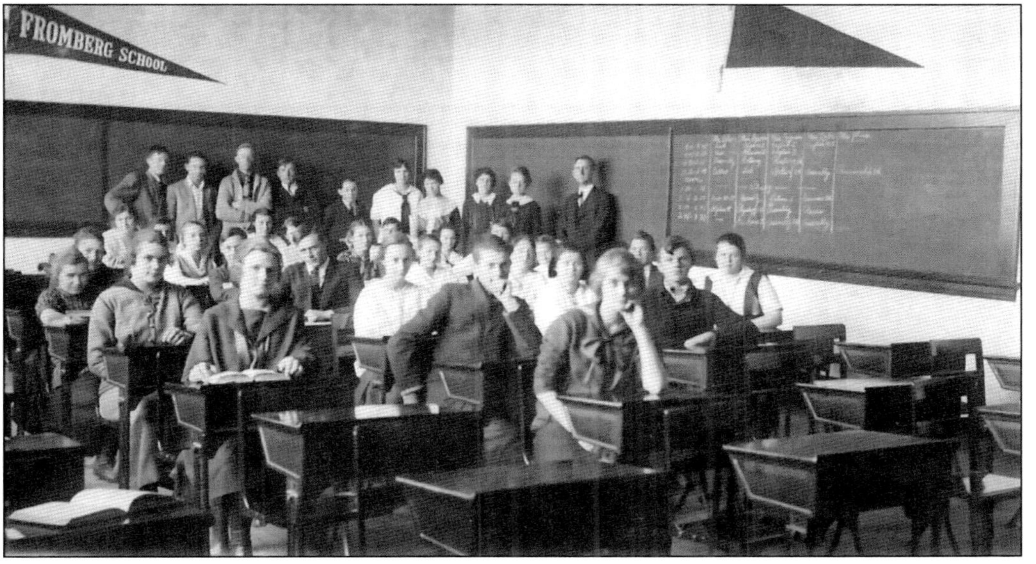

The Fromberg High School's student body posed for this 1915 photograph in the first brick school building. The following year, six of these students became Fromberg's first graduating class and the first class to graduate from the new brick school building. The 1916 graduates included Katherine Foss, Helen McCall, Neil McDonough, Alice Nerlin, Vida Nerlin, and Alfred Parker. (CFVM.)

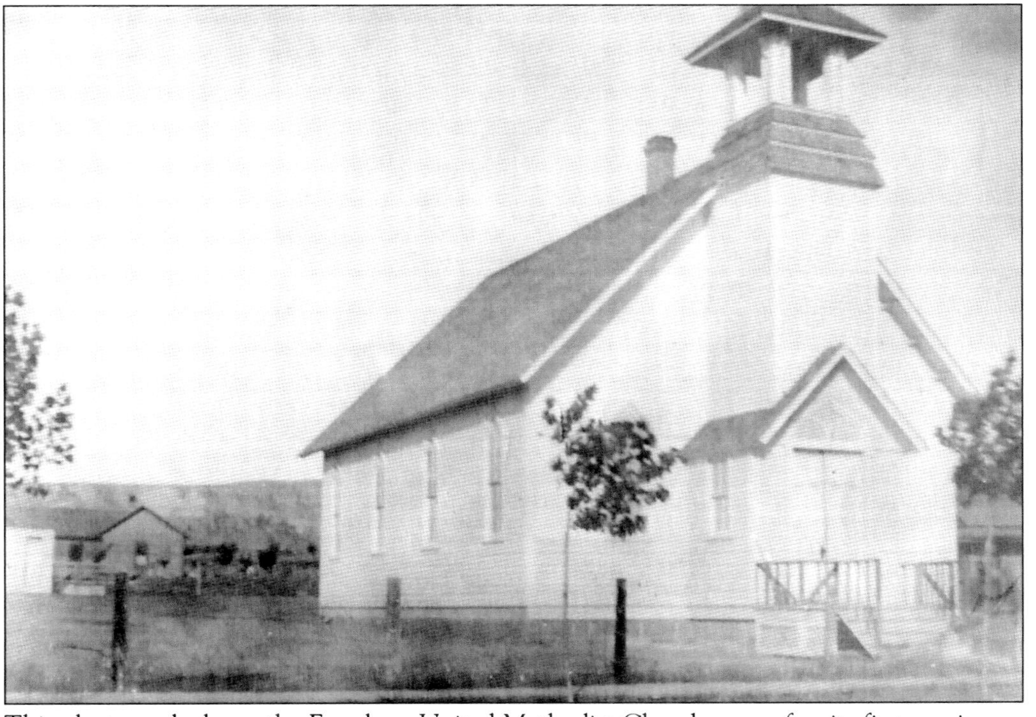

This photograph shows the Fromberg United Methodist Church soon after its first service on January 26, 1908. The roots of this church started in Gebo when Red Lodge's Rev. John G. Clark held the first Protestant service there on June 13, 1897, in a boardinghouse tent. The Fromberg Methodist Church is listed on the National Register of Historic Places. (CFVM.)

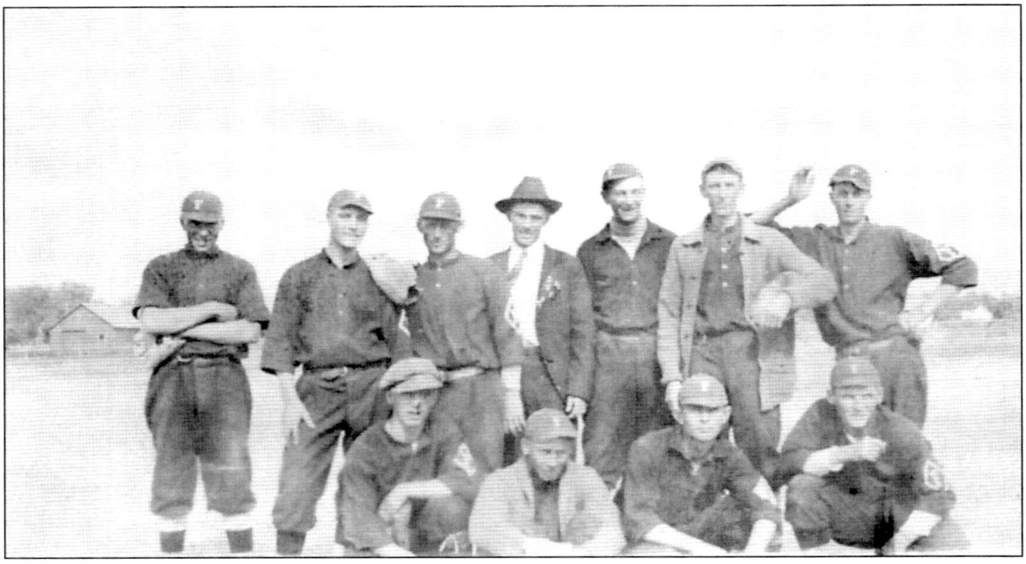

Baseball provided essential relief from the day-to-day struggles of building Carbon County into the agricultural and mining powerhouse it became. Every town in Carbon County fielded a squad, and teams and fans traveled by railroad to attend out-of-town games. The photograph above illustrates an early-1900s Fromberg baseball team on what is likely Fromberg's first baseball field. (Andersen.)

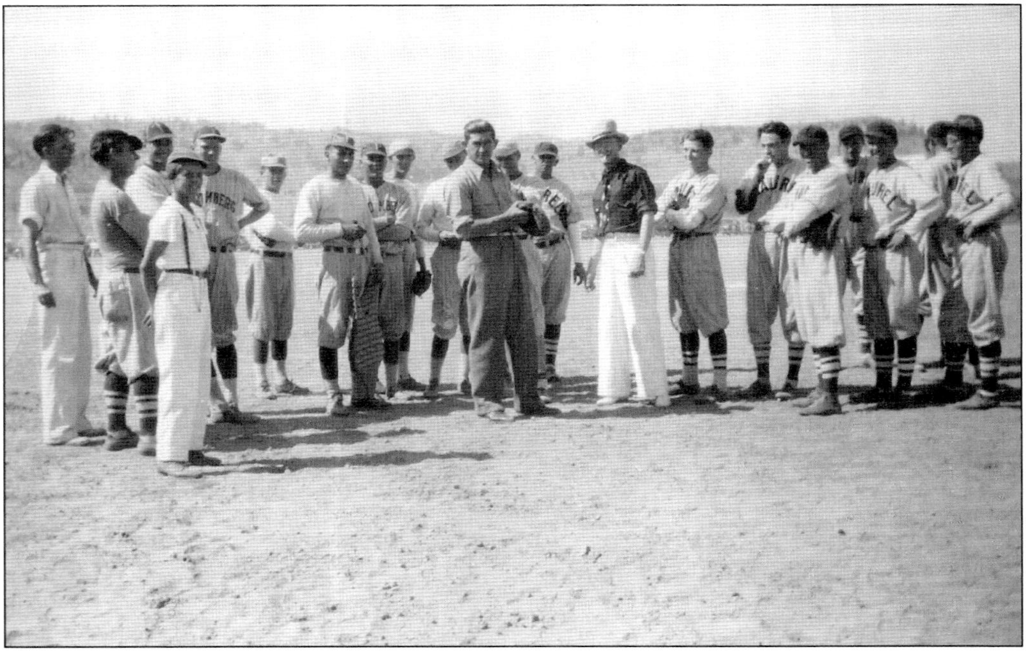

In this 1940s photograph, Gordon Stanley "Mickey" Cochrane, Baseball Hall of Fame member and three-time World Series winner, stands in dark pants between the Fromberg (left) and Laurel (right) baseball teams in Fromberg. After retiring from baseball, Cochrane and his family came to Montana. Mickey ran a dude ranch in the Beartooth Mountain foothills, and his brother Archie built a successful Ford dealership in Billings. (CFVM.)

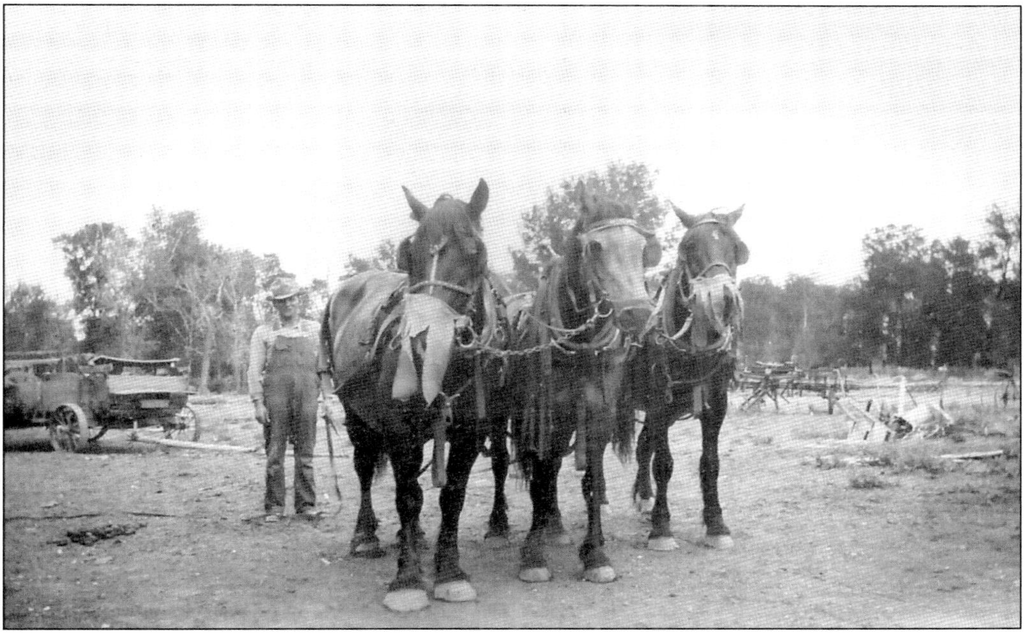

Otto Yedlicka poses with a team of three draught horses in this 1930s photograph. Otto's parents, James and Marie, homesteaded near Gebo in April 1897. Like the descendants of so many other homesteaders in Clark's Fork Valley, the Yedlicka family continues over a century of farming heritage in the Clark's Fork Valley. (Andersen.)

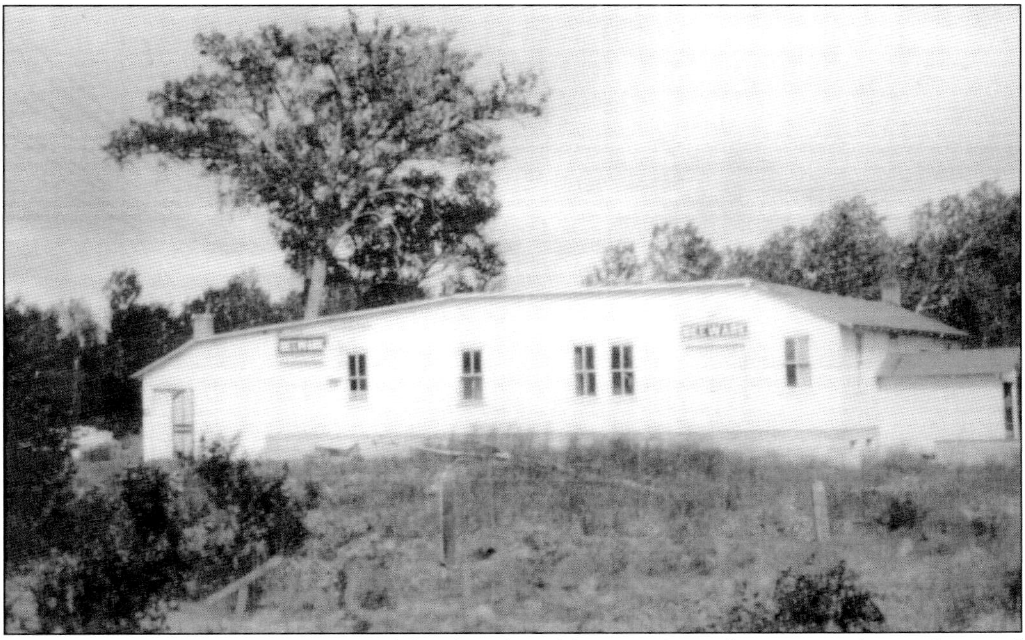

Several apiaries, taking advantage of the abundant foliage in the valley, operated in and around Fromberg throughout the years. This photograph shows the Charles Phillips honey house. This building held equipment to extract and purify the honey collected from hives placed around the Fromberg area. The building also acted as a warehouse for the purified honey. (CFVM.)

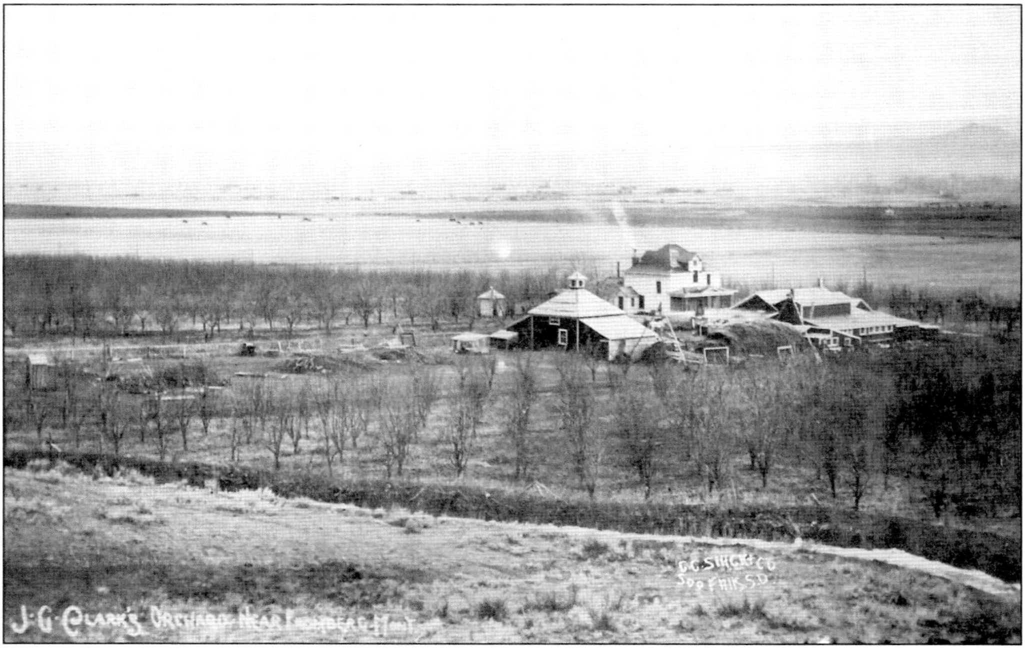

Methodist minister John G. Clark began his Carbon County ministry in Red Lodge during the 1890s, relocated to Joliet for a time, and finally settled on 40 acres of land south of Fromberg while holding church services in Gebo. Reverend Clark purchased the land in 1897 and planted one of the Clark's Fork Valley's first commercially successful orchards. The early-1900s photograph above shows Clark's home and surrounding orchards. By 1909, a local paper reported that Clark's orchard proved that the Clark's Fork Valley could sustain fruit agriculture. In the photograph below, Reverend Clark (left) hauls apples to market. (Above, K. Hergenrider; below, CFVM.)

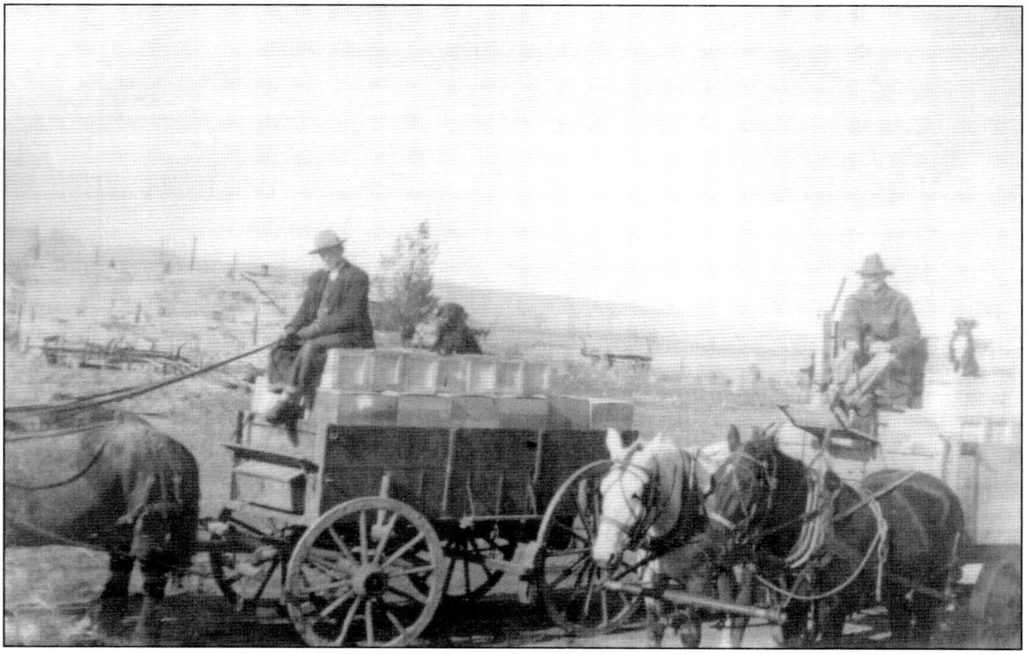

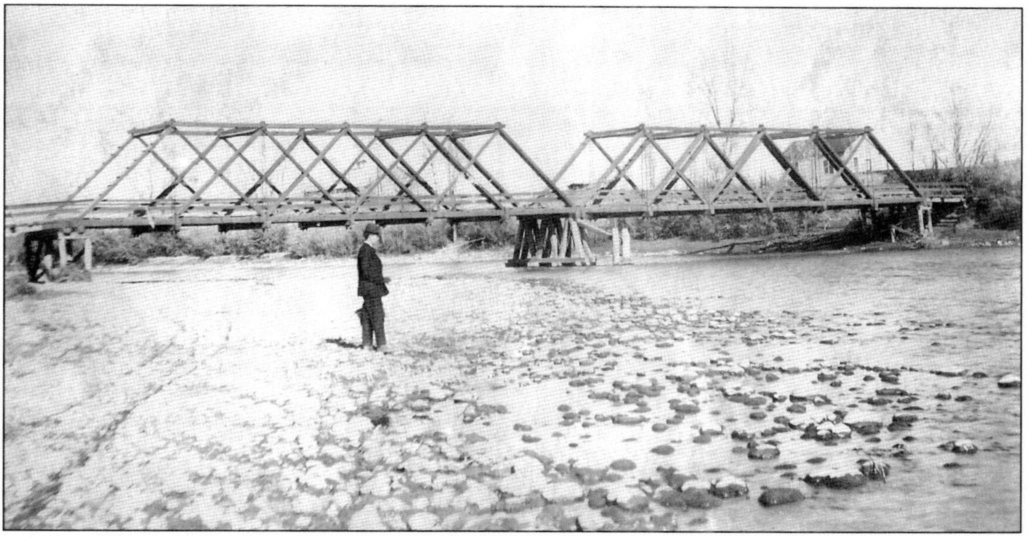

When Carbon County officials condemned the original timber truss bridge spanning the Clark's Fork River at Fromberg (above), work started immediately to replace it with a reinforced concrete span (below), using concrete from Fromberg's Gibson Concrete Company. The new bridge opened in January 1915. John Gibson's Concrete Company spurred Carbon County to begin replacing and constructing new bridges out of reinforced concrete. From 1911 to 1931, Carbon County replaced over half of its 129 bridges with reinforced concrete. John Gibson's company constructed 23 of these bridges and supplied concrete for most of the others. The original concrete bridge is listed on the National Register of Historic Places. (Both, CFVM.)

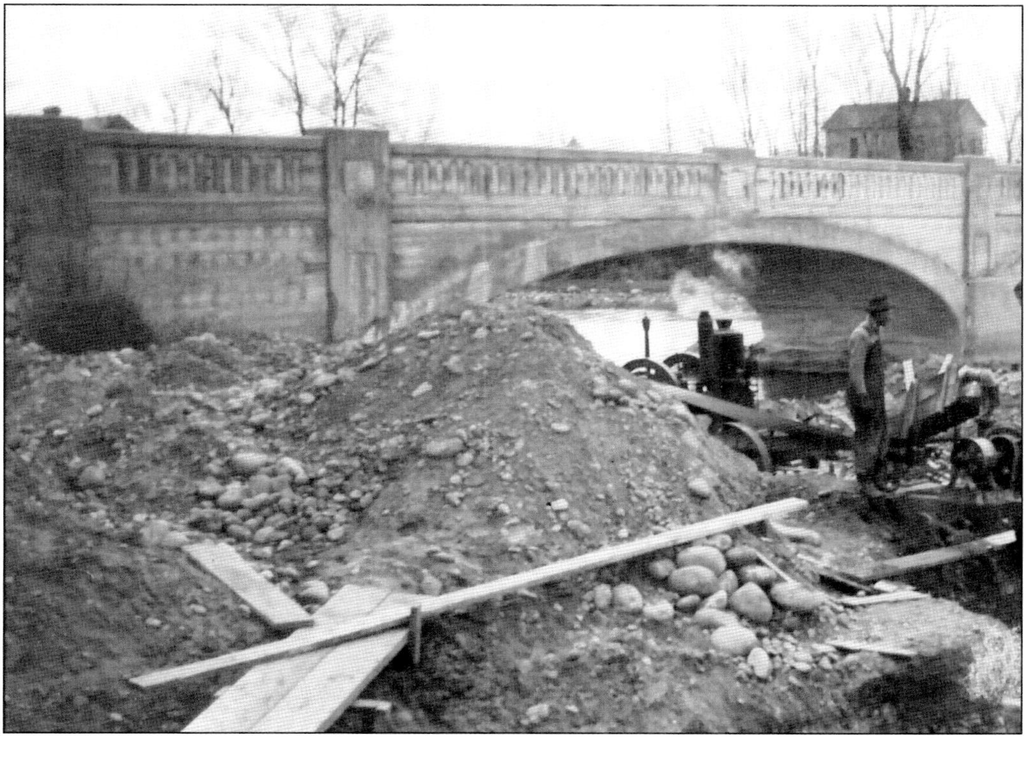

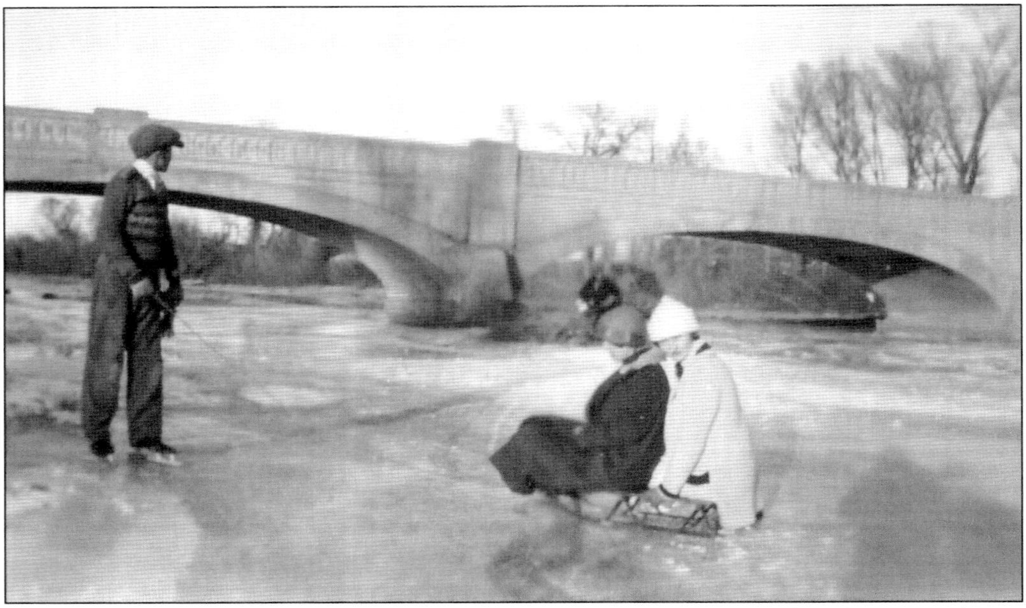

The Clark's Fork Valley winters provided a thick layer of river ice to harvest for refrigeration during the summers. The ice also provided valley children with skating and sledding opportunities as shown in the 1910s photograph above. The thick river ice also proved dangerous at times. As the ice began to break up in the spring, it dammed the Clark's Fork River, forcing it to overflow its banks and flood low-lying areas with water and large pieces of ice. The photograph below shows the aftermath of one such flood as a house stands surrounded by blocks of ice after the floodwaters receded. (Above, CFVM; below, Andersen.)

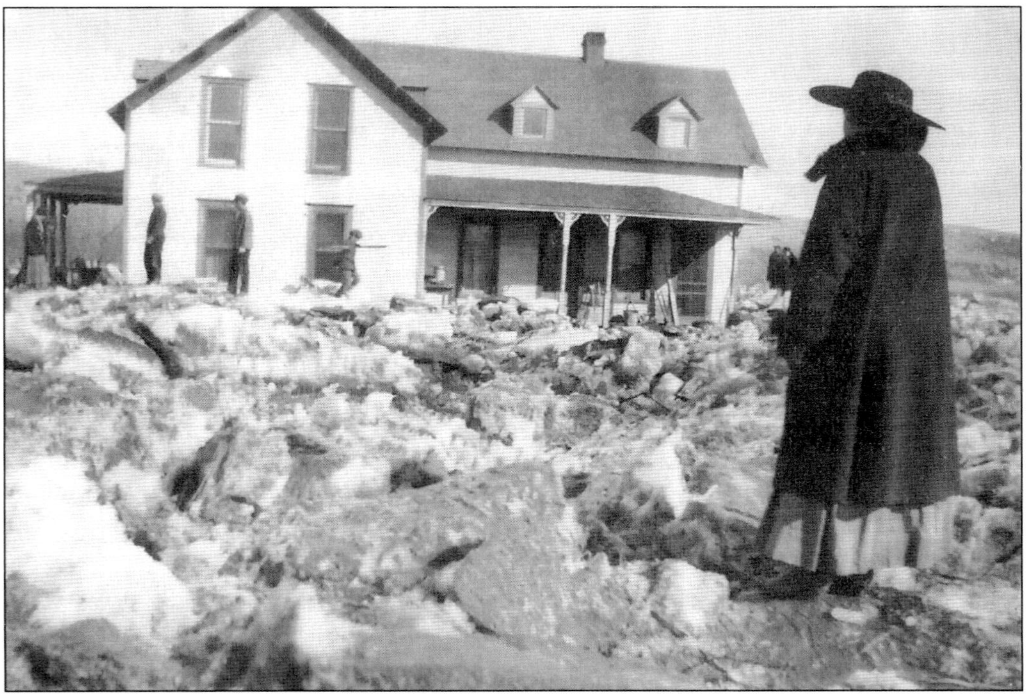

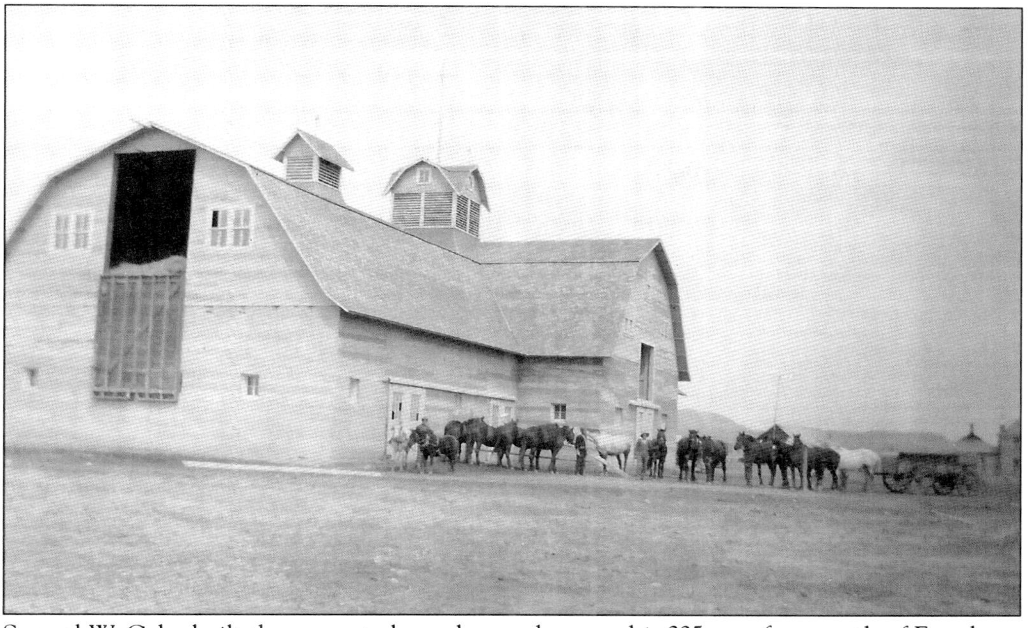

Samuel W. Gebo built the concrete barn shown above on his 335-acre farm south of Fromberg. Gebo used the barn to house his stable of purebred Belgian workhorses. Built between 1907 and 1909 of Gibson Concrete, the barn still stands and is listed on the National Register of Historic Places. (CCHS.)

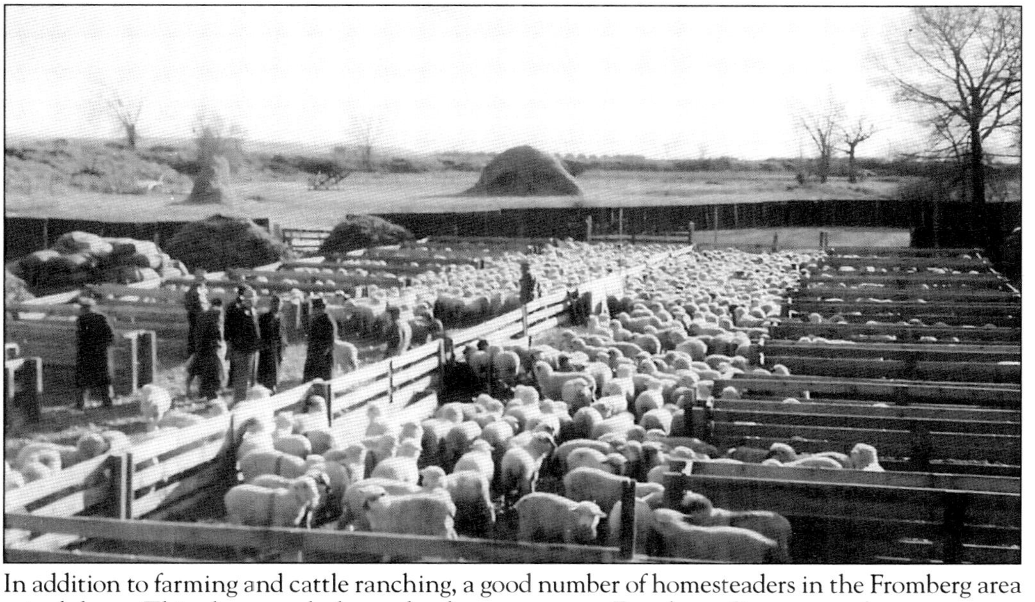

In addition to farming and cattle ranching, a good number of homesteaders in the Fromberg area raised sheep. This photograph shows the sheep pens near Fromberg. Once a year, buyers came to the area to purchase wool from these farmers. (CFVM.)

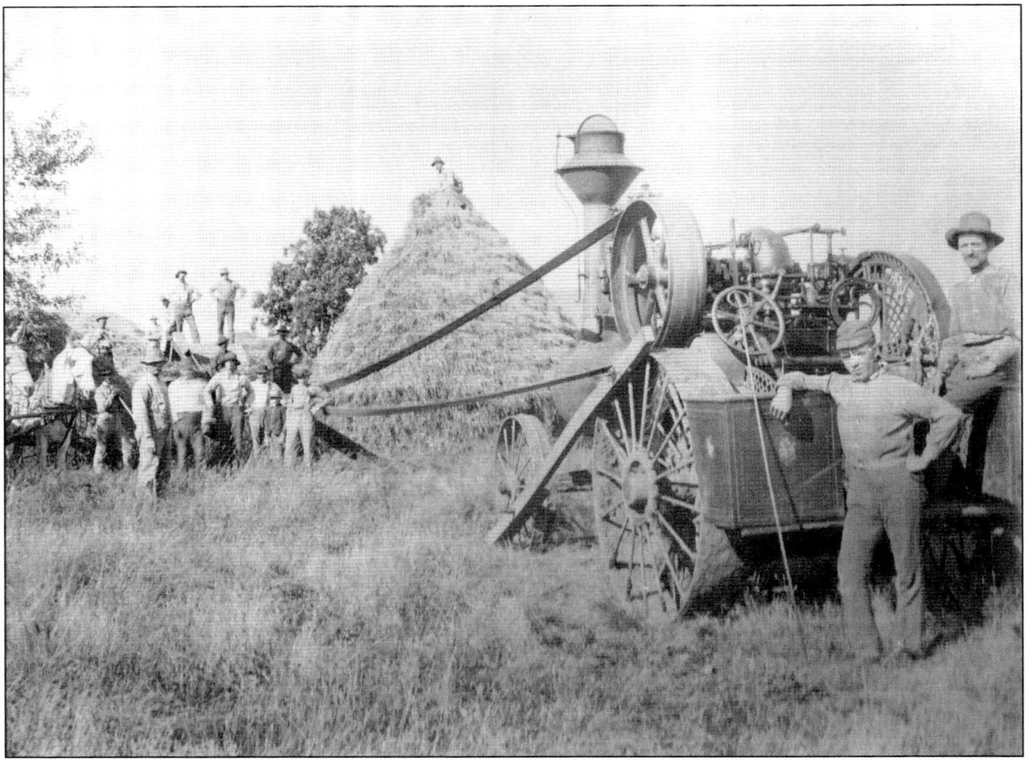

Providing feed for their livestock over the long Montana winters dominated the summertime activities of ranchers. This 1910s photograph shows a haying crew near Fromberg using an early steam-powered tractor to help stack hay for feeding their herds over the winter. (CFVM.)

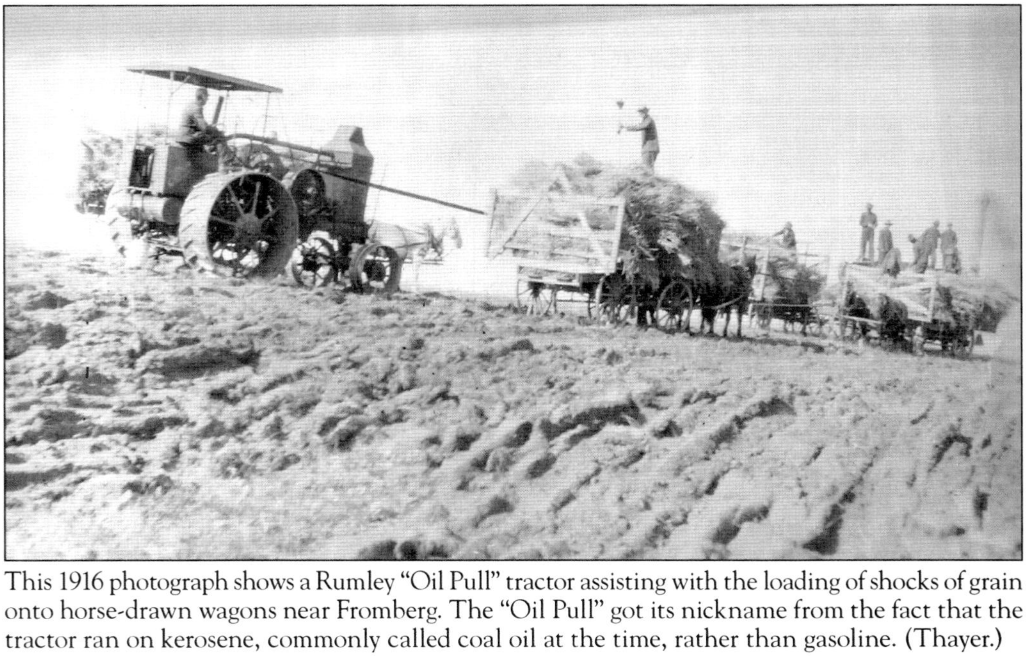

This 1916 photograph shows a Rumley "Oil Pull" tractor assisting with the loading of shocks of grain onto horse-drawn wagons near Fromberg. The "Oil Pull" got its nickname from the fact that the tractor ran on kerosene, commonly called coal oil at the time, rather than gasoline. (Thayer.)

Six

Bridger and the Dry Creek Oil Camp

The town of Bridger began its modern history in 1864, when Jim Bridger blazed a wagon route through the Clark's Fork Valley to provide a less dangerous alternative to the Bozeman Trail from Denver, Colorado, to the Virginia City, Montana, goldfields. This trail crossed the Clark's Fork River at what was known as "Bridger's Crossing" and followed the river north. In 1898, Butte Copper King William A. Clark helped finance the Northern Pacific Railroad's expansion of its line from Fromberg, Montana, to his nearby coal mine. That same year, a post office was opened to serve the community. With the opening of Clark's coal mine, an informal community formed nearby. Going by the names of Georgetown and Stringtown, the name Bridger, suggested by George "Daddy" Town, a friend of Jim Bridger's and the first to mine coal in the area, eventually stuck. Bridger was platted on February 27, 1902, by A. H. Wethey. With the closing of the Bridger coal mine around 1915, homesteaders of the late 1890s and early 1900s supported the quickly growing town. They raised cattle, sheep, dryland wheat, pinto beans, and sugar beets. Bridger soon grew to be the second largest city in Carbon County. Throughout its lifetime, Bridger housed a bank, an elementary school and a high school, hotels, several mercantile stores, lumber mills, and a 300-seat opera house. The 1920s discovery of oil on Dry Creek, southwest of Bridger, further mitigated the loss of the Clark's Fork Valley's coal industry. Developed by the Ohio Oil Company, later Marathon Oil, and situated on land initially owned by Dr. Samuel Mott Souders of Red Lodge, a fully operational camp soon emerged to support workers of the drilling operation. Bridger housed Carbon County's only Civilian Conservation Corps camp during the Great Depression. An array of churches served members of the Bridger community. These churches included the Church of the Good Shepherd, Sacred Heart Catholic Church, Saint Paul's Lutheran Church, the Seventh Day Adventist Church, the United Methodist Church, and the Bridger Baptist Church.

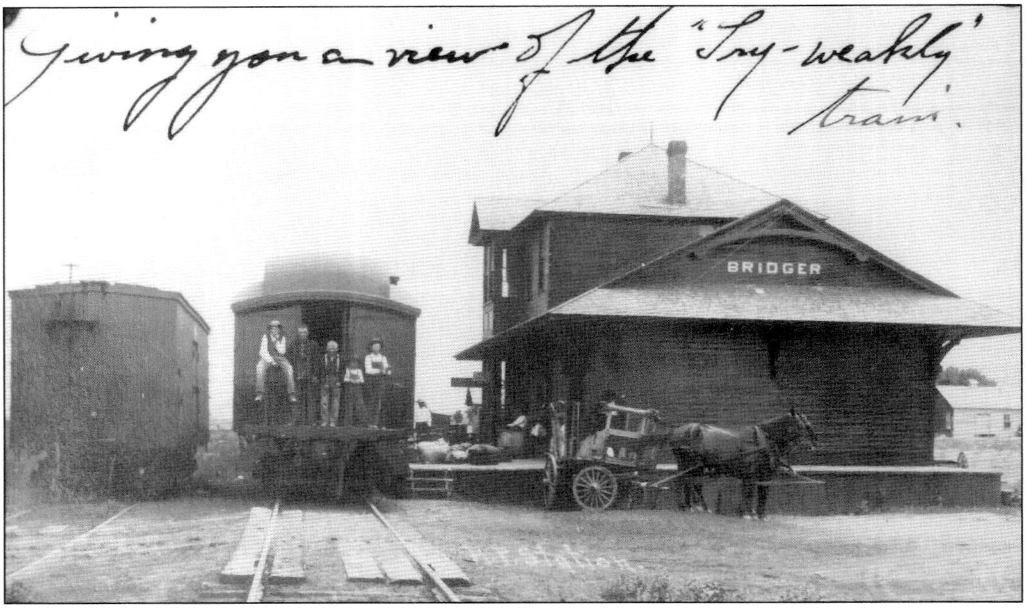

With a clever twist of words, the sender of this May 31, 1910, postcard clearly indicates his opinion of early passenger train reliability. By 1910, railroad passenger service ferried Clark's Fork Valley residents from all valley towns to bigger cities, such as Billings, to the north and Cody and Lovell, Wyoming, to the south. (CCHS.)

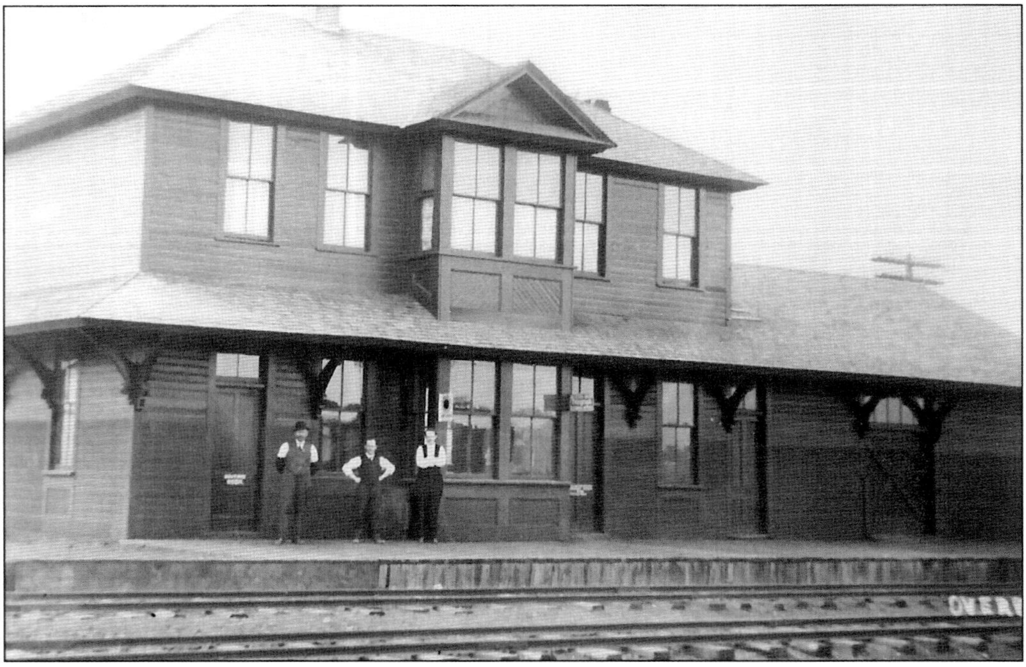

This early-1900s photograph shows a trackside view of the third Bridger train station located on East Broadway Avenue. The Northern Pacific Railroad arrived in Bridger thanks to the financing of Butte Copper King William A. Clark. To make his coal mine holdings near Bridger viable, Clark financed construction of the grade and bridges from Gebo to Bridger. (CCHS.)

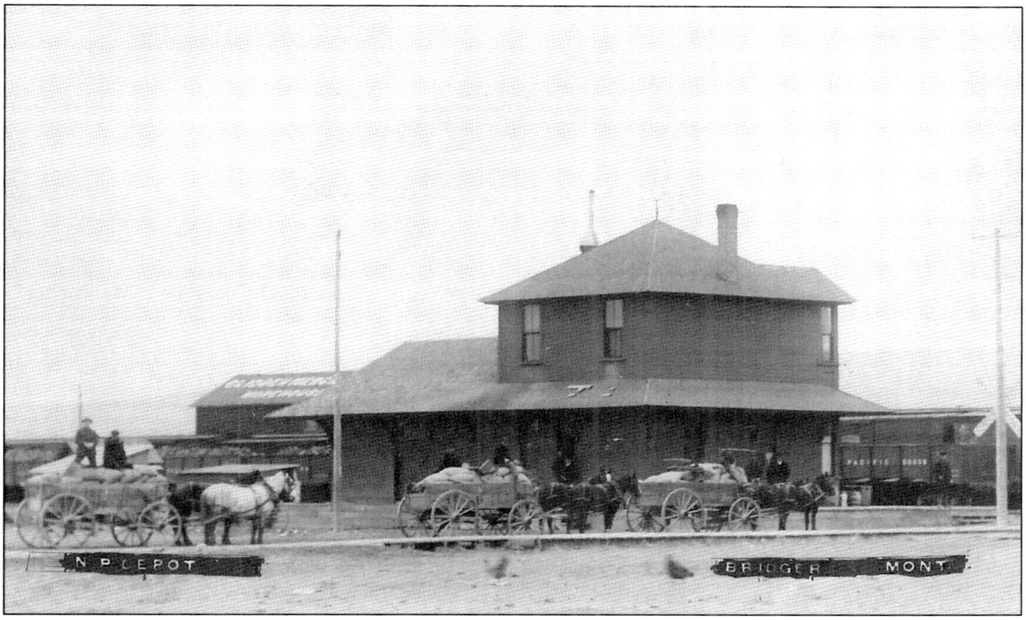

This early-1900s photograph shows the town-side view of the third Bridger train. In exchange for William A. Clark's financing of the Northern Pacific Railroad's line from Gebo to Bridger, Clark's coal company received reduced rates on several services such as railcar weighing and preparing bills of lading. (K. Hergenrider.)

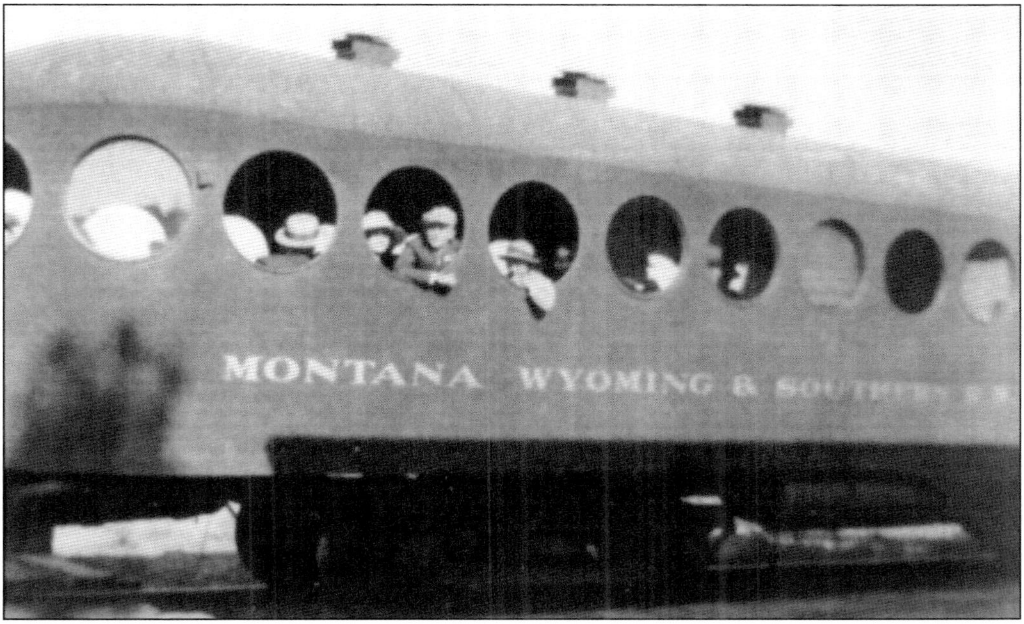

In 1917, The Montana, Wyoming, and Southern Railroad purchased a McKeen Motor Car Company passenger car for service between Bridger and Washoe. McKeen passenger cars had their own engines. Although officially named the Bear Creek, valley residents soon referred to the car as the "Submarine" or the "Galloping Goose." The Bear Creek ceased operation in 1933 due to mounting competition from automobiles. (CCHS.)

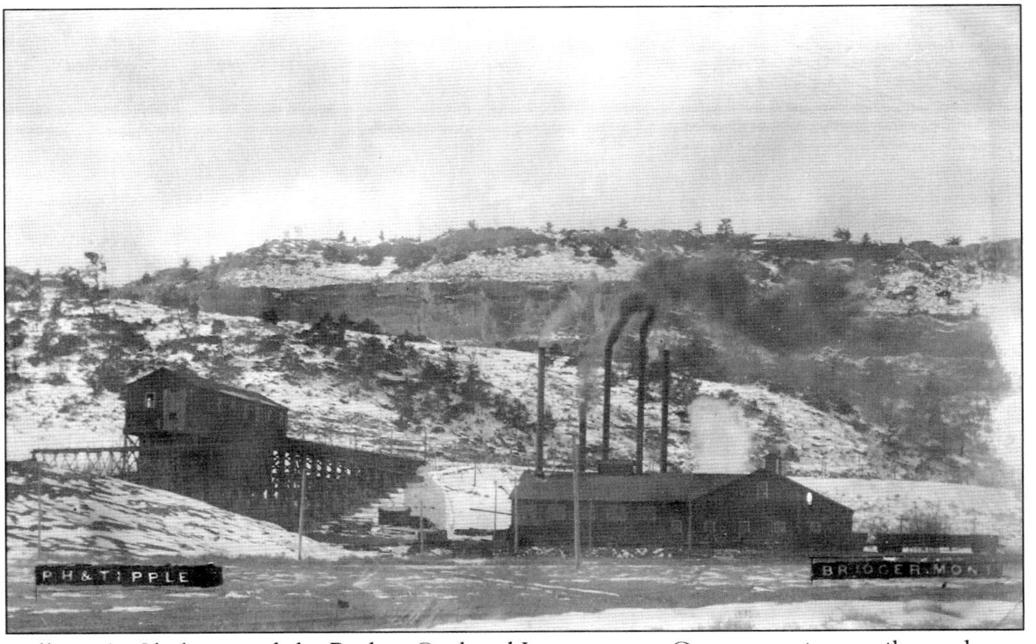

William A. Clark opened the Bridger Coal and Improvement Company mine a mile northwest of Bridger in 1897. This 1900 photograph shows the mine's tipple (left) and powerhouse (right). In 1906, the mine reserved 20 percent of its coal production for use by the power plant to provide electricity for mine operations and the town of Bridger. (Author's collection.)

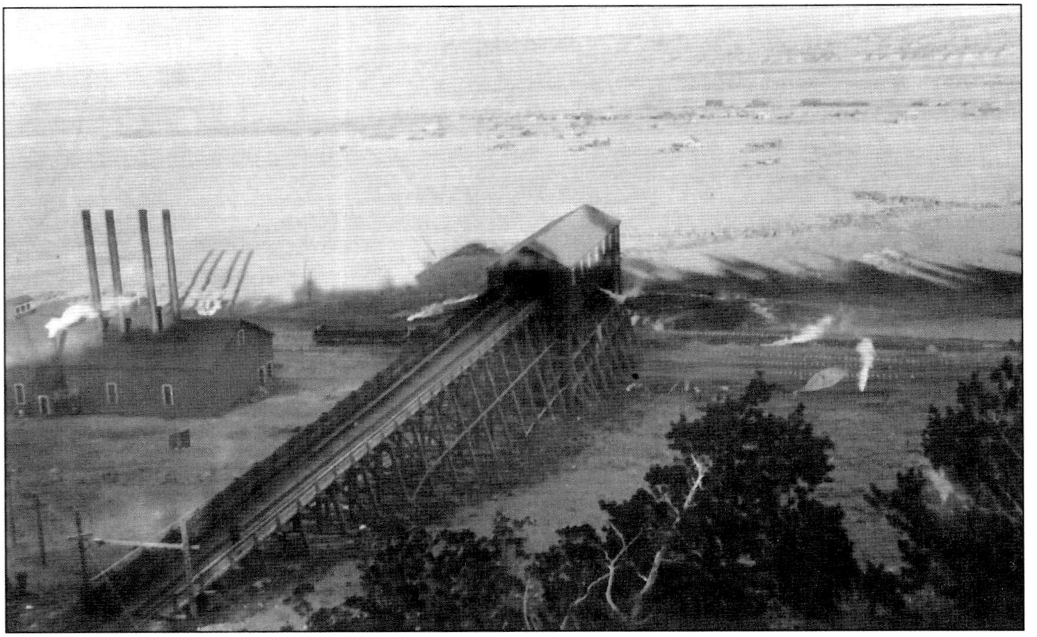

This 1906 photograph looks east from the Bridger Coal and Improvement Company mine toward the fledgling town of Bridger. In the foreground, the power plant (left) and tipple (right) represent some of the mine's aboveground coal-processing structures. The tracks leading to the tipple run .75-mile west to the mine's entrance. (CCHS.)

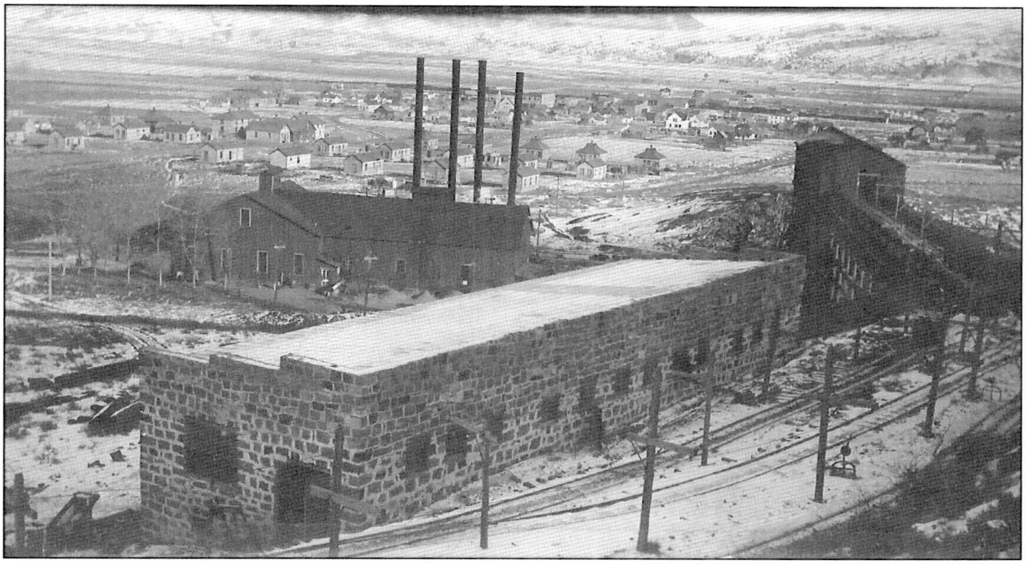

The Bridger Coal and Improvement Company mine and neighboring Bridger grew greatly between 1906 and 1912. In this 1912 photograph, a stone mine shop is visible in the foreground, and miners' homes and boardinghouses fill the mile-wide gap between the mine and the town of Bridger in the distance. (CCHS.)

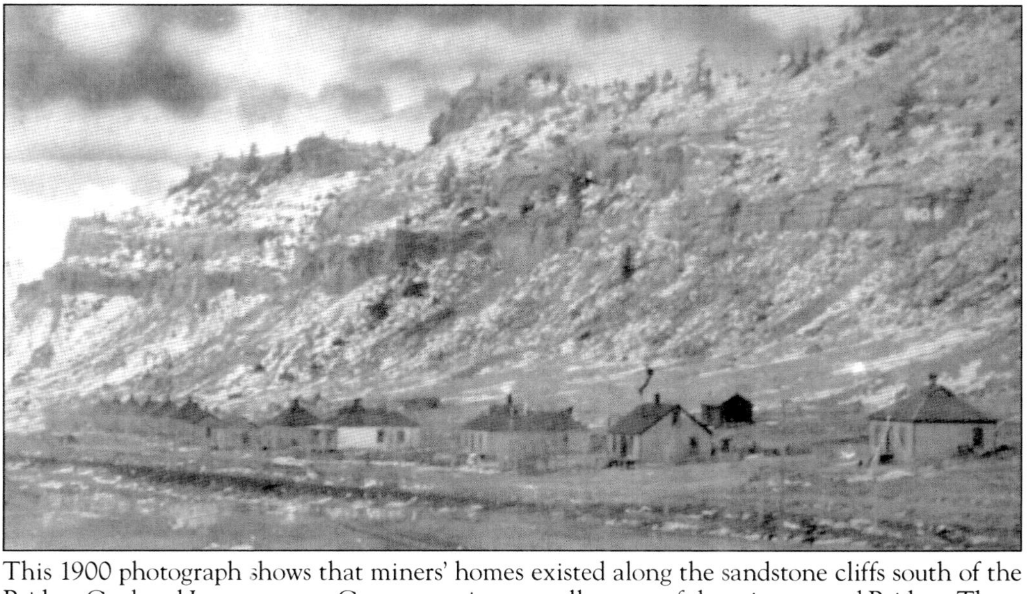

This 1900 photograph shows that miners' homes existed along the sandstone cliffs south of the Bridger Coal and Improvement Company mine, as well as east of the mine toward Bridger. These homes bear a striking similarity to the homes William A. Clark built for the miners on his Washoe property in Bear Creek Valley seven years later. (CCHS.)

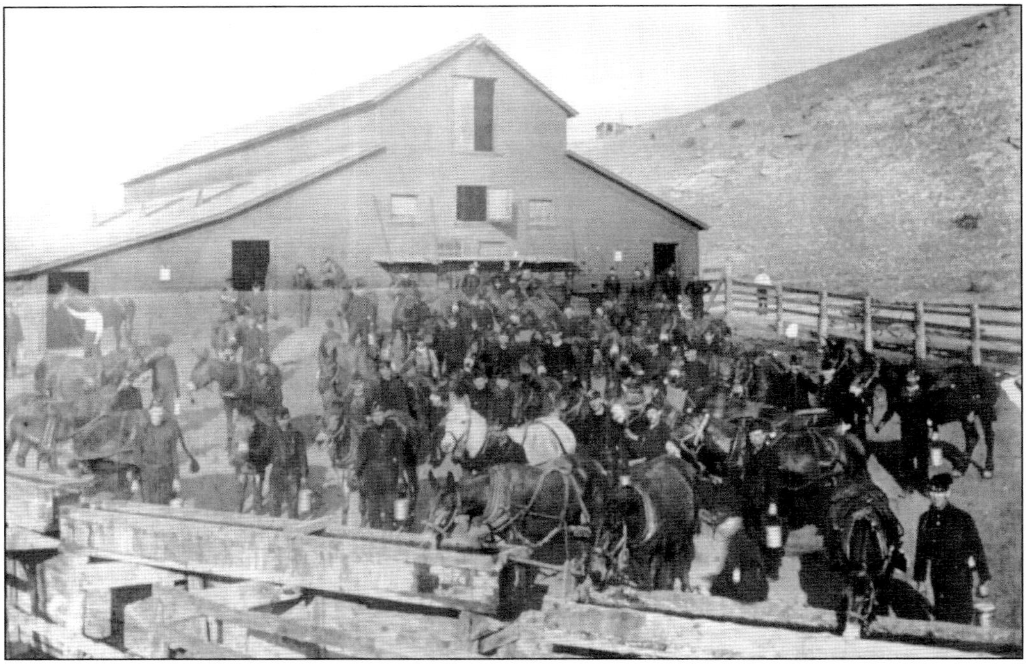

While the Bridger Coal and Improvement Company mine used electricity to power underground implements such as coal-cutting machines and ventilation fans, the use of mules and horses for hauling the mined coal underground continued until the mine's closure in the mid-1910s. This photograph shows teamsters gathering their animals at the start of a shift. (CCHS.)

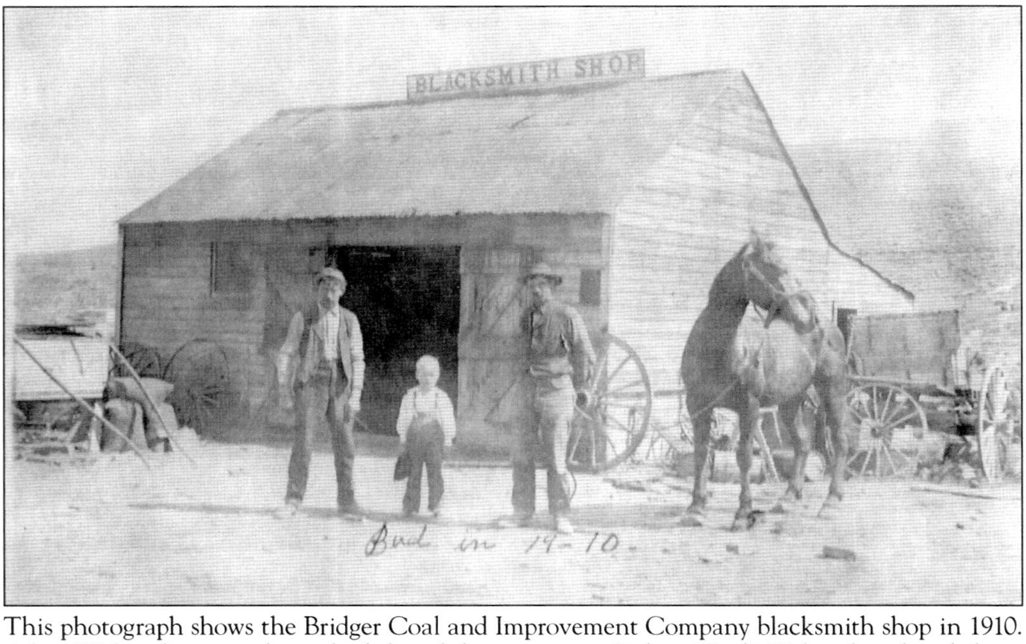

This photograph shows the Bridger Coal and Improvement Company blacksmith shop in 1910. Adam Wakenshaw stands on the left with his young son Robert "Bud" Wakenshaw beside him. Thirty-three years later, father and son became victims of Montana's worst coal mining accident while working in nearby Bear Creek Valley's Smith Mine. (Wakenshaw.)

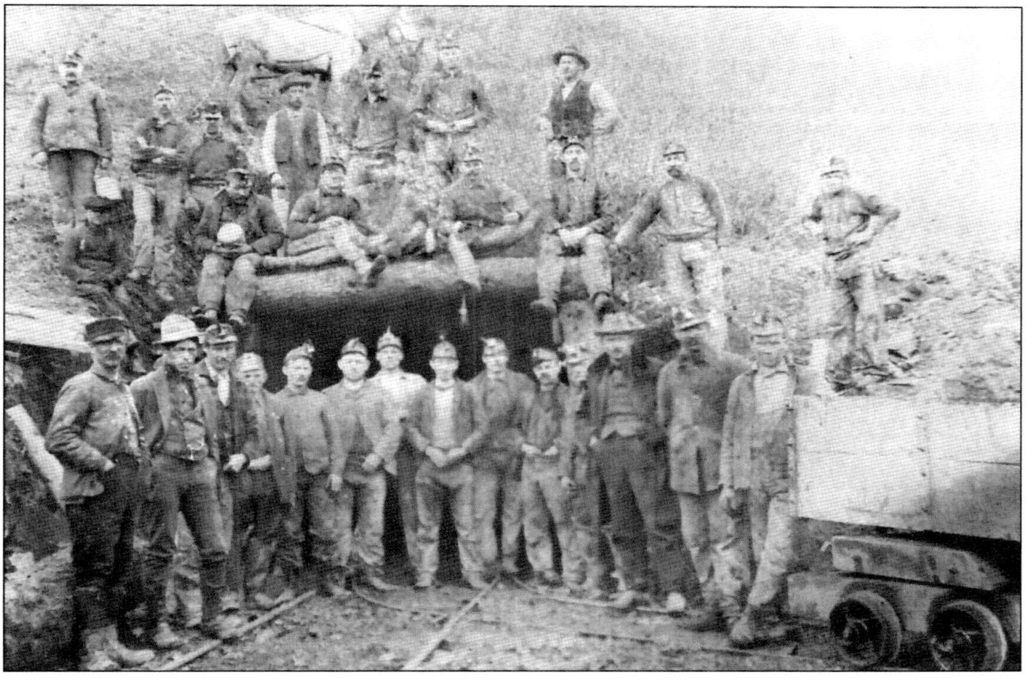

Bridger Coal and Improvement Company (BCIC) miners pose near a mine entrance for this c. 1900 photograph. In 1907, the BCIC paid miners $1 per 2,000 pounds of screened coal and $1 per foot of pick work done in advancing the mine. At this same time, the BCIC charged miners $2.50 per 2,000 pounds of coal for domestic use. (CCHS.)

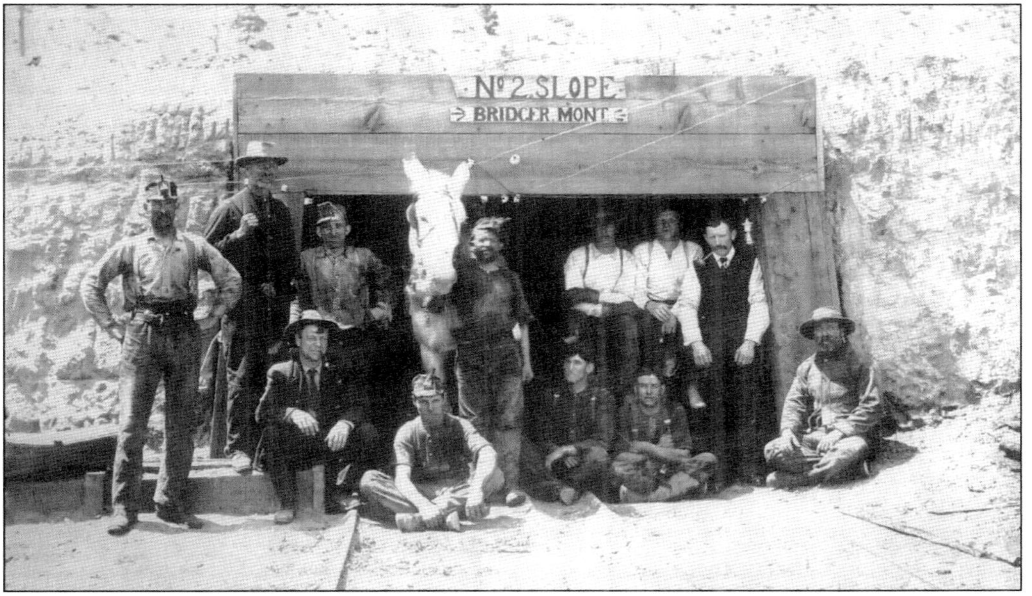

This photograph shows a group of Bridger Coal and Improvement Company employees standing in front of the mine's second entrance. The company opened this entrance in 1908 to supplement the original opening created in 1897. The only person identified in this photograph is Adam Wakenshaw. Adam stands third from left next to the white mule. (Wakenshaw.)

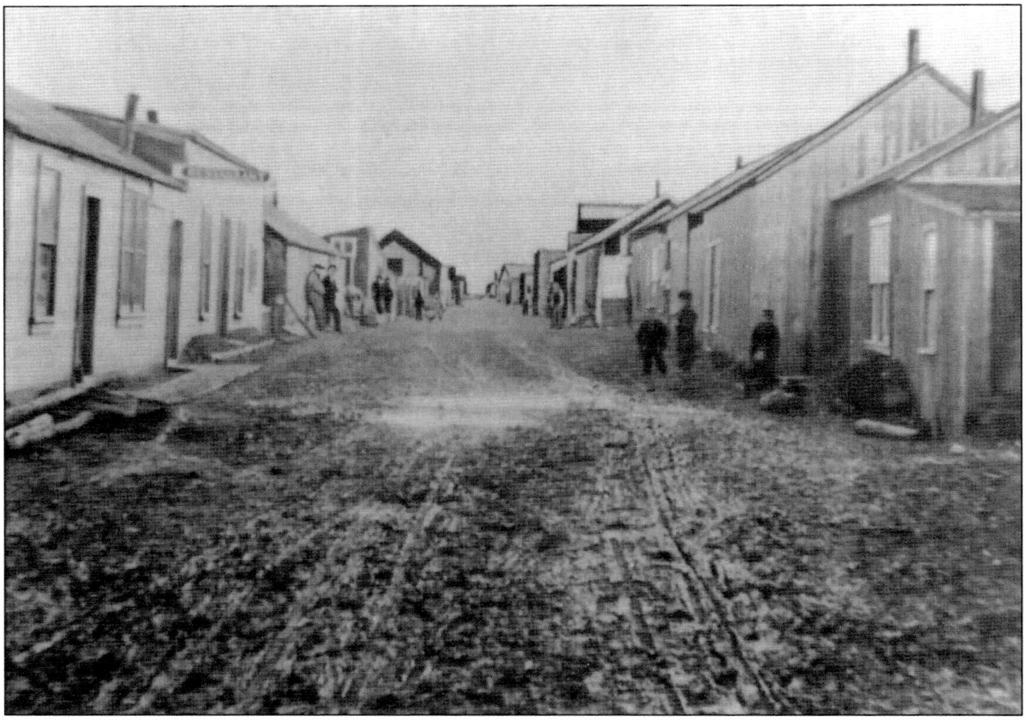

One of the earliest-known photographs of Bridger's Main Street shows homes and businesses lining a narrow muddy road. Still known as "Stringtown" at the time of this photograph, a sign reading "restaurant" on the second structure on the left provides the only identifiable business. (CCHS.)

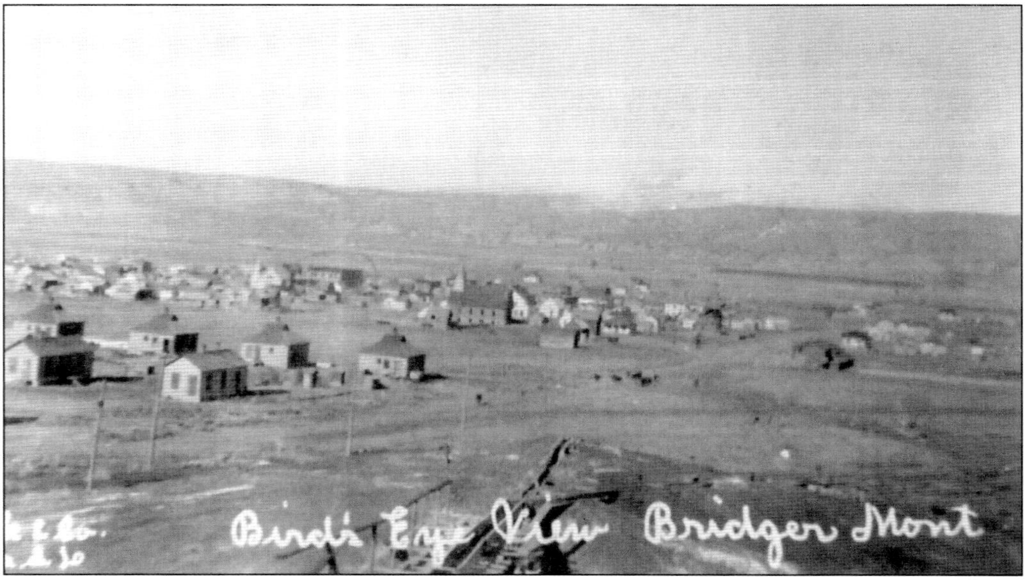

This photograph documents Bridger's growth compared to its early days as Stringtown. Looking east, this photograph shows the Bridger Coal and Improvement Company mine dump (lower right) and miners' homes (left foreground) with a string of utility poles bringing electricity from the mine to Bridger in front of them. (CCHS.)

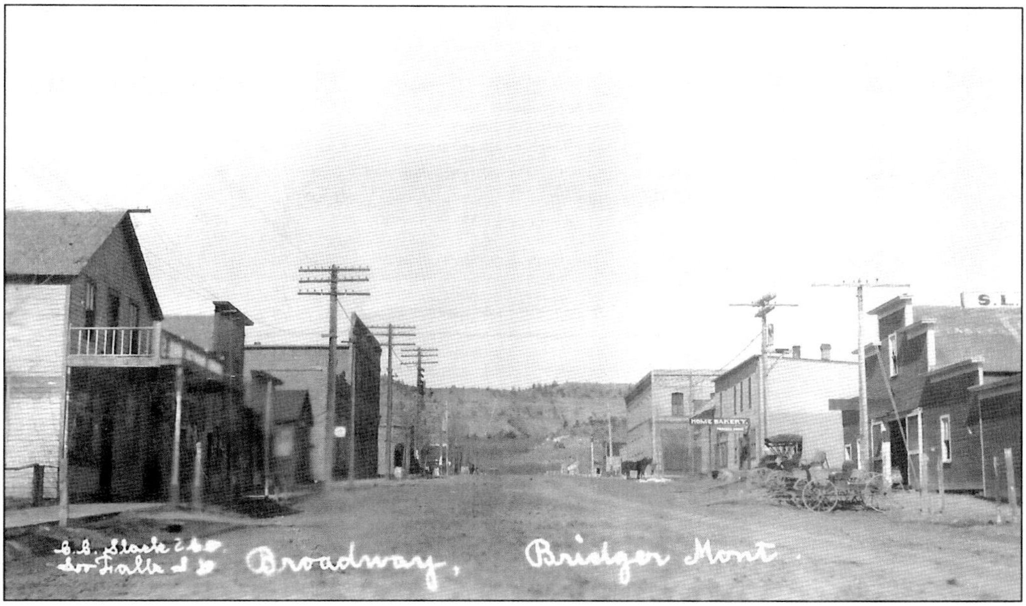

Early Bridger businesses occupying the western end of Broadway Avenue included, on the left from foreground to background, the Montana Hotel; two unidentified establishments; the Stockman Bar; and the Amoretti, Barclay, and Company Bank building then occupied by town dentist Dr. Carl Marcus. Businesses on the right include, from foreground to background, Star Dray and Transfer; Bridger National Bank, Bridger's second bank; and the Glidden Mercantile. (CCHS.)

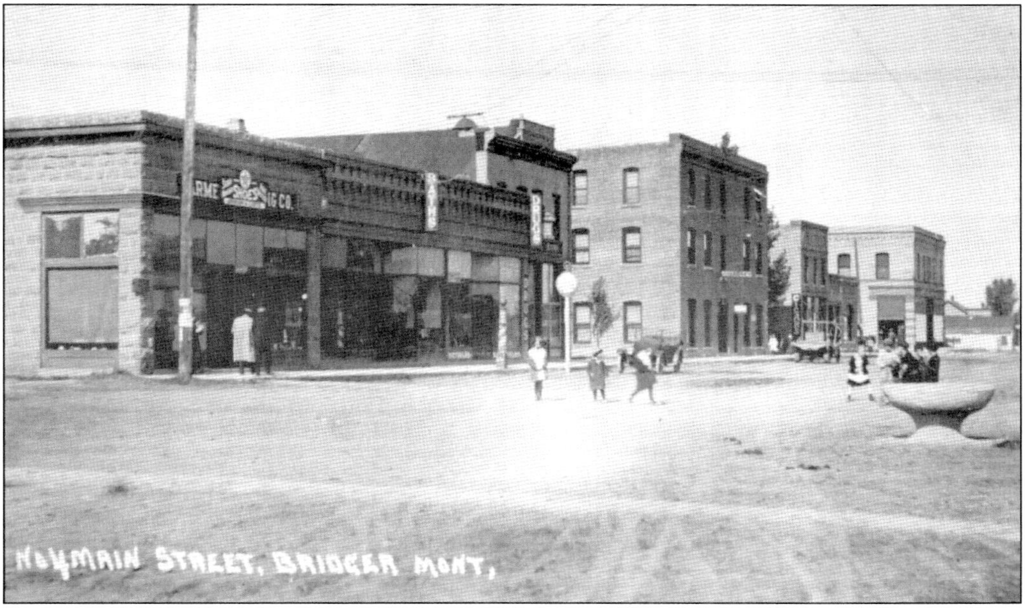

Businesses in this photograph of the southwest side of Bridger's Main Street are, from left to right, Farmer's Trading Company; a bathhouse; a barbershop; a grocery store; unidentified; the Lens Hotel; a confectionery; the post office; the Amoretti, Barclay, and Company Bank; and the Glidden Mercantile. The large concrete object to the right once served as the intersection's roundabout center point. (CCHS.)

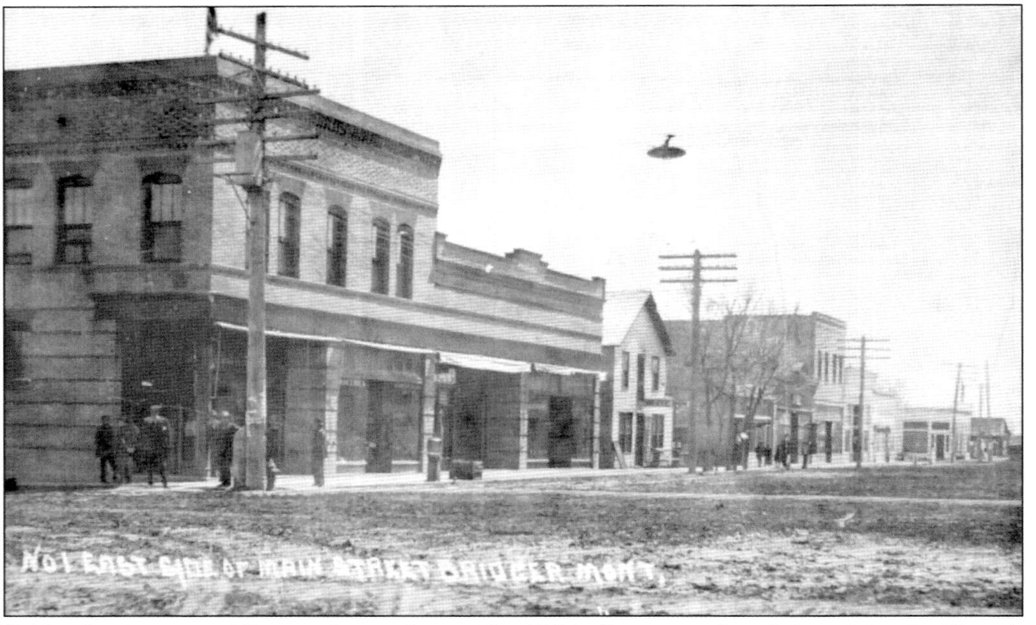

Bridger businesses residing on the southeast side of Main Street are, from left to right, the Shupak and Kuchinski Building housing the Stockman Bar, Homik Cash Grocery, a boardinghouse, the Star Theater, Duffy's Tavern with apartments on the second floor, the current Masonic Temple building, a bar, the Baldwin Lumber Company, unidentified, and unidentified. (CCHS.)

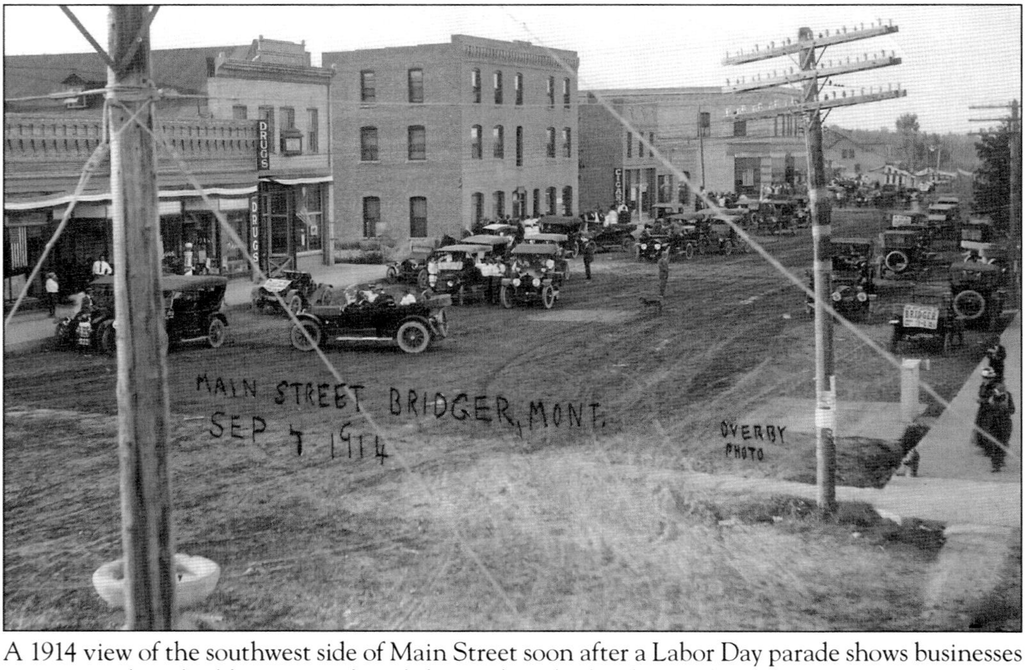

A 1914 view of the southwest side of Main Street soon after a Labor Day parade shows businesses occupying these buildings were, from left to right, a barbershop, a drugstore, a grocery store with apartments on the second floor, the Lens Hotel, the Bridger Post Office, the Bridger National Bank, the Glidden Mercantile, and unidentified. (CCHS.)

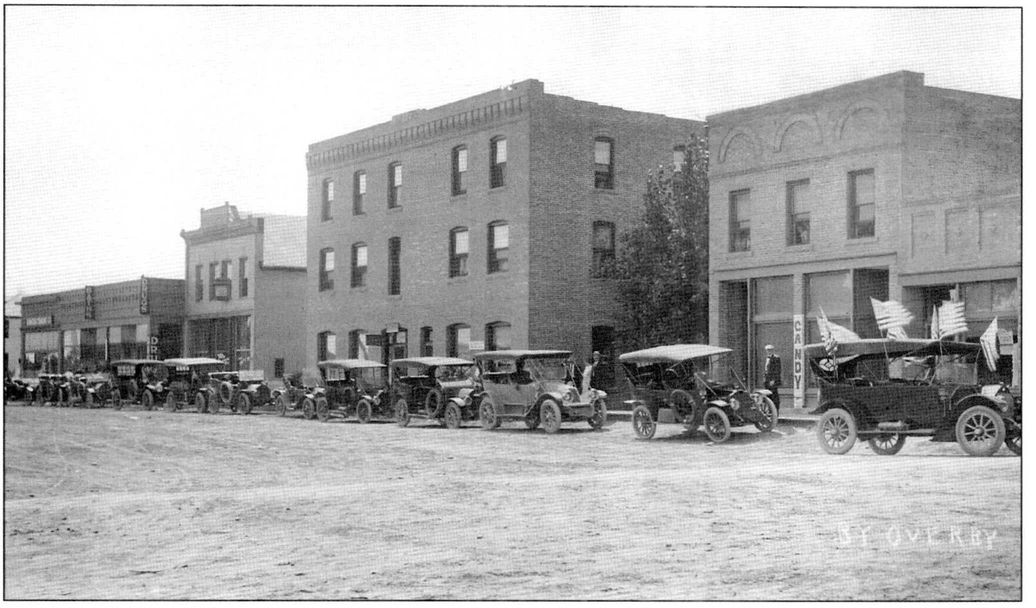

Cars line up on the west side of Main Street between Sunnyside Avenue and Broadway Avenue for a 1914 Bridger parade. Businesses in this photograph are, from left to right, a mercantile, a bathhouse, a drugstore, unidentified, the Lens Hotel, Harold Shepherd's Confectionery, and the Bridger Post Office. Bars were not allowed west of Main Street due to the close proximity to local churches. (CCHS.)

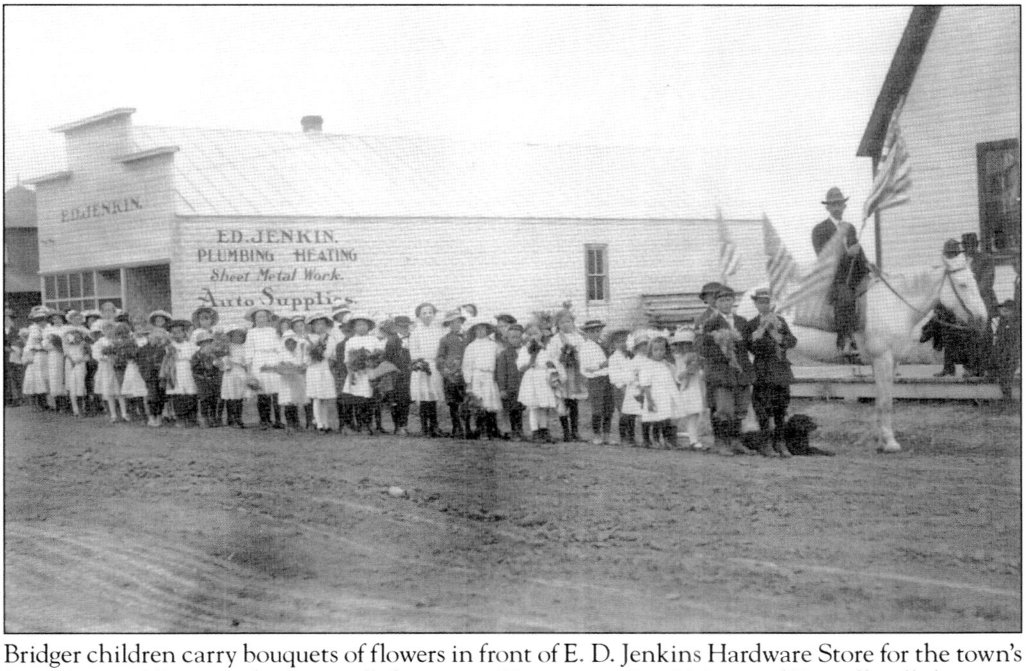

Bridger children carry bouquets of flowers in front of E. D. Jenkins Hardware Store for the town's first Memorial Day parade. Originally known as "Decoration Day," Memorial Day officially began in 1868 to honor the Union dead of the Civil War. After World War I, the holiday changed to honoring all American war dead and eventually to today's more general form of remembrance. (CCHS.)

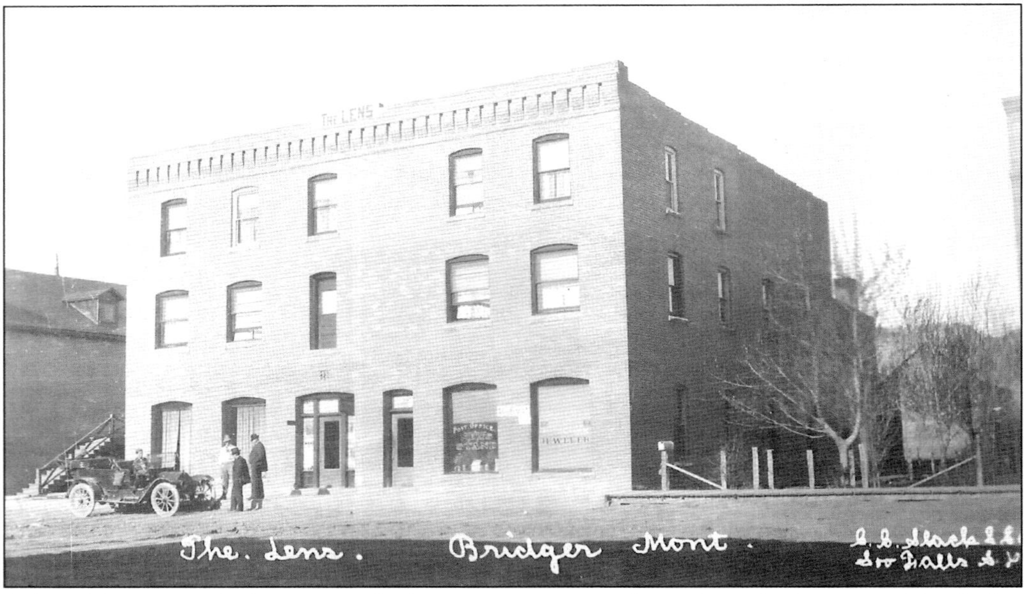

Officially known as the Lens Hotel, Bridger residents soon took to calling this hotel the "Nola," after Nola Jones, wife of the Bridger banker. The Joneses owned and operated the Lens Hotel. The building to the left is the Raymond Haugh Grocery, which housed a bowling alley downstairs. (CCHS.)

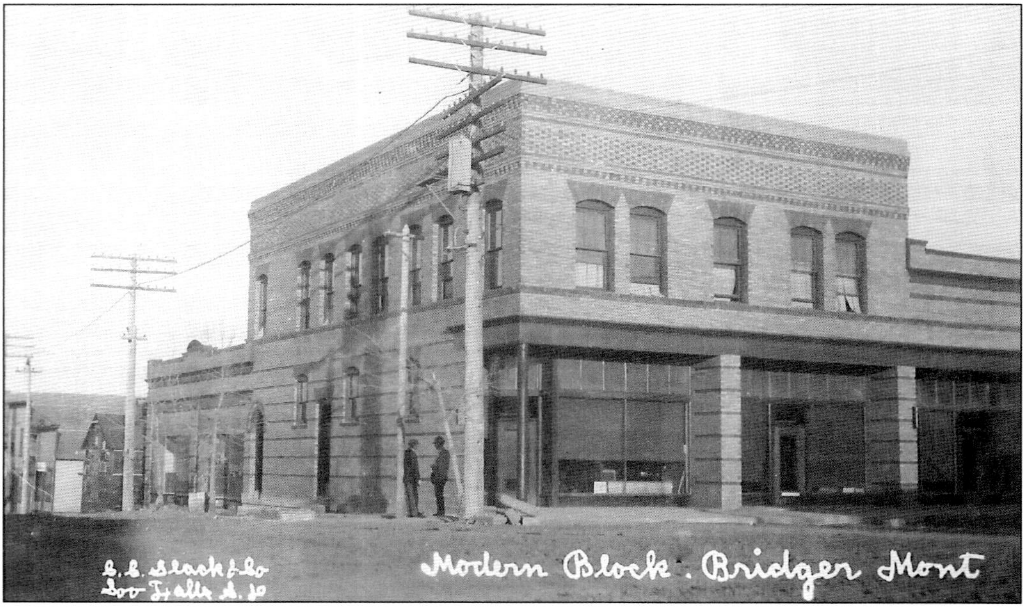

The second Shupak and Kuchinski building shown in this early-1900s photograph replaced the original structure, which burned around 1900. Located at the southeast corner of Broadway Avenue and Main Street, this building housed the Stockman Bar. Part of Homik Cash Grocery can be seen to the far right. (CCHS.)

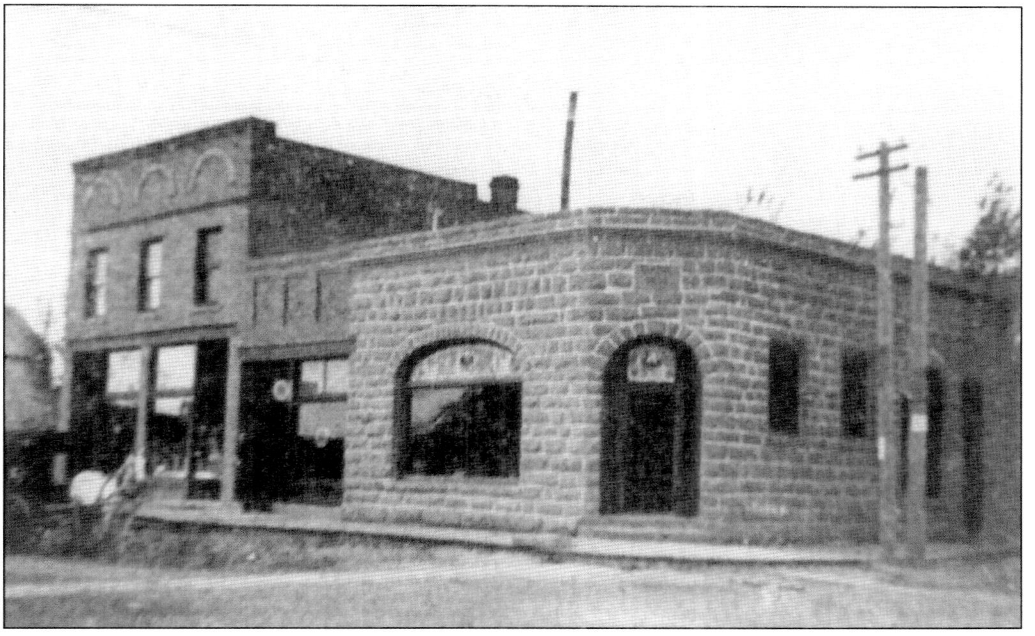

This 1909 photograph shows three businesses on the west side of Main Street south of Broadway Avenue. These businesses are, from left to right, Bridger Drug Store; the Bridger Telephone Office, later a confectionery; and Amoretti, Barclay, and Company Bank. Built in 1903, this bank provided the first financial services in Bridger. Bridger dentist Dr. Carl Marcus later practiced in this building. (CCHS.)

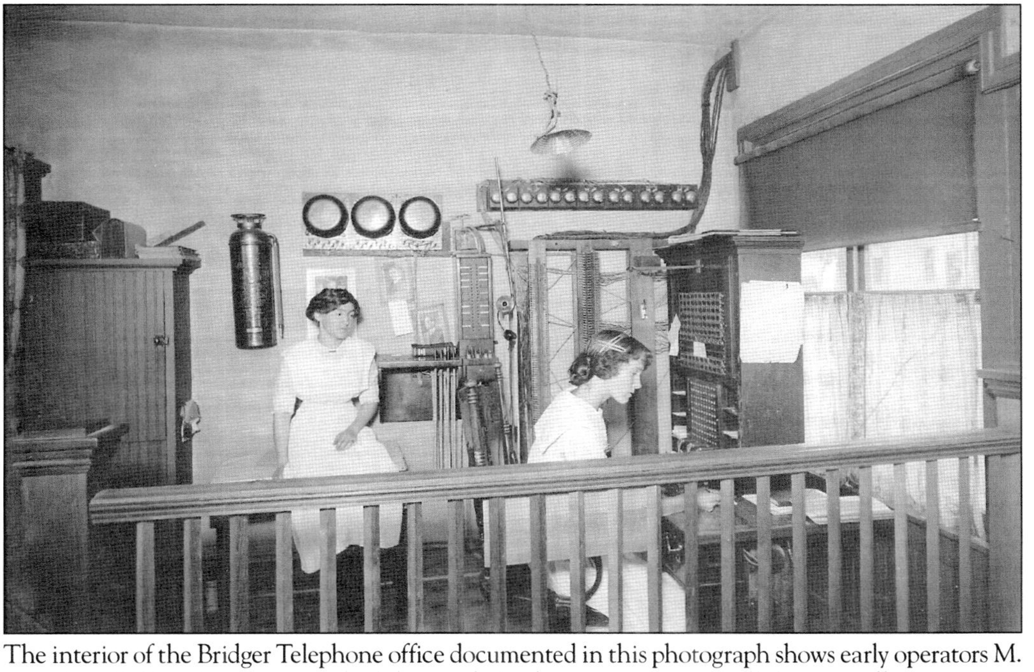

The interior of the Bridger Telephone office documented in this photograph shows early operators M. Hamilton (left) and Ruth Simon (right) at work. Ruth routes incoming calls by manually connecting the wire carrying the incoming call with the wire leading to its intended destination. (CCHS.)

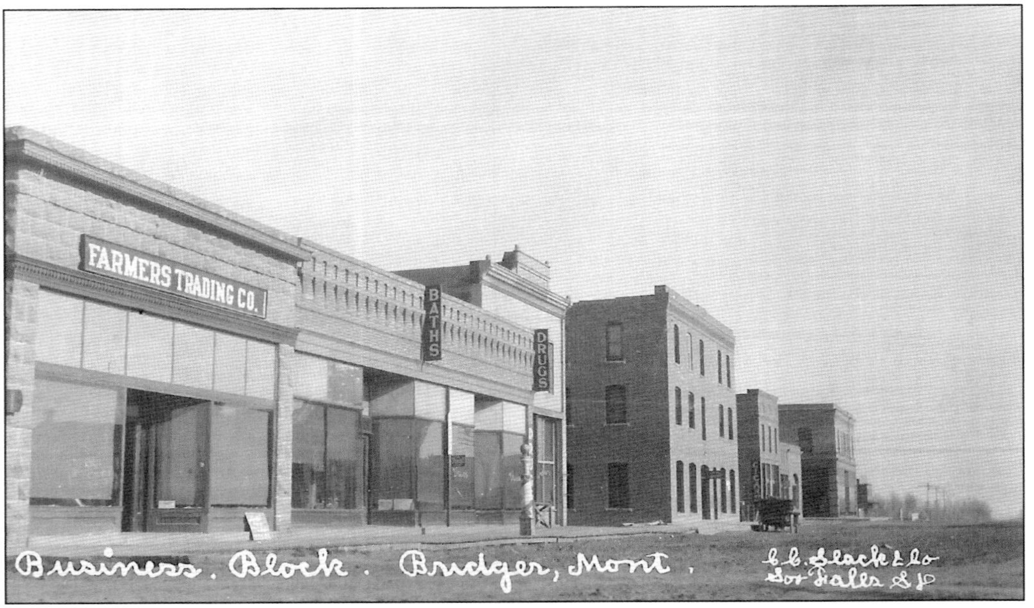

This early-1900s photograph documents businesses along the west side of Main Street north of Sunnyside Avenue towards Broadway Avenue. These businesses are, from left to right, the Farmers Trading Company; the Hughes-Keppler Building; Raymond Hall; the Lens Hotel; the Bridger Times Building; the Amoretti, Barclay and Company Bank; and the Glidden Mercantile. (CCHS.)

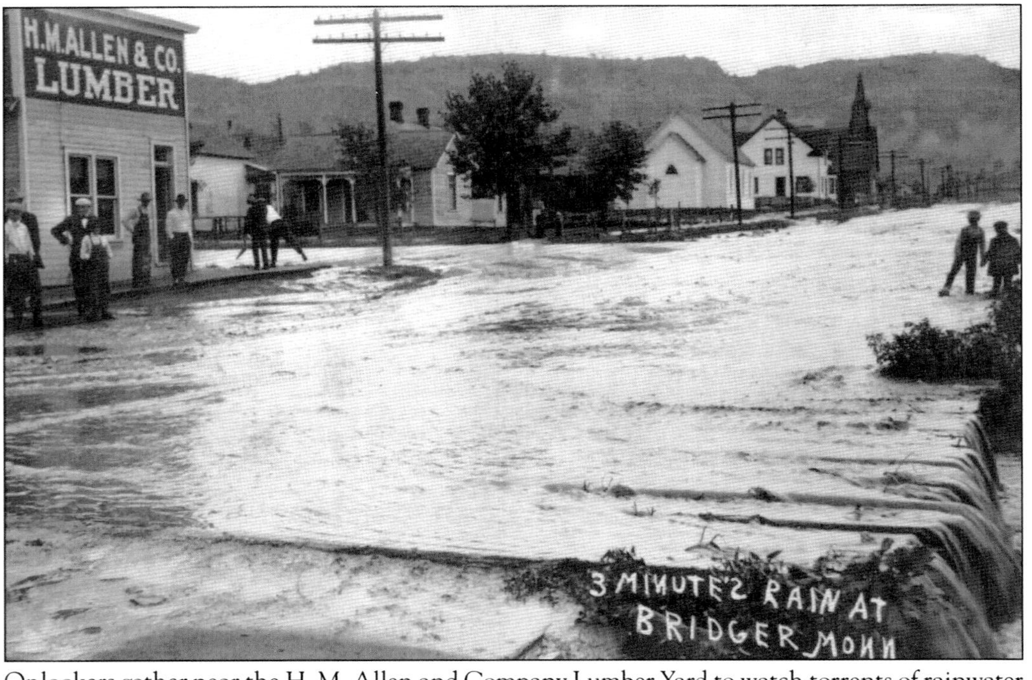

Onlookers gather near the H. M. Allen and Company Lumber Yard to watch torrents of rainwater sweep through Bridger's Sunnyside Avenue. A three-minute deluge resulted in the flooding seen in this photograph. The buildings next to the lumber store are, from left to right, the Terry Dravekski home, the Episcopal church, and the Catholic church. (CCHS.)

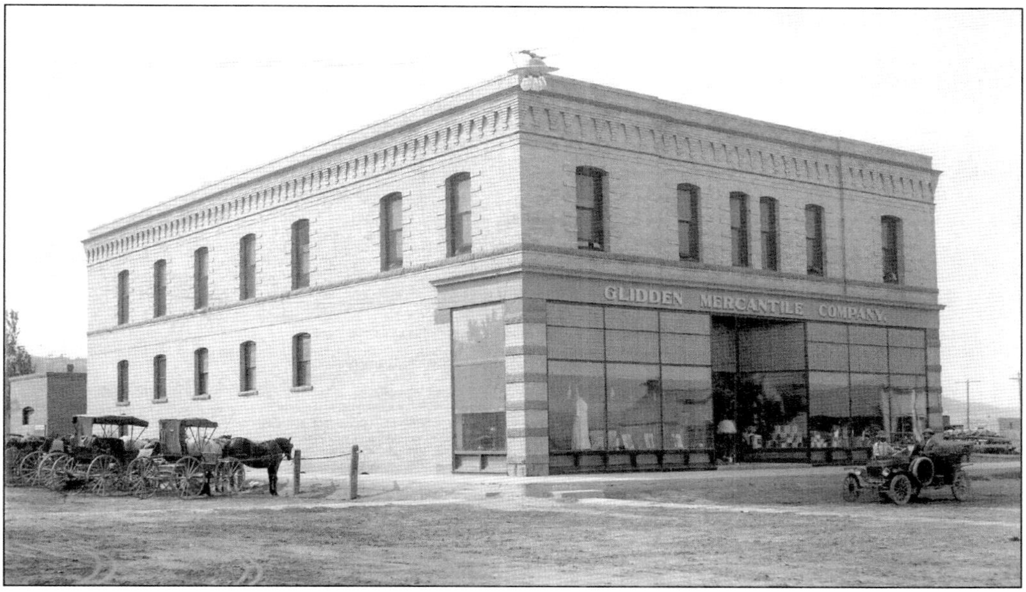

The second Glidden Mercantile Company store, seen in the 1910 photograph above, still resides at the intersection of Main Street and Broadway Avenue in Bridger. Sam Glidden began his mercantile company in Bridger in 1903, but within six months built a new store to accommodate a surge in business. Builders used half a million pressed yellow bricks made in Bridger and large red sandstone blocks quarried in nearby Bridger Canyon to complete the building in 1905. In 1915, Sam Glidden's involvement with the mercantile ended. This resulted in the renaming of the company to the Bridger Mercantile Company. The Bridger Mercantile Company operated until 1957. The photograph below illustrates a small sampling of items sold in the Glidden Mercantile Company's dry goods department in the late 1910s. (Both, CCHS.)

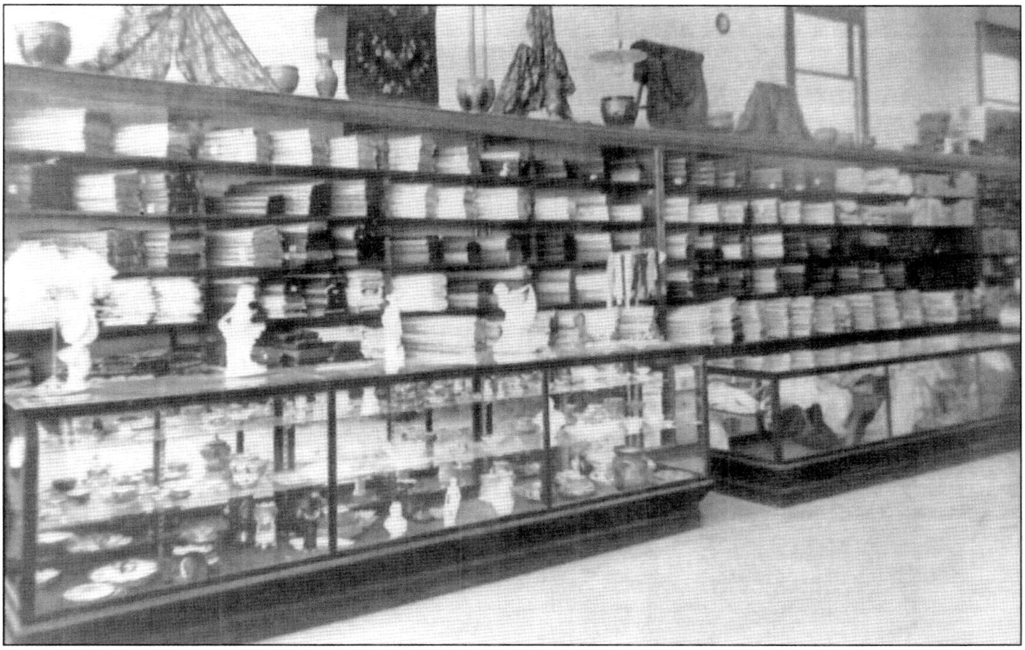

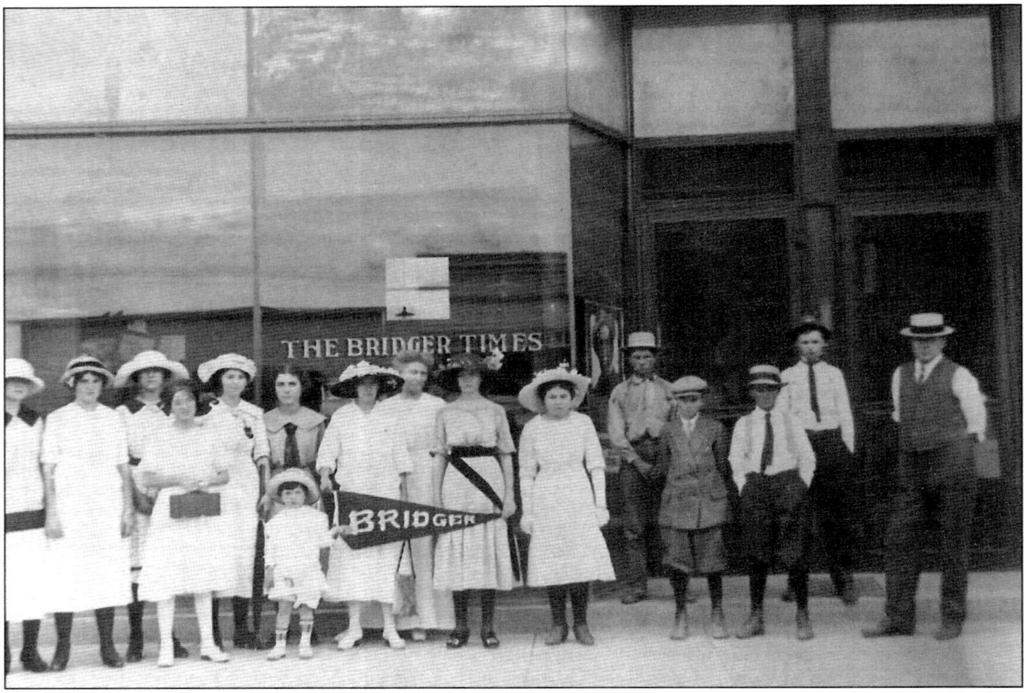

Taken in front of the Glidden Mercantile Building, this August 15, 1913, photograph shows *Bridger Times* newspaper employees waiting to attend a traveling circus show. Many newspapers operated over the years in Bridger. These newspapers were the *Bridger Tribune* (1904–1905); *Bridger Advocate* (1906–1907); *Bridger Times* (1909–1959); *Bridger News* (1961–1961); *Valley Voice*; *Bridger Record*; *Bridger Bonanza* (1965–1976); and *Clarks Fork Pioneer* (1995–2000). (CCHS.)

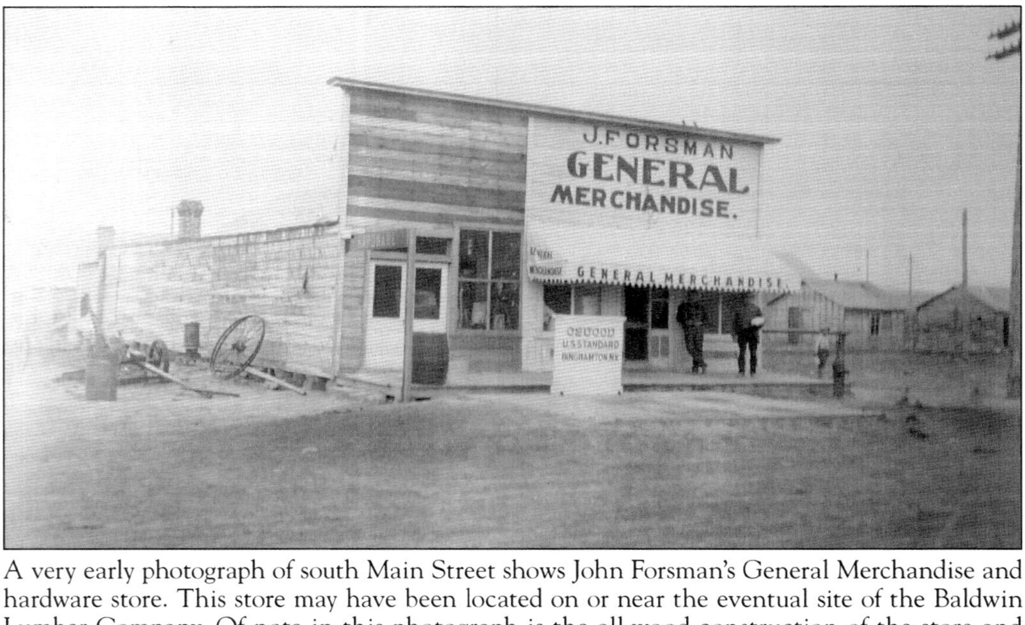

A very early photograph of south Main Street shows John Forsman's General Merchandise and hardware store. This store may have been located on or near the eventual site of the Baldwin Lumber Company. Of note in this photograph is the all-wood construction of the store and neighboring homes to the right. (CCHS.)

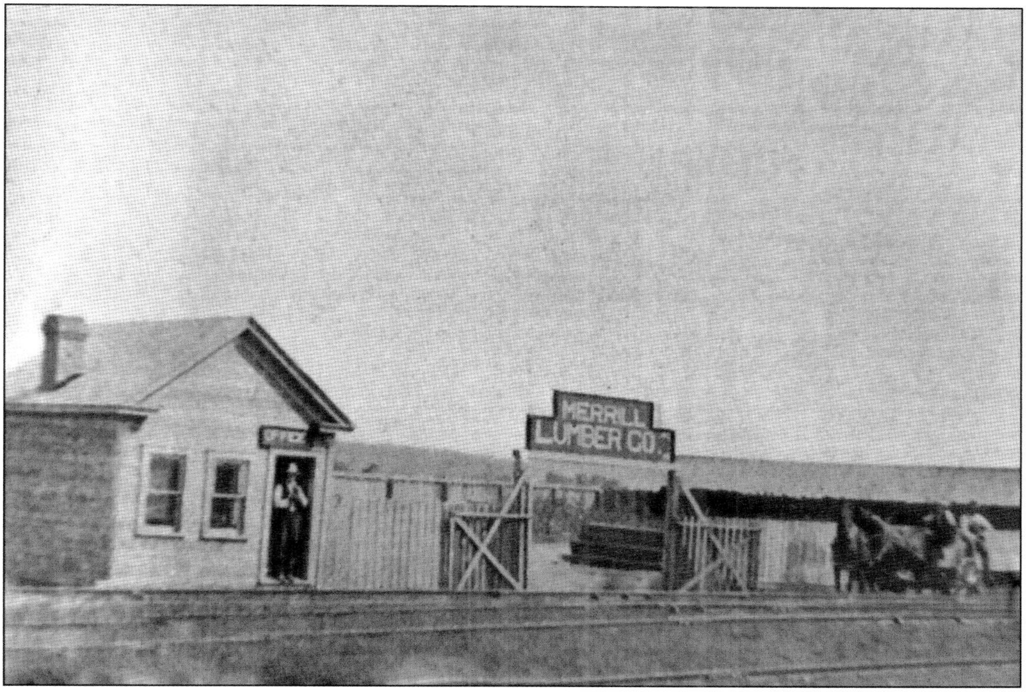

Lumber companies proved lucrative to their owners in the early days of Clark's Fork Valley. The demand for lumber came from homesteaders, coal companies, new businesses, and new workers arriving in the valley's towns. Fromberg, Belfry, and Bridger all supported at least one lumberyard, with the nearby Pryor Mountains providing their raw material. These pre-1907 photographs show two of Bridger's early lumber companies: the Merrill Lumber Company (above) and the Baldwin Lumber Company (below). (Both, CCHS.)

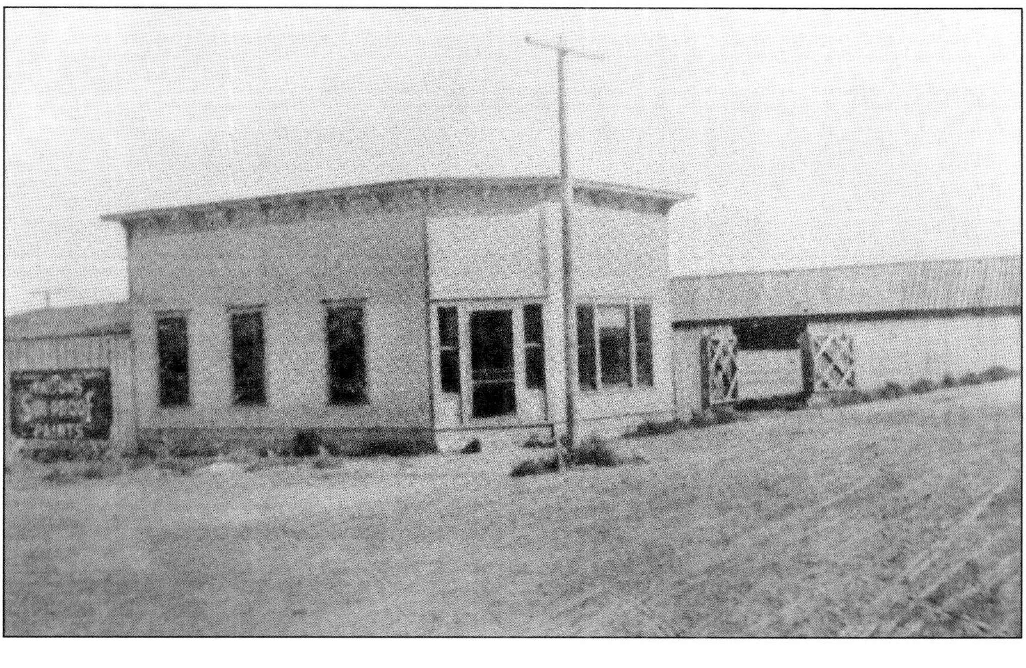

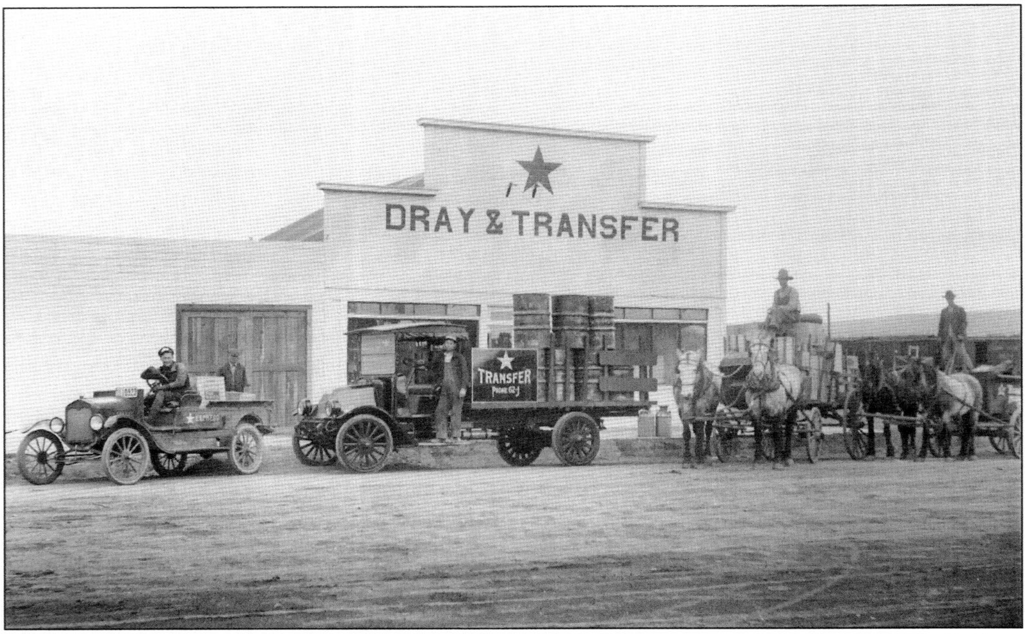

Dray, or delivery, companies provided good business opportunities in the Clark's Fork Valley's early days. Dray companies delivered everything imaginable to the valley's many rural inhabitants. These photographs show an early version of Noel J. Montgomery's Star Dray and Transfer Company looking south on Main Street (below), when it also served as a livery and stable, and the 1920s facility (above) after it moved closer to the railroad tracks, possibly on Broadway Avenue. Even this late in the 20th century, dray companies used a mixture of automobiles and horse and wagons to make their deliveries. In the photograph above are, from left to right, Happy Jordan, unidentified, Noel J. Montgomery, Gus Boehn, and Lee Shelmardine. (Both, CCHS.)

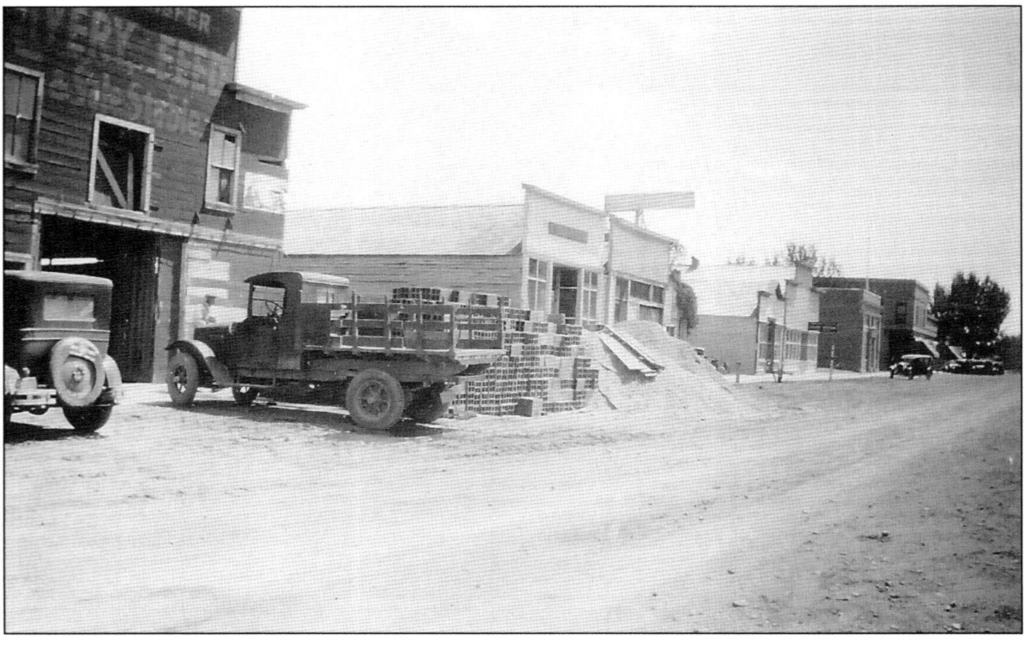

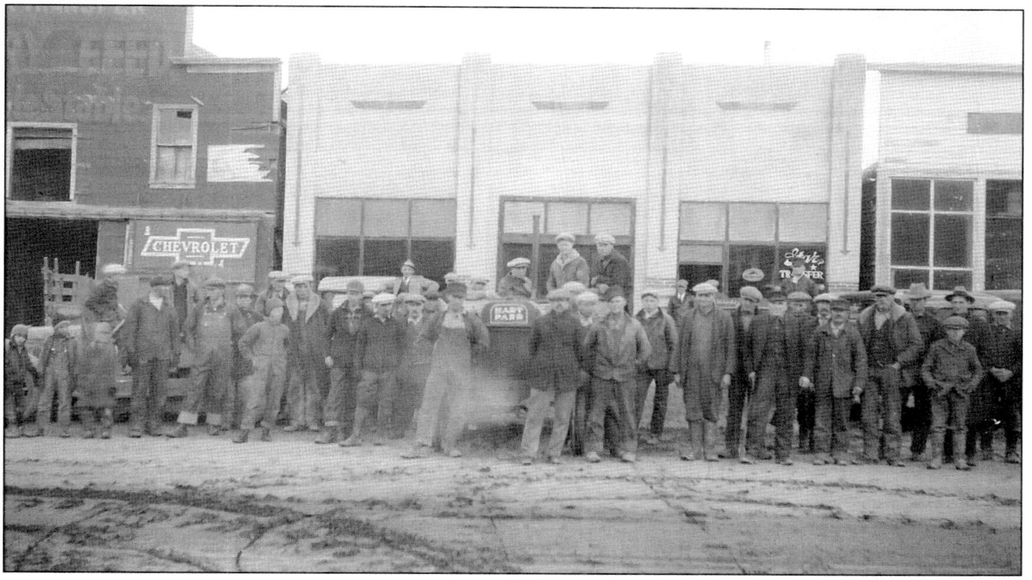

A group of Bridger residents gathered in front of Gordon Anderson's garage (center) soon after the completion of its construction. Businesses flanking the garage are Star Dray and Transfer (left) and John Kanvick's Blacksmith Shop (right). (CCHS.)

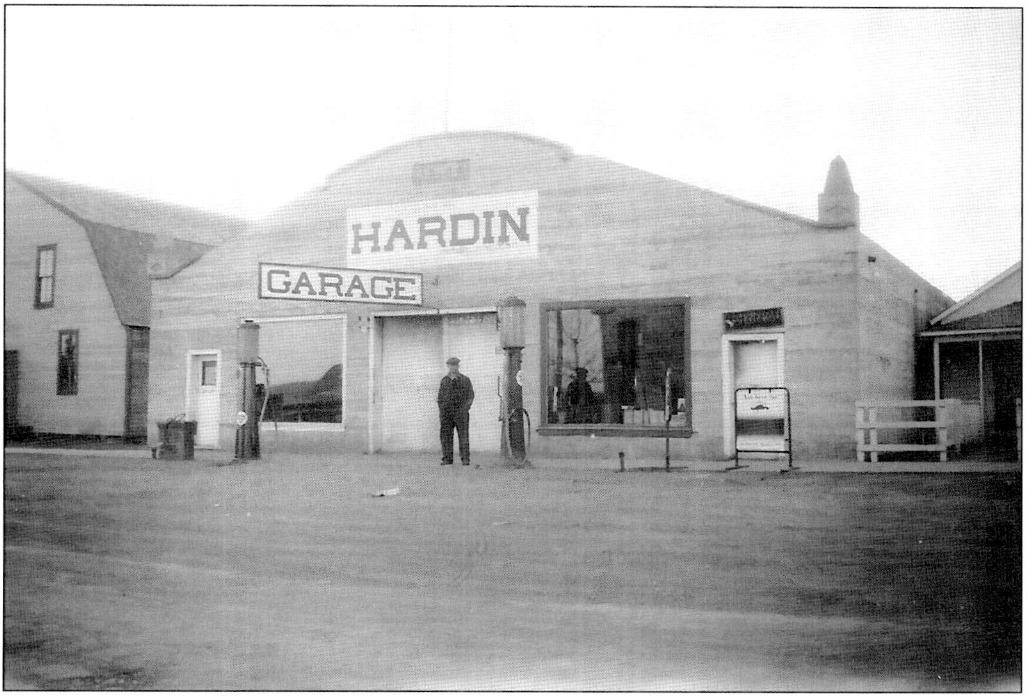

This 1917 photograph shows George Hardin's Garage. Built in 1914 and constructed of concrete, the garage measured 50-by-100 feet in size. In addition to repairing automobiles, George Hardin also provided gasoline from two glass-topped pumps in front of the business. To the left of the photograph is the Bridger Opera House. (CCHS.)

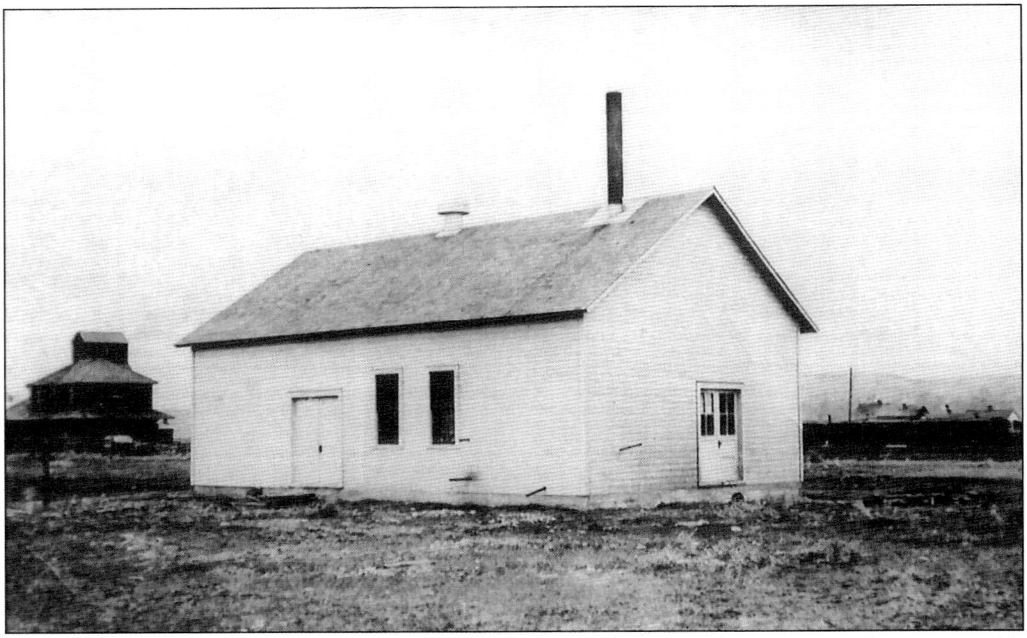

This 1910 photograph shows the Bridger Creamery, originally an icehouse, at the corner of B Street and Sunnyside Avenue, east of the Northern Pacific Railroad (NP) tracks. The NP train depot, with the top of the pinto bean elevator behind it, can be seen on the left side of this photograph. (CCHS.)

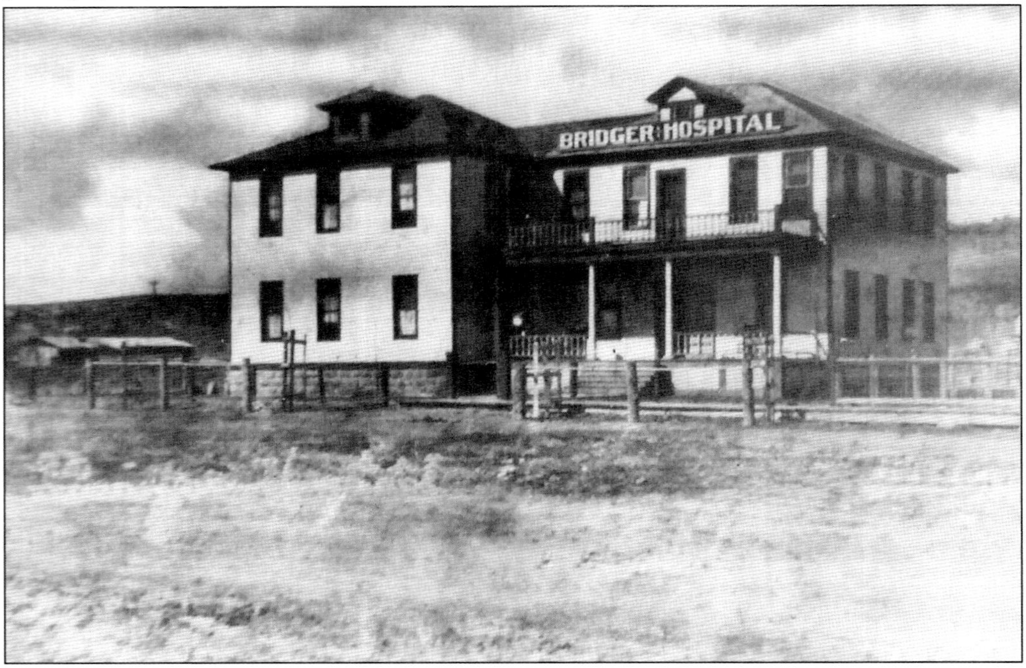

The Bridger Hospital once stood on Main Street near Sunnyside Avenue where the Civic Center is now located. Founded by Dr. Arthur J. Movius, the Bridger Hospital ceased operating when it burned down, and Dr. Movius relocated his practice to Billings, Montana. (CCHS.)

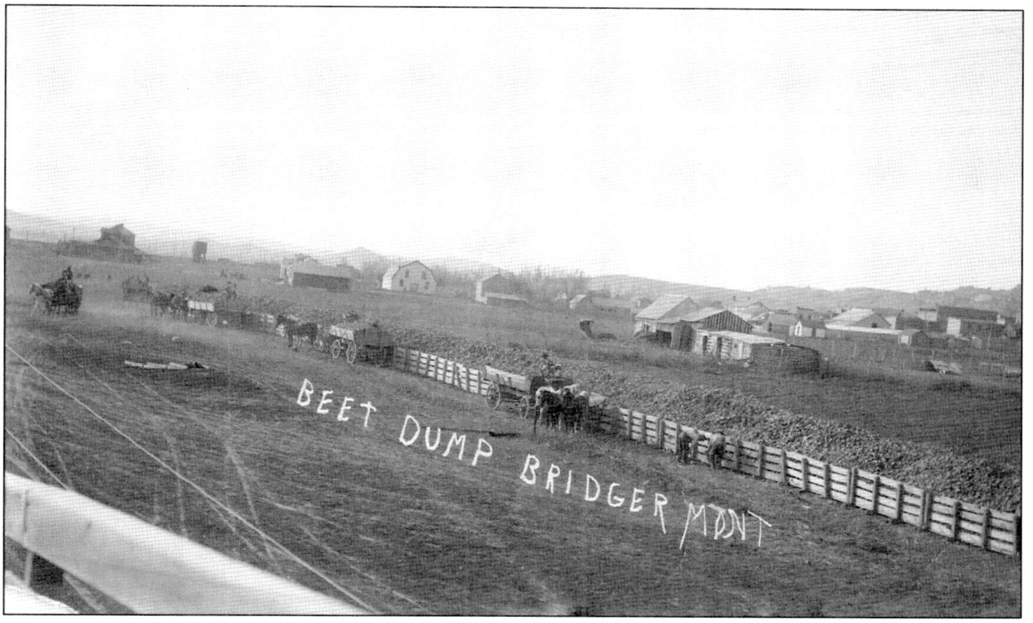

This *c.* 1910 photograph shows the Bridger beet dump. Farmers harvested the first Clark's Fork Valley sugar beet crops in 1906 and built the dump in 1907. The large structure in the left background is the Northern Pacific Railroad train depot. The large, white, four-window building in the center is the Bridger Opera House. (CCHS.)

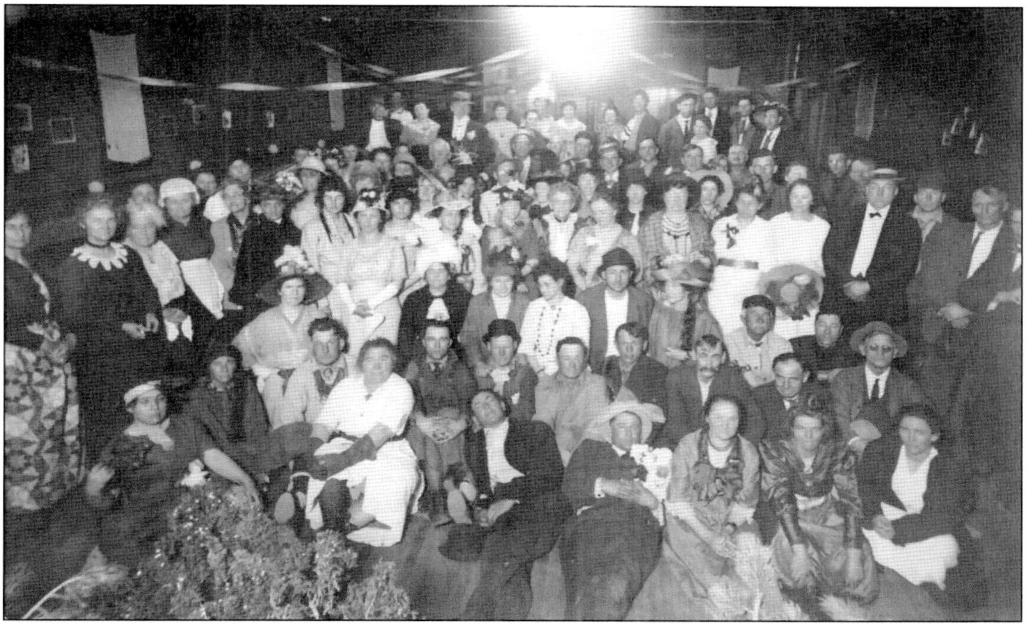

Community dances provided a primary source of entertainment for residents of Clark's Fork Valley. In this 1920 photograph, over 100 dancers took a break from the festivities to pose for this photograph in the Bridger Opera House. Dances often lasted until the early morning with at least one meal served during the course of the evening. (CCHS.)

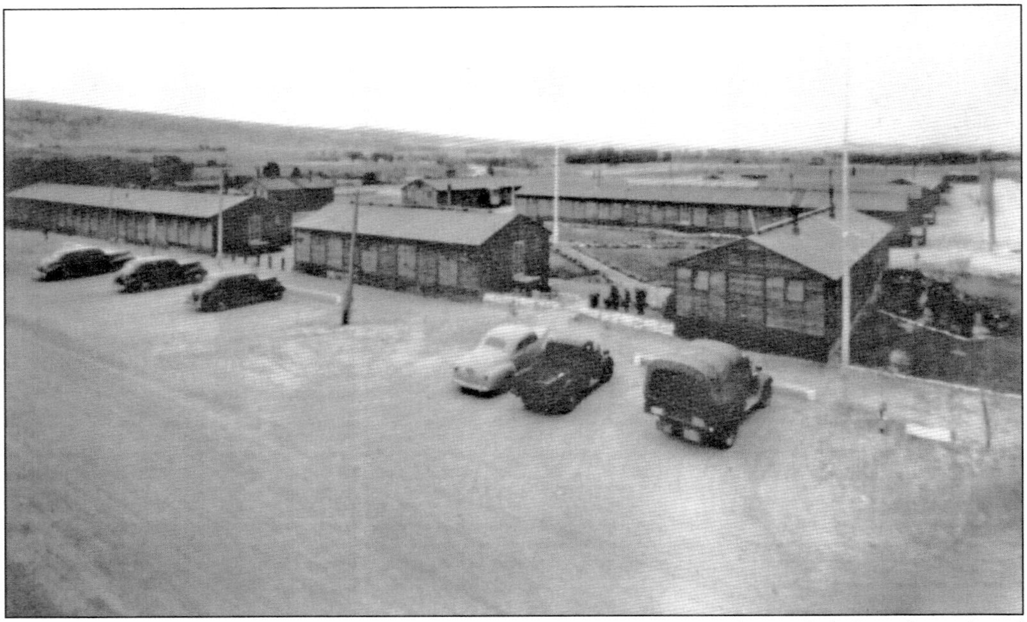

The Depression-era Civilian Conservation Corps (CCC) program housed, fed, and employed out-of-work young men in the conservation and development of natural resources. The CCC built camps across the country, and Montana alone housed 113 camps with the only Carbon County camp located in Bridger. CCC workers built dams in the Pryor Mountains, bridges on the Beartooth Highway, and new ski runs near Red Lodge. (CCHS.)

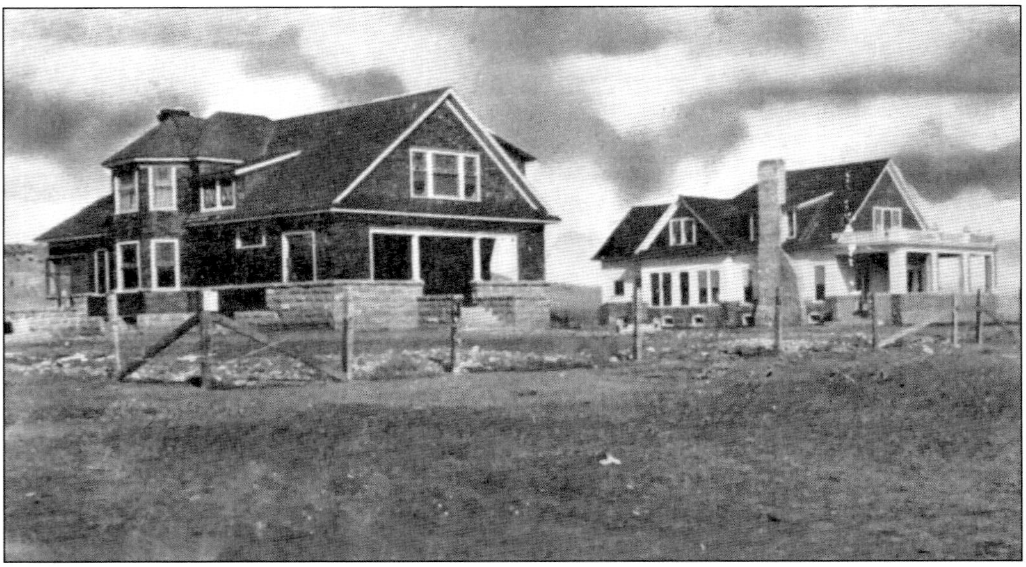

This 1907 photograph shows the homes of L. E. Corey and his brother-in-law Sam Glidden soon after their construction in 1906. Prominent Bridger businessmen, Corey owned the Bridger Stucco Works and Bridger Canyon Oil Company. Sam Glidden owned the Glidden Mercantile and purchased the entire Bridger Coal and Improvement Company holdings from William A. Clark. (CCHS.)

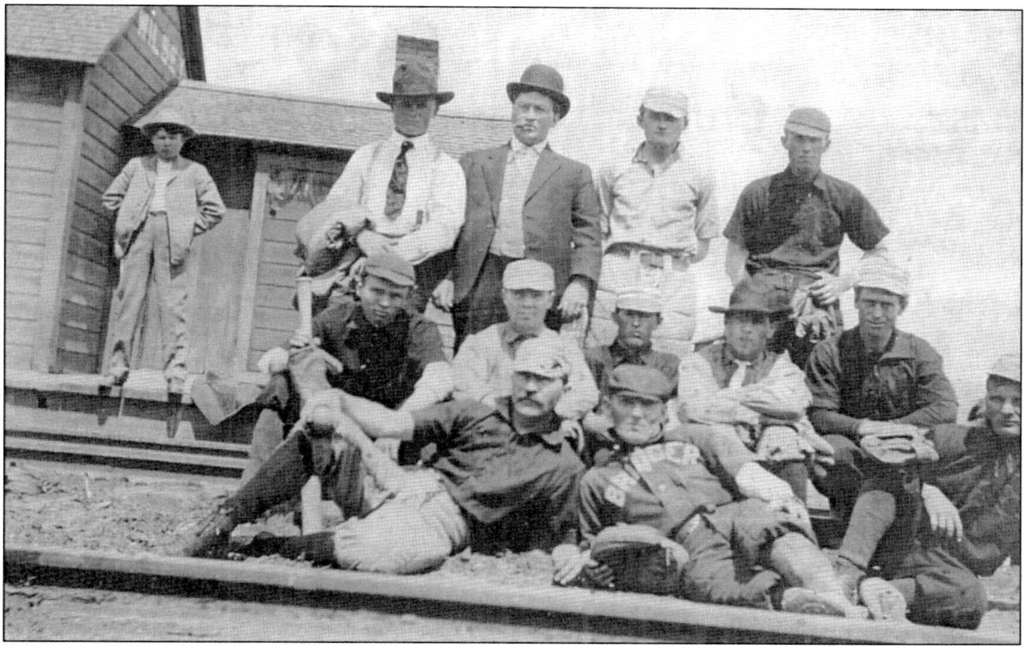

The Bridger baseball team poses for a photograph at the Wilsey train stop near Carbon County's Montaqua Hot Springs. Known team members are (first row) an unidentified Arrington at far left and an unidentified Stark on the far right; (second row) Mark Yoakim on the far left; (third row) Charles Kearns at far left and Charles Buzzetti, wearing a derby hat. (CFVM.)

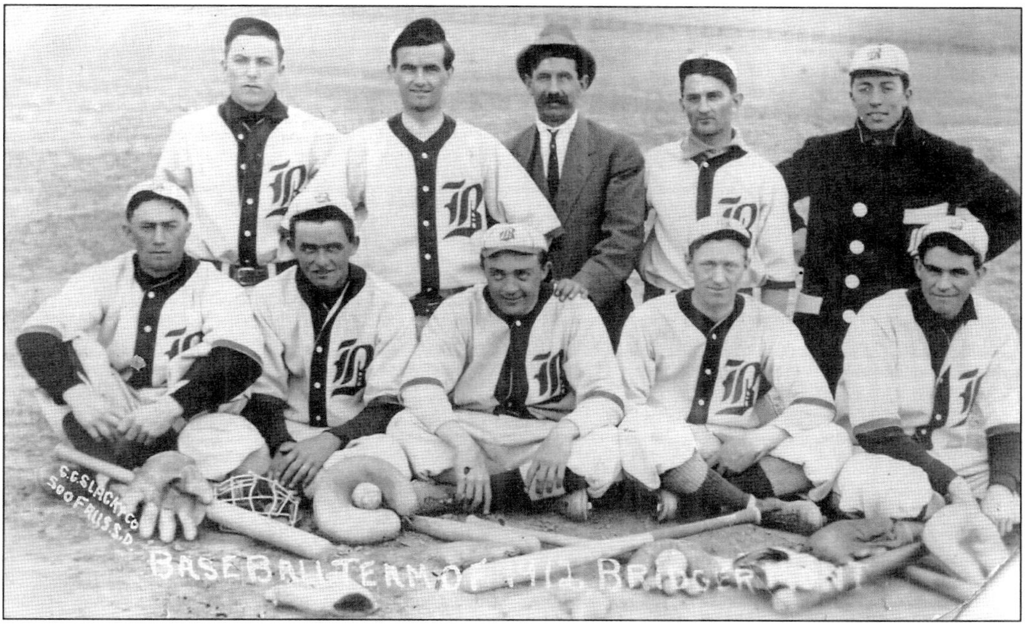

The Bridger baseball team poses in full uniform, and with all of their equipment, in this 1912 photograph. Shown are Jack Henderson, Jim Hanley, Ben Boyer, ? Cherrie, Ray Barlow, unidentified, Clarence Hanley, unidentified, Henry Johnson, and Bill Hanley. Unfortunately, the location of each man in the photograph is unknown. (CCHS.)

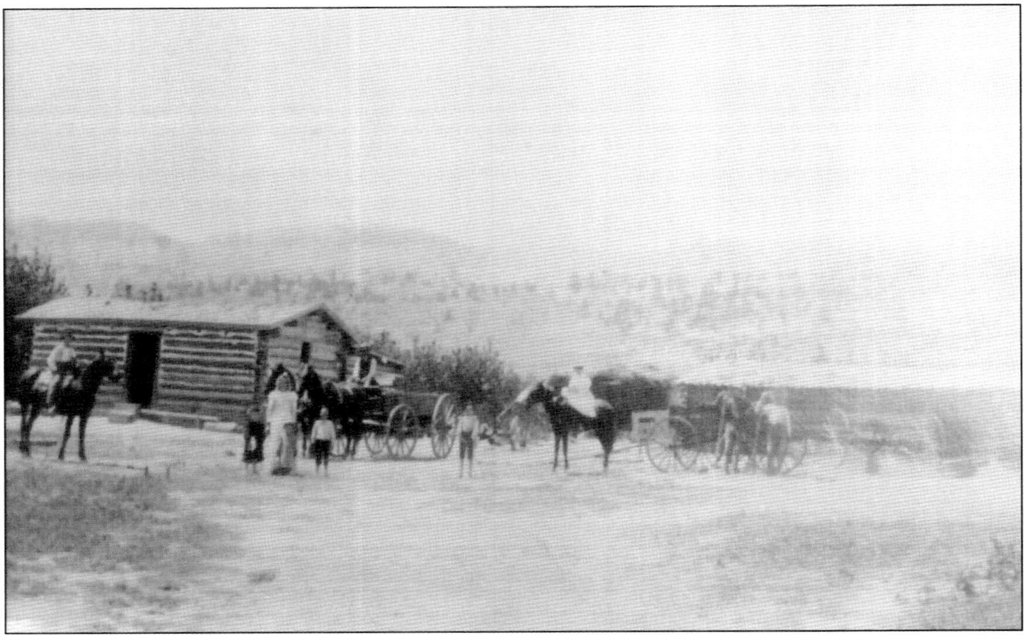

Martha Jane "Calamity Jane" Canary lived in Stringtown from 1898 to 1899. She cooked for a restaurant on Stringtown's Main Street and lived in a small shack behind it. She also took in washing to earn extra money. From time to time, Calamity Jane stayed in the root cellar of either the Foust (above) or Teesdale homes just north of Stringtown. (CCHS.)

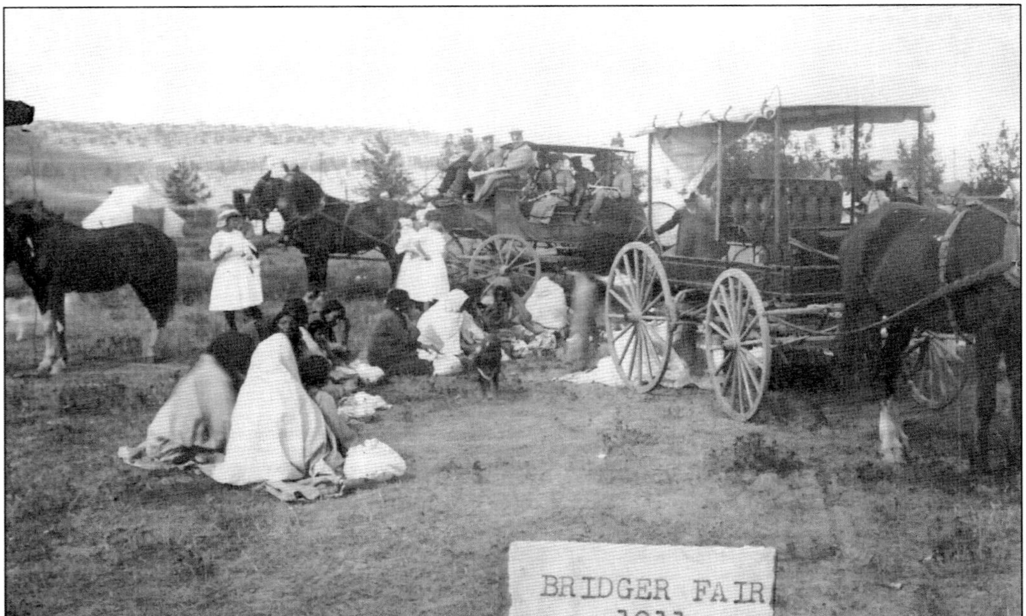

This 1911 Bridger Fair photograph shows a group of Crow resting between events near the fairgrounds. A wagon behind them transports the Bridger Band in full uniform. The Crow attended many fairs and parades in Carbon County as spectators and participants. Unfortunately, few photographs of this participation exist today. (CCHS.)

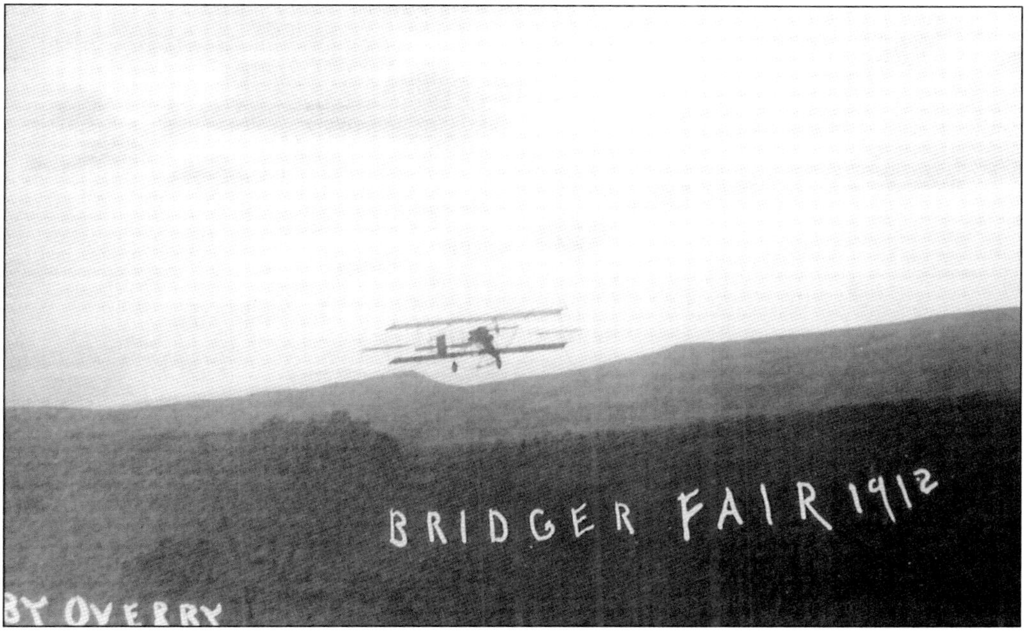

The 10th annual Bridger Fair held September 7, 1912, featured aviation as its theme. The photograph below shows a group of local residents helping inflate a hot air balloon as spectators look on from the grandstands in the background. Early barnstorming pioneer and renowned aviator Robert "Lucky Bob" St. Henry provided the keynote event with flights of his Glenn Curtiss biplane (above). Just nine years after the Wright brothers' first flight near Kitty Hawk, North Carolina, this flight by St. Henry may have been the first successful one in Carbon County. The annual Bridger Fair also included horse races and chariot races among its events. (Both, CCHS.)

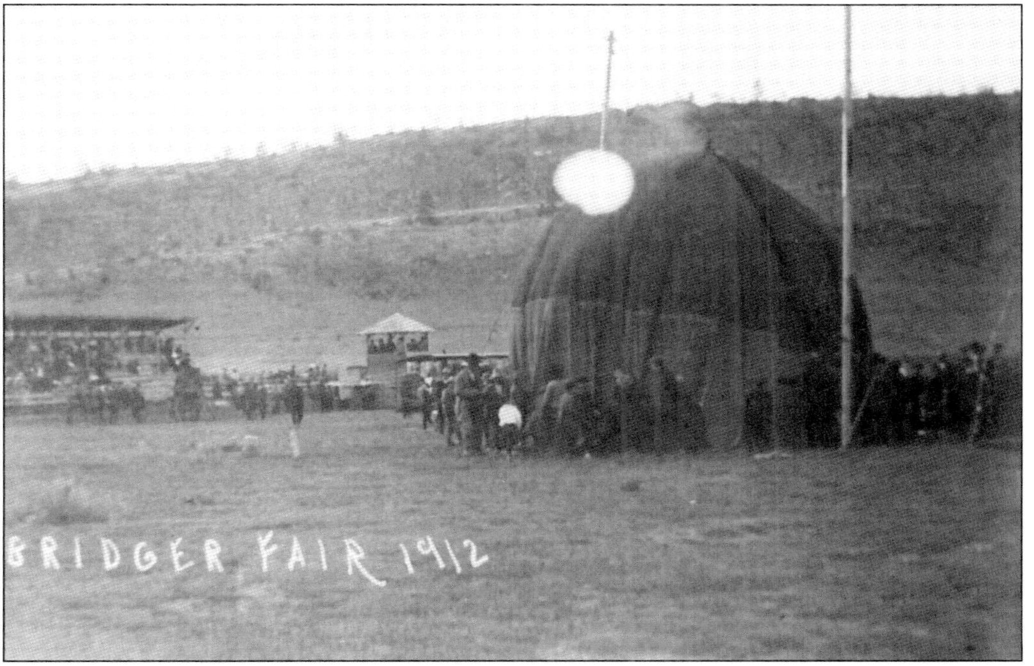

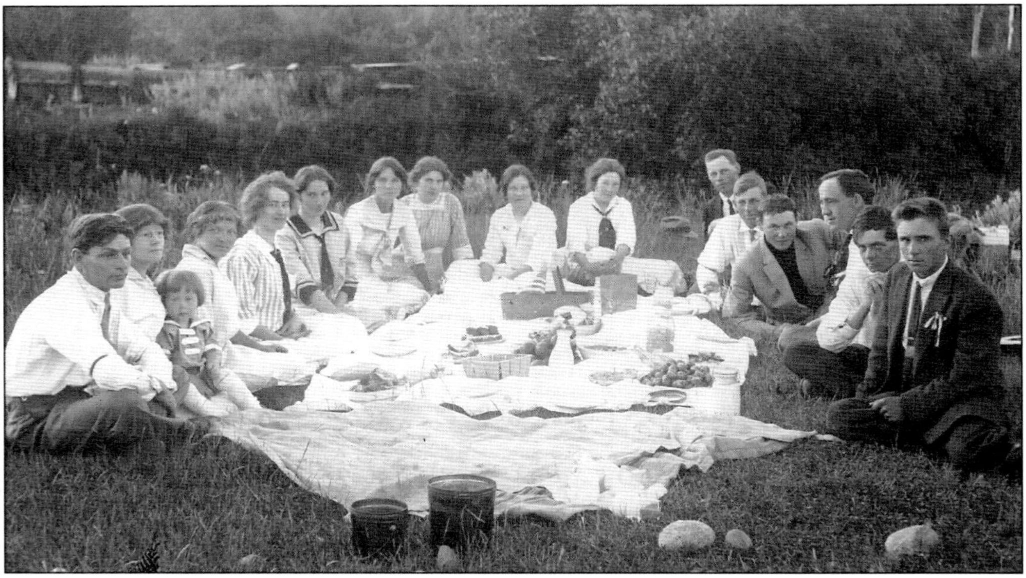

A local chapter of the Epworth League gathered for a picnic in this 1920s photograph. The Epworth League is a young adult organization of the United Methodist Church. Locally grown food on the picnic blankets included bottles of fresh milk, fried chicken, sandwiches, cakes, pies, plums, and apples. (CCHS.)

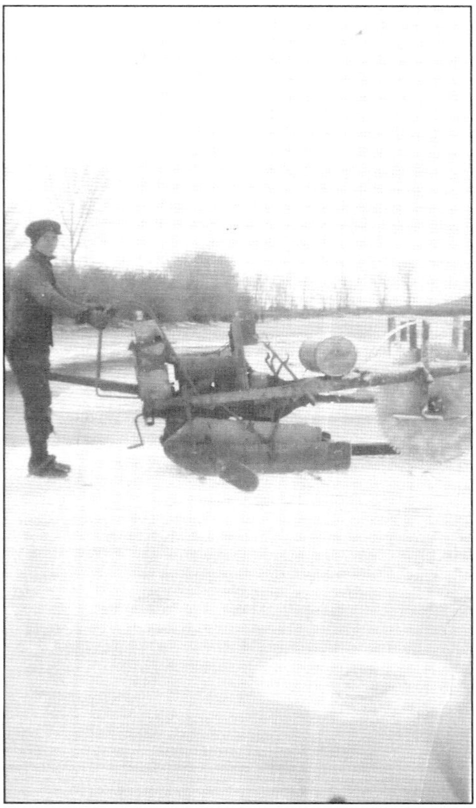

Noel J. Montgomery, owner of Star Dray and Transfer, saws ice on the Clark's Fork River east of Bridger in this 1920s photograph. Montgomery harvested ice during the winter and stored it in his North D Street icehouse. During the summer, he sold it to area residents and used his dray business to make the deliveries. (CCHS.)

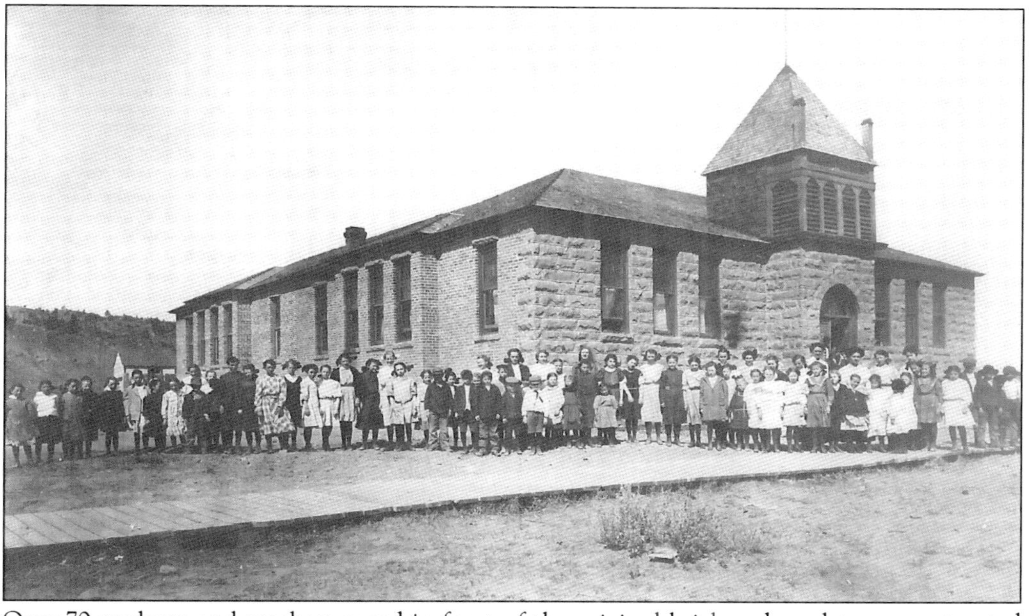

Over 70 students and teachers posed in front of the original brick-and-sandstone constructed Bridger Elementary School in this August 25, 1911, photograph. Like so many other buildings in the Clark's Fork Valley's early days, the Bridger Elementary School burned to the ground in the late 1910s or early 1920s. (CCHS.)

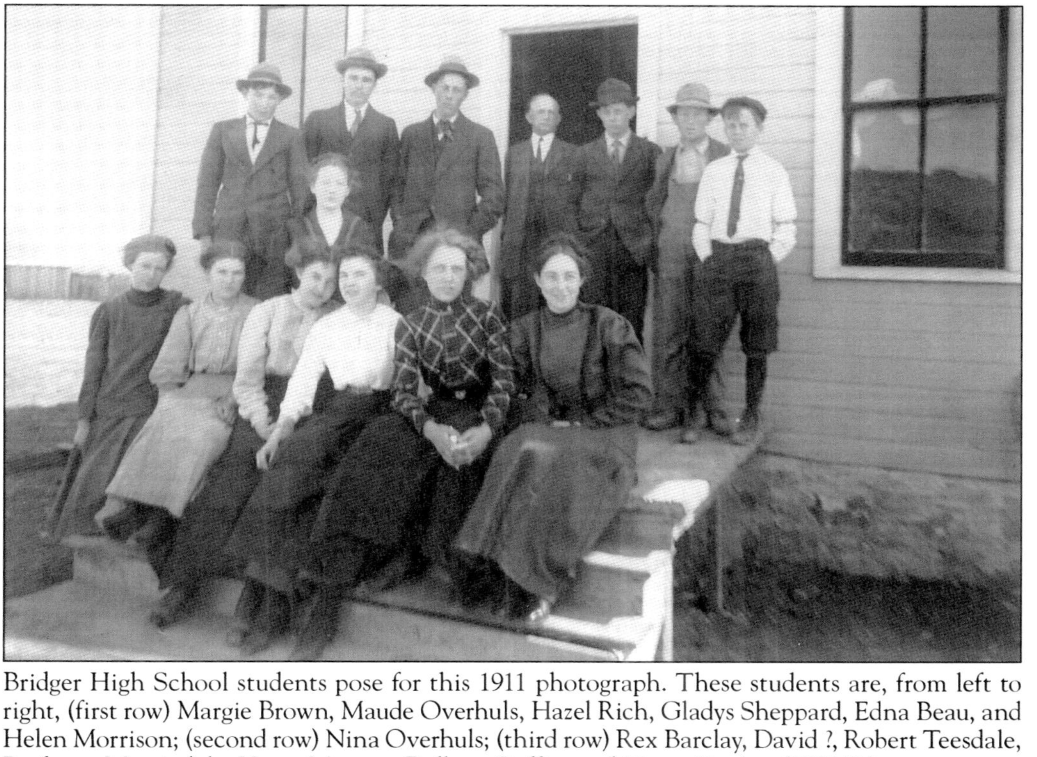

Bridger High School students pose for this 1911 photograph. These students are, from left to right, (first row) Margie Brown, Maude Overhuls, Hazel Rich, Gladys Sheppard, Edna Beau, and Helen Morrison; (second row) Nina Overhuls; (third row) Rex Barclay, David ?, Robert Teesdale, Professor Martindale, Harry Morrow, Delbert Coffin, and Harry Hauley. (CCHS.)

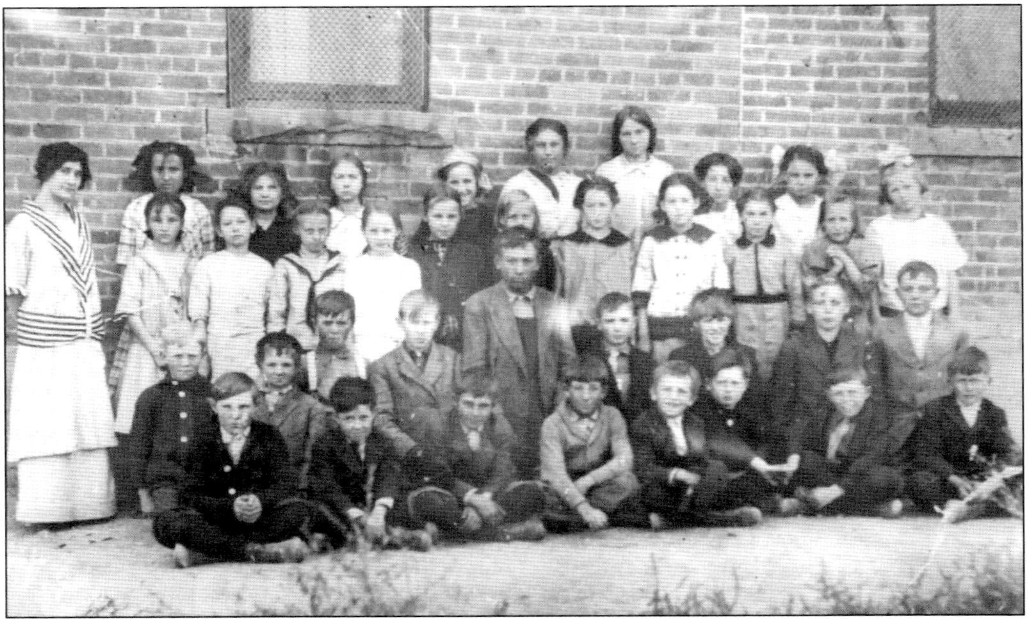

The third through fifth grade Bridger Elementary School classes posed for the 1914 photograph above. The students are, from left to right, (first row) Bob Bruce, Henry Hough, William Thormahlen, Corwin Rule, Louis Kuechler, Morgan Gottschalk, William Simon, and Frank Kuechler; (second row) Earnest Forsman, Robert Moody, Clark Simon, Walter Culbertson, Godfrey Adolph, William Ryan, Frank Kuechler, ? Lookingbill, and Harold Bourett; (third row) Hazel Moody, Nellie Folkins, Ora Rollins, Thelma Bourett, Iva Walters, Gloria Walters, Viola Culbertson, ? Hough, Millecent Young, and Thera Moore; (fourth row) teacher Emma Duvall, Helen Adolph, Mildred Rich, Elsie Foust, Valley Barns, unidentified, Sadie Foust, Edith Rule, Helen Spencer, and Edith Rife. The 1916 photograph below shows the interior of a Bridger High School classroom. (Both, CCHS.)

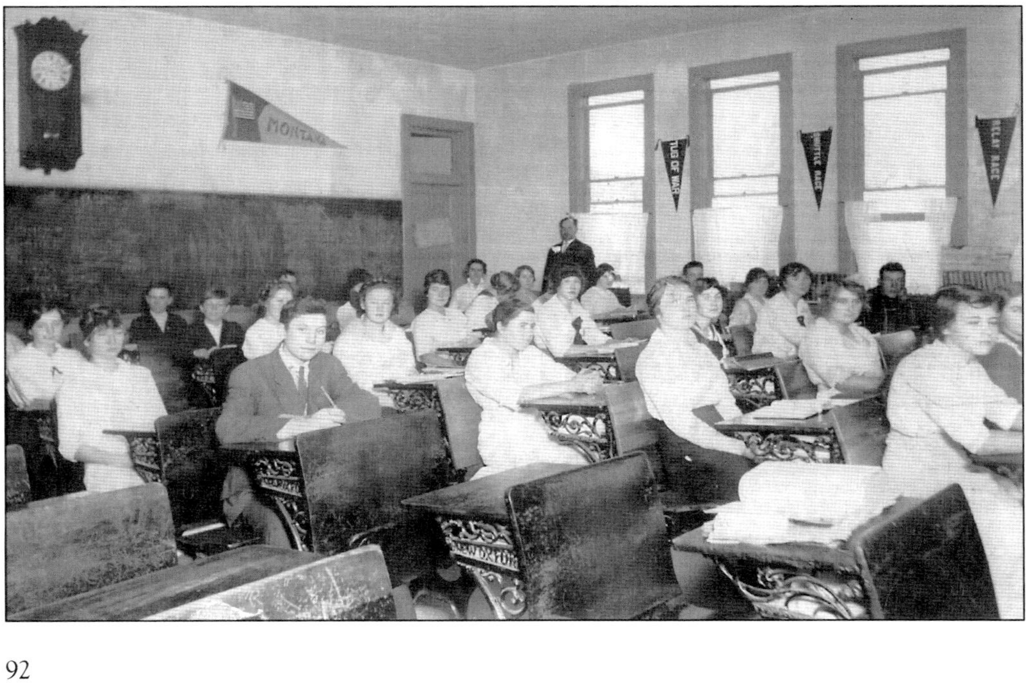

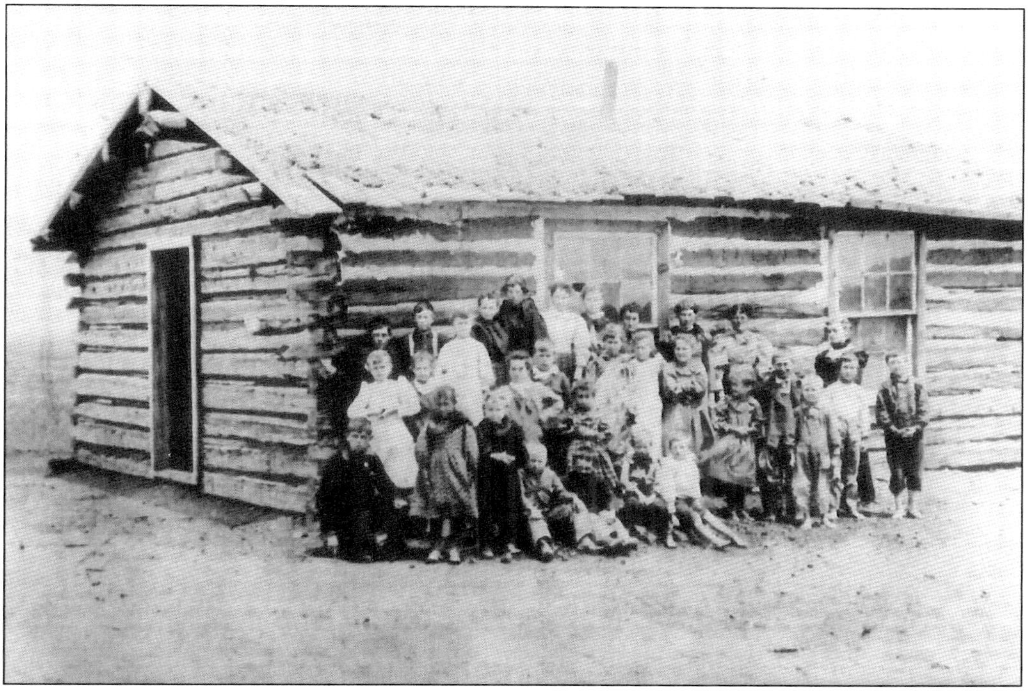

A group of children gathered for an 1897 class photograph above. This rural school stood across the road from the old Teesdale place, and the only student identified in the image is Art Foust, third from right in the first row. (CCHS.)

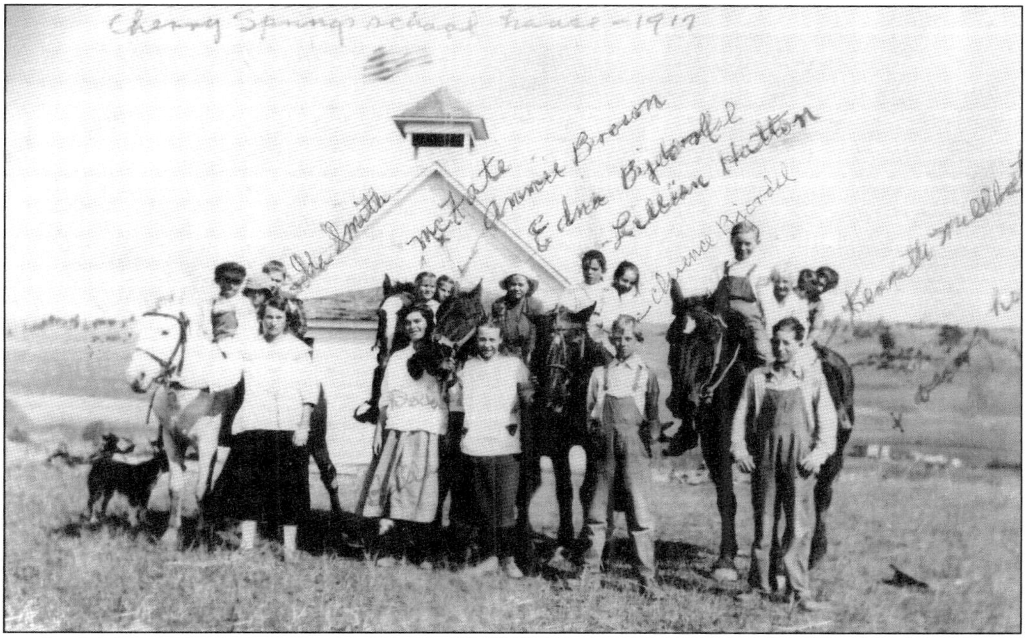

A 1917 photograph of the students attending the rural Cherry Springs School shows that many of them commuted to school on horseback. Cherry Springs School operated from 1915 through 1939 and also served as a voting place for farmers and ranchers living west of Bridger. (CCHS.)

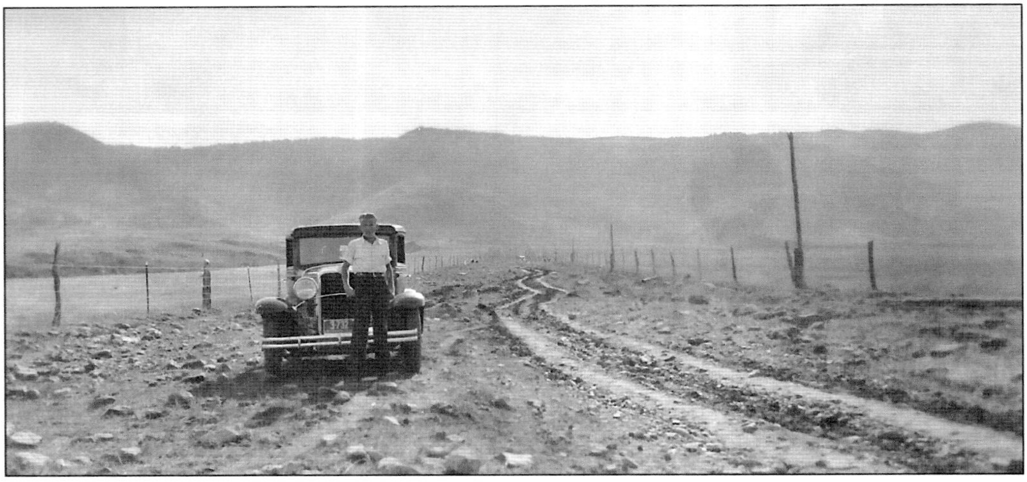

These photographs illustrate the conditions of Clark's Fork Valley roads (above) and the efforts implemented to improve them (below). Automobile travel over these unimproved roads proved impossible at times. Heavy rains left the roads too muddy to use or just passable enough to leave large pieces of mud and rock in the wake of drivers daring enough to traverse them. When the rains stopped, the sun baked the displaced mud into rock-hard obstacles that forced drivers to navigate around them. The 1922 photograph below shows Walt Owen (left) and Clif Helt (right) improving a road by grading it with a four-horse team. (Both, CCHS.)

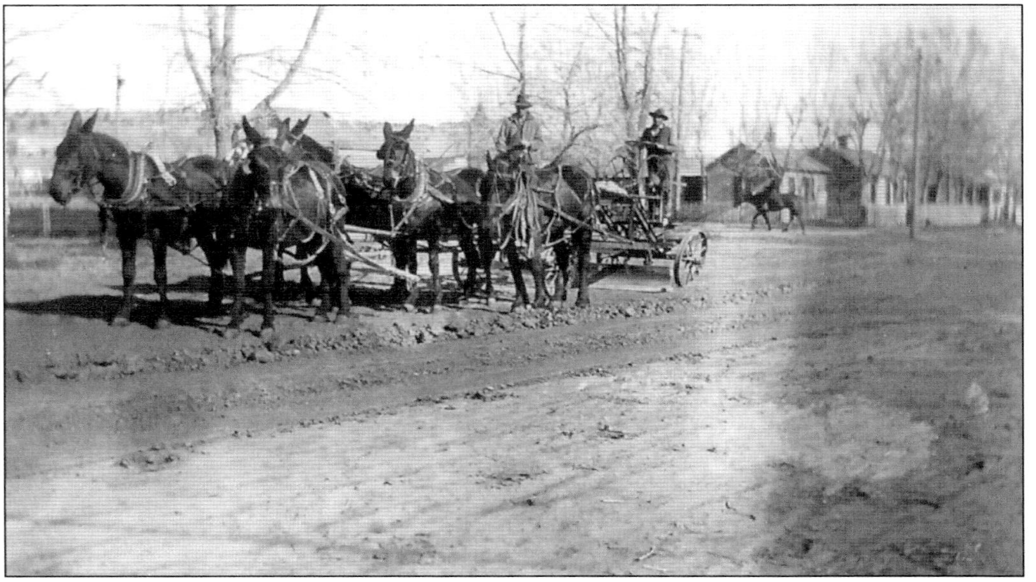

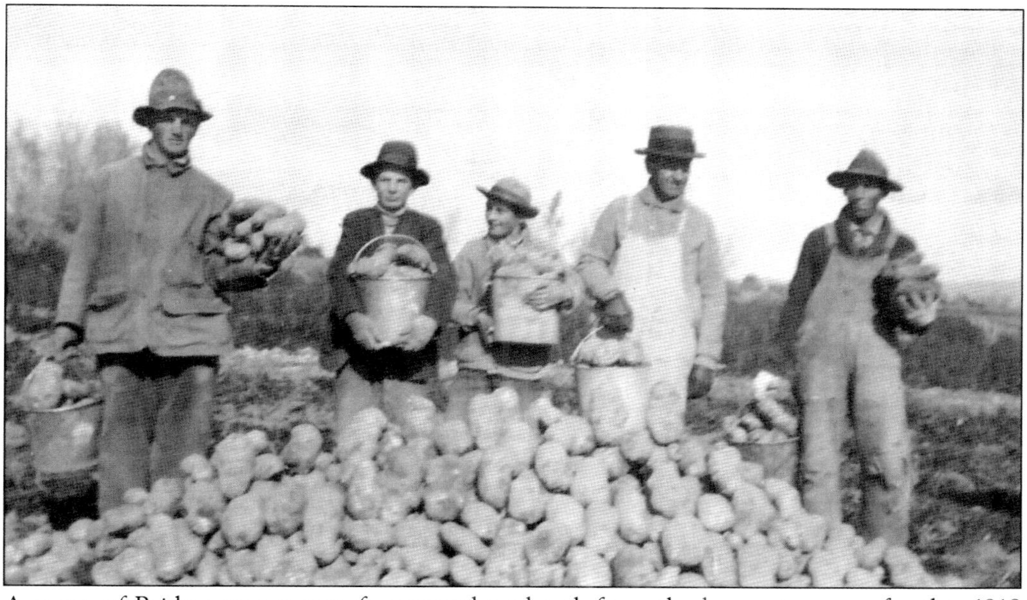

A group of Bridger area potato farmers take a break from the harvest to pose for this 1918 photograph. The soil of Clark's Fork Valley produced potatoes of exceptional size. Potato farming proved so successful that valley producers formed a potato cooperative and even developed a new variety of potato in Fromberg. (CCHS.)

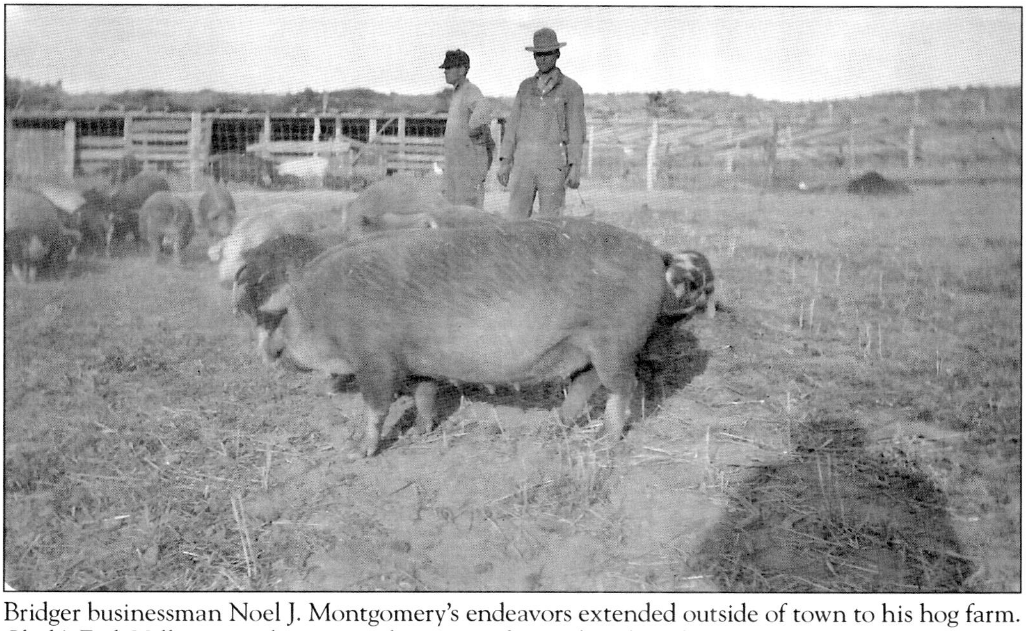

Bridger businessman Noel J. Montgomery's endeavors extended outside of town to his hog farm. Clark's Fork Valley not only supported an array of agricultural products, it also supported a livestock industry that produced hogs, sheep, and cattle. In this photograph, Montgomery (right) displays a small number of his prime hogs. (CCHS.)

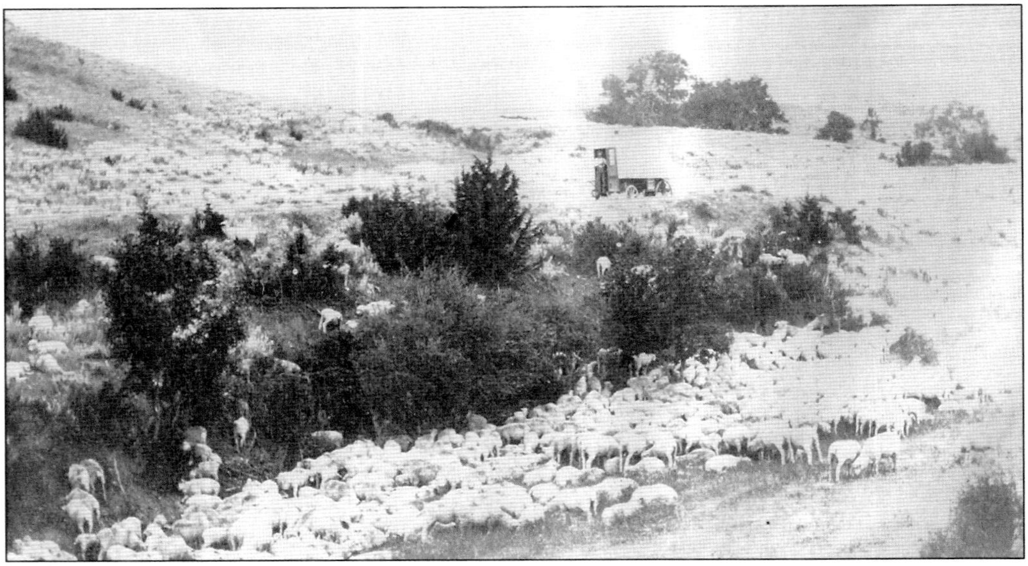

These photographs illustrate activities associated with the two primary types of livestock raised in Clark's Fork Valley, particularly in the Bridger area. Above, a large herd of sheep grazes under the watchful eye of the sheepherder standing in his sheep wagon (center, top). Sheepherders spent many long days alone watching over their herds while living in sheep wagons, an early-day version of camper trailers. Below, a group of Bridger cowboys break for lunch during a day of branding cattle. These cowboys are, from left to right, Clyde Hawks, Norwood Siesen, Irvin Ellis, Mike Kapor, Bill Schwend, Midford "Mid" Knight, cook Gordon Walcott, Walt Owen, Walt Torsk, hired man Jess Schwend, Gerald Ellis, Martin Ellis, Joe O'Brien, Fred Jeffers Sr., and unidentified. (Above, K. Hergenrider; below, CCHS.)

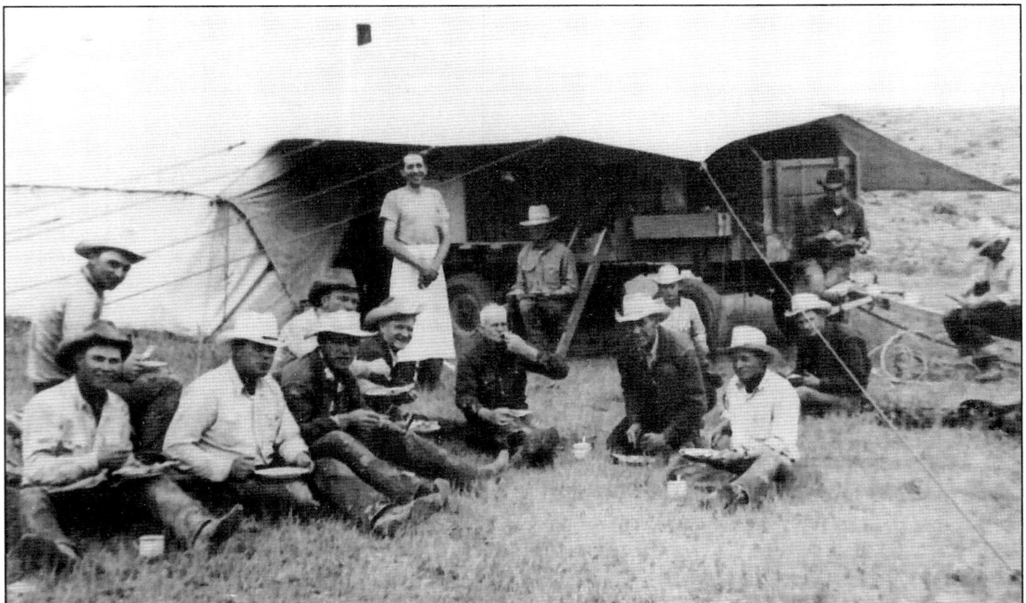

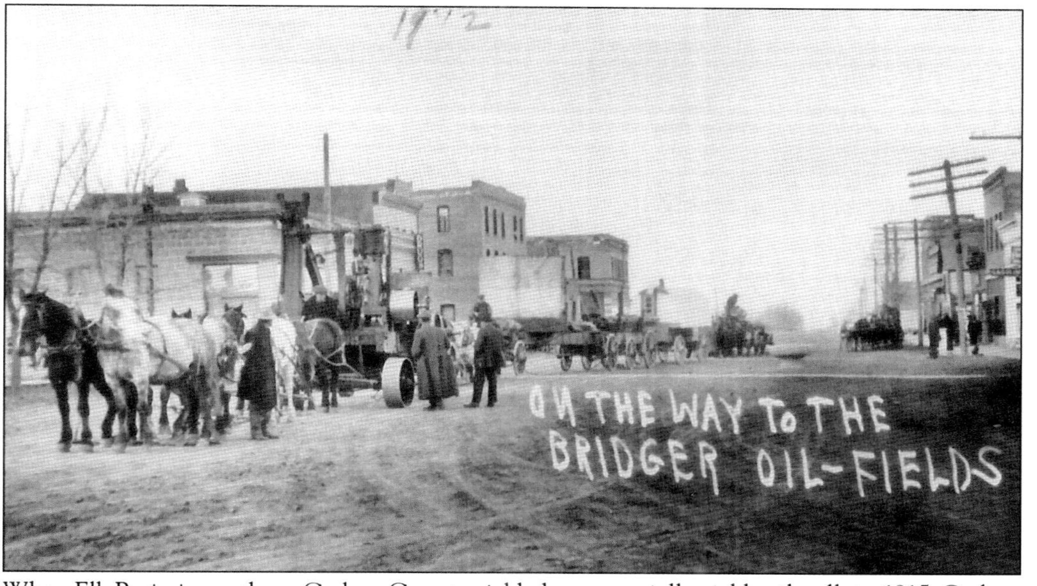

When Elk Basin in southern Carbon County yielded commercially viable oil wells in 1915, Carbon County oil prospecting began immediately. In 1916, test drilling started on Dry Creek near Bridger, at Golden near Belfry, and at Moser Dome east of Silesia. This early-1920s photograph shows steam-powered equipment on its way through Bridger to the Dry Creek Oil Field. (CCHS.)

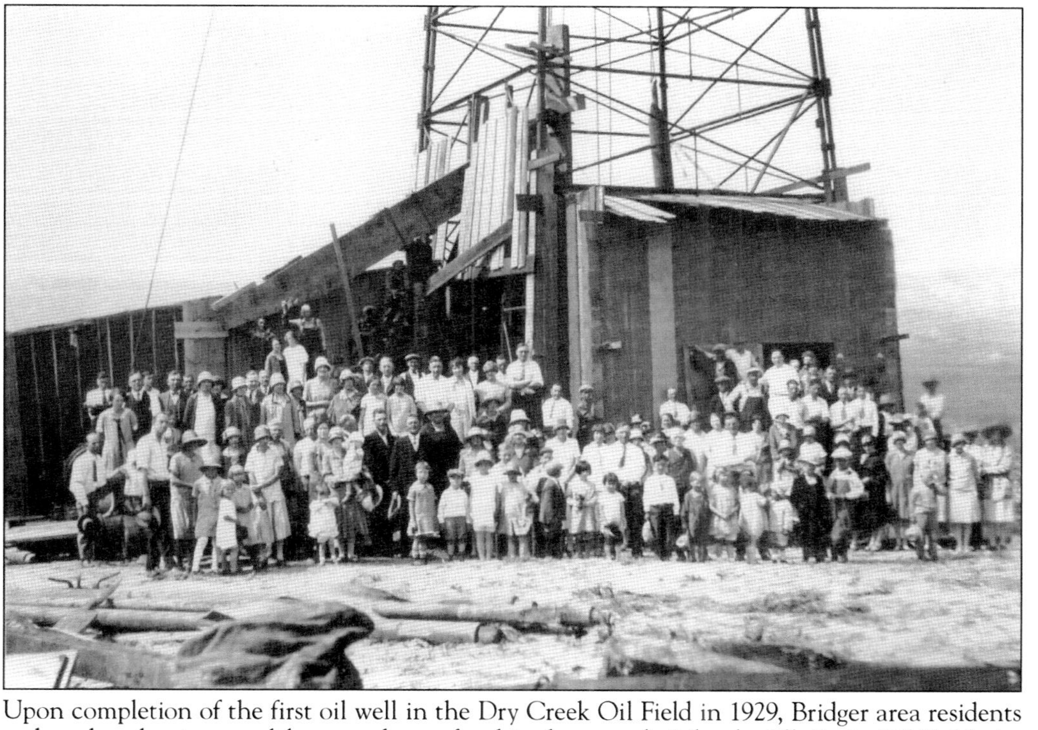

Upon completion of the first oil well in the Dry Creek Oil Field in 1929, Bridger area residents gathered at the site to celebrate and pose for this photograph. Like the Elk Basin Oil Field, the Ohio Oil Company eventually installed a camp to house the Dry Creek Oil Field workers and their families. (CCHS.)

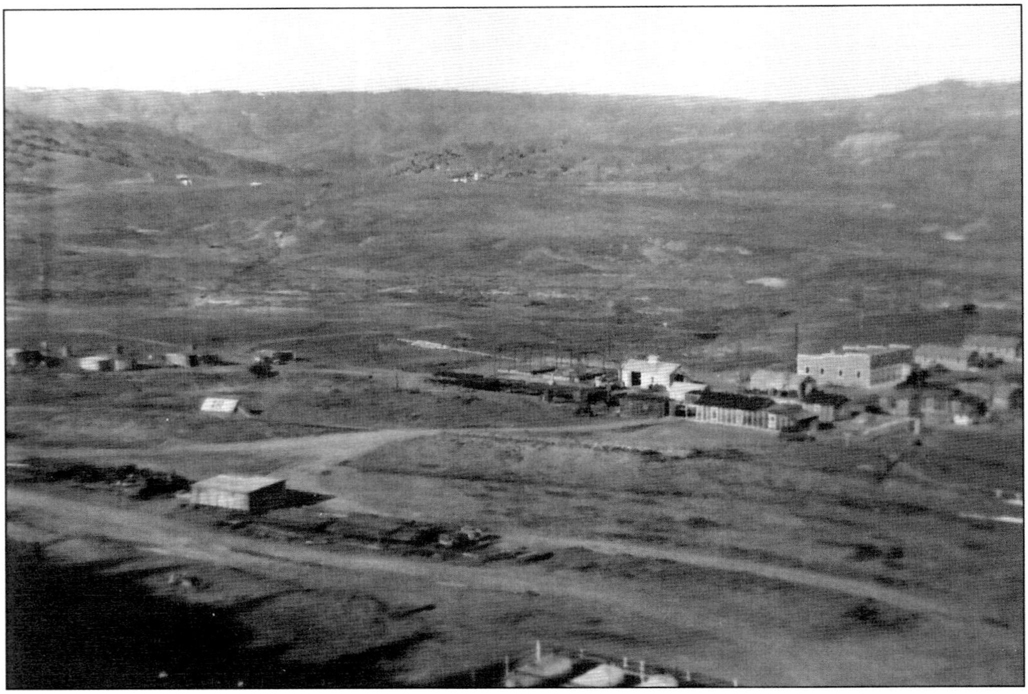

A late-1950s aerial view of the Marathon Oil Company's Dry Creek Oil Camp shows the camp's growth in the nearly 30 years since oil production began. In addition to many oil and gas wells, the camp contained a drilling-core house, a machine shop, a garage, a compression plant, a gas station, homes for workers and their families, and a swimming pool. (CCHS.)

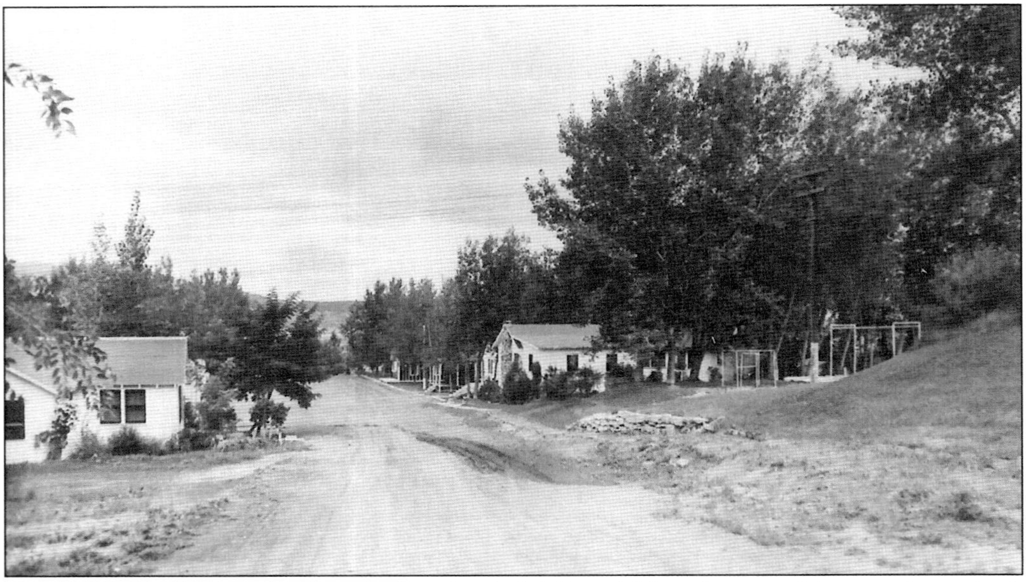

This late-1950s photograph shows the Dry Creek Oil Camp's Main Street with housing lining both sides. Ivan John "Toby" Hares's home is the first one on the right. Around 1960, Hares purchased the Dry Creek Oil Camp homes from the Marathon Oil Company and continued renting them out to oil field workers. (CCHS.)

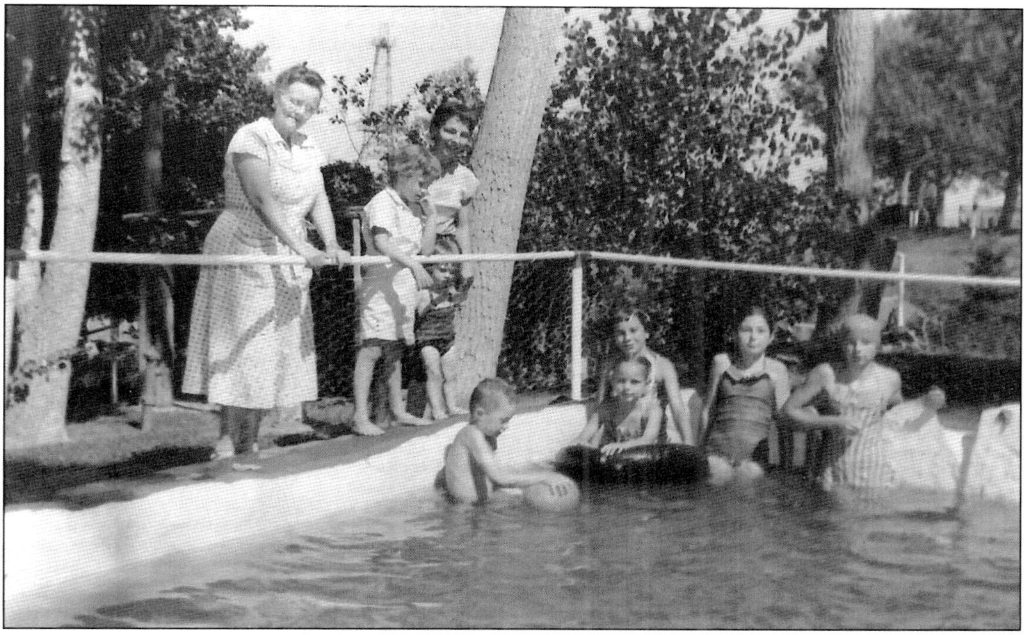

After purchasing the residential portions of the Dry Creek Oil Camp, Ivan John "Toby" Hares installed a swimming pool for the camp's residents (above). The two adults in this photograph are Irma Hares (left) and Helen McCann (right). The four girls in the pool are Helen McCann's daughters. Of note in this photograph is the oil derrick rising in the distance. (CCHS.)

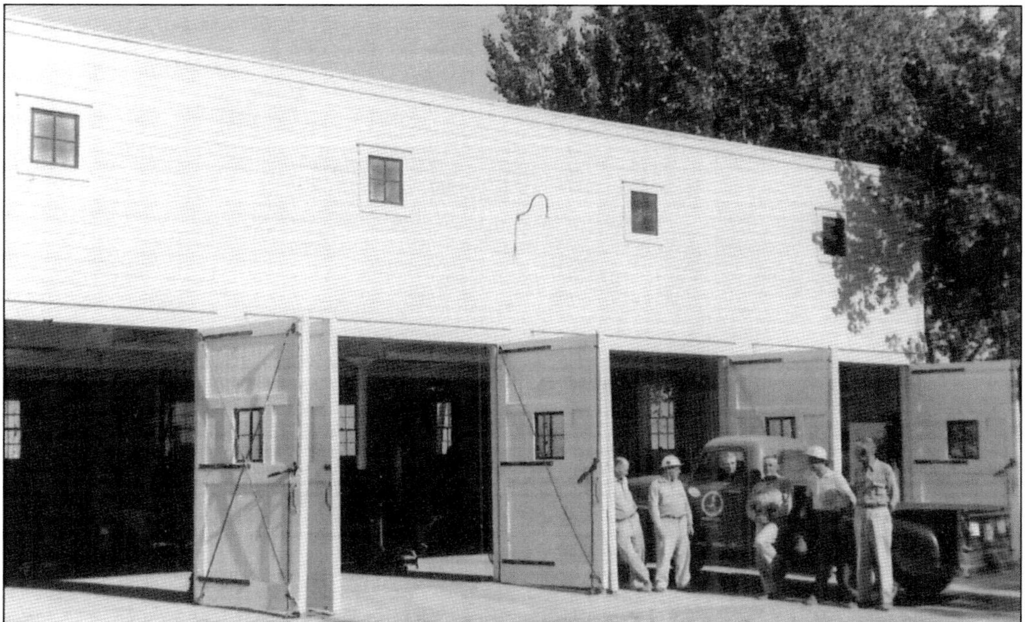

This 1958 photograph shows the expansive Marathon Oil Dry Creek Garage. These six men shown in this photograph are, from left to right, Ivan John "Toby" Hares, Shorty Dunn, Tuffy Hilliard, Jim Upton, Kenny Outland, and Gerald Merrill. Hilliard sits in a truck with the Marathon Oil Company logo on it. (CCHS.)

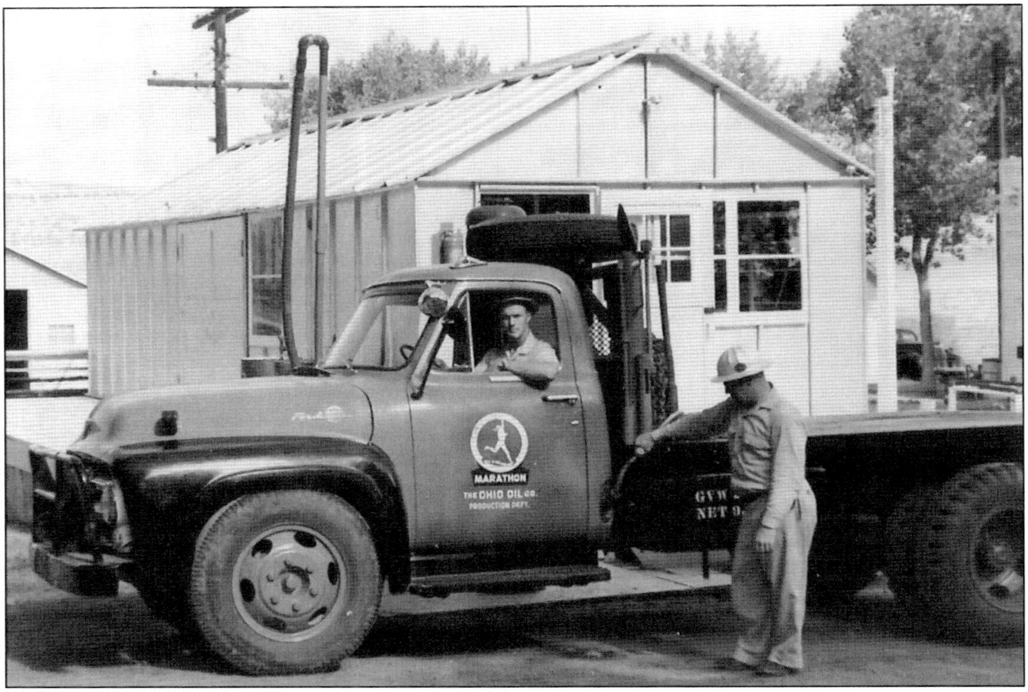

This photograph depicts the gas station at the Marathon Oil Dry Creek Camp. Kenny Outland sits in a company truck while Shorty Dunn fills its gas tank. (CCHS.)

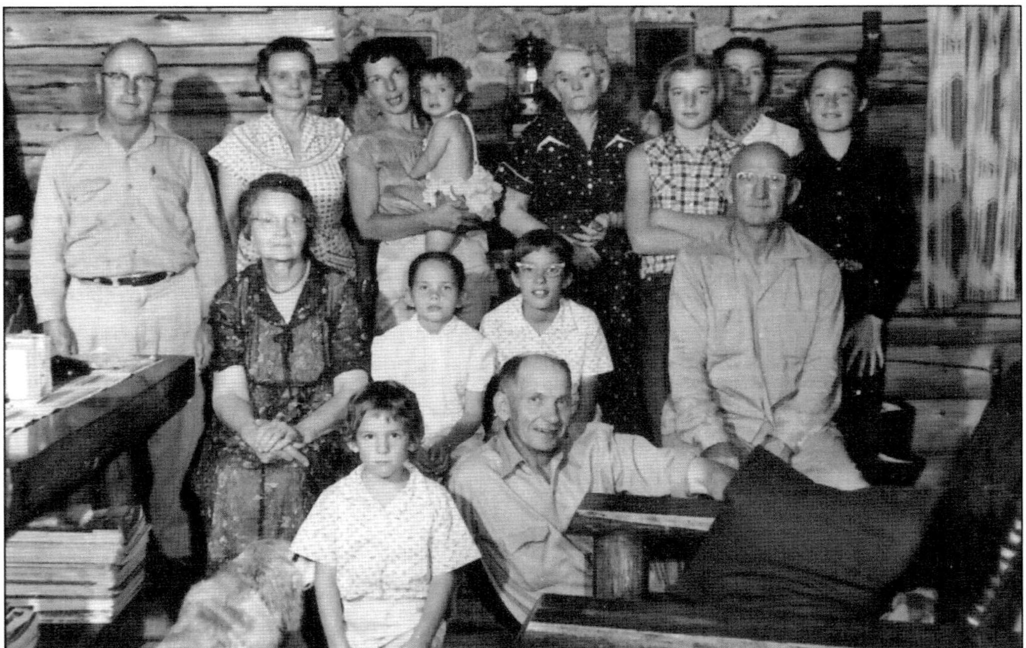

Thirteen Dry Creek Oil Camp residents posed for this 1958 photograph. Included among this group is Shorty Dunn, Maude Davis, Irma Hares, Irma Dunn, Mrs. Gibbs, Anita Black, Frank Gibbs, Mary Lou Dunn, Ivan John "Toby" Hares, and Buttons the dog. (CCHS.)

Seven

BELFRY, CHANCE, AND THE ELK BASIN OIL CAMP

Like neighboring Bearcreek and Washoe to the west, Belfry owes its existence to the construction of the Yellowstone Park Railroad (YPRR), later renamed the Montana, Wyoming, and Southern Railroad (MW&S). The YPRR, under the direction of F. A. Hall, president of the Belfry Townsite Committee, platted the town on July 26, 1905, and named it after Pennsylvania investor Dr. William Belfry. The town served as headquarters for the YPRR/MW&S until 1954, when the company folded. At its peak, Belfry housed several hotels, bars, and grocery stores; a lumber mill; and a drugstore. These businesses served railroad workers living in town, rural ranchers, residents of nearby Chance, and, later, workers from the Elk Basin Oil Camp. Belfry residents built several schools and three churches over the years. The churches served the United Methodist, Lutheran, and Church of Jesus Christ of Latter Day Saints denominations. The small village of Chance lies 8 miles south of Belfry along Montana Highway 72, and just 2 miles from Wyoming's northern border with Montana. Chance began as a stage stop along the Meeteetse Trail, a wagon route skirting the northern flank of the Beartooth Mountains between Red Lodge, Montana, and Meeteetse, Wyoming. Chance takes its name from early homesteader and postmaster Nathan Chance, who also constructed the first toll bridge across the Clark's Fork River. Chance served a mostly rural population of farmers and ranchers and offered a post office from 1898 to 1921 as well as a school. Butcher Creek in western Carbon County has the distinction of being the site of the first, although unsuccessful, oil well in Carbon County. In 1915, Elk Basin yielded Carbon County's and Montana's first commercially productive oil well under the ownership of the Ohio Oil Company. The Elk Basin Oil Field straddles the Montana-Wyoming border, with oil production in both states. Soon after the Elk Basin discovery, a small camp was erected on the Montana side of the field to house oil field workers. This camp was approximately 11 miles east of Chance.

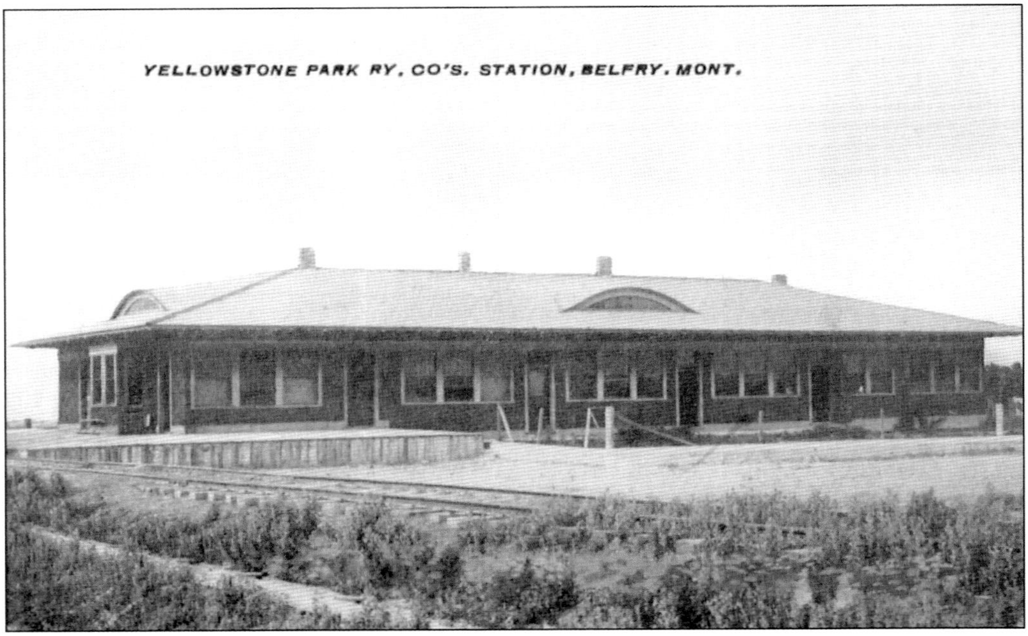

The Montana, Wyoming, and Southern Railroad (MW&S) began life as the Yellowstone Park Railroad (YPRR). The MW&S brought Belfry to life when it needed a rail stop along the Clark's Fork River before turning west toward the Bear Creek Valley's coal mines. The photograph above shows the Belfry depot soon after its construction in 1907. The YPRR/MW&S located its headquarters in Belfry, building many other railroad support buildings such as the machine shop pictured below. Local residents referred to the shop and surrounding area as the "roundabout." The railroad provided many jobs to Belfry and Bear Creek Valley residents. (Above, author's collection; below, Wolchesky.)

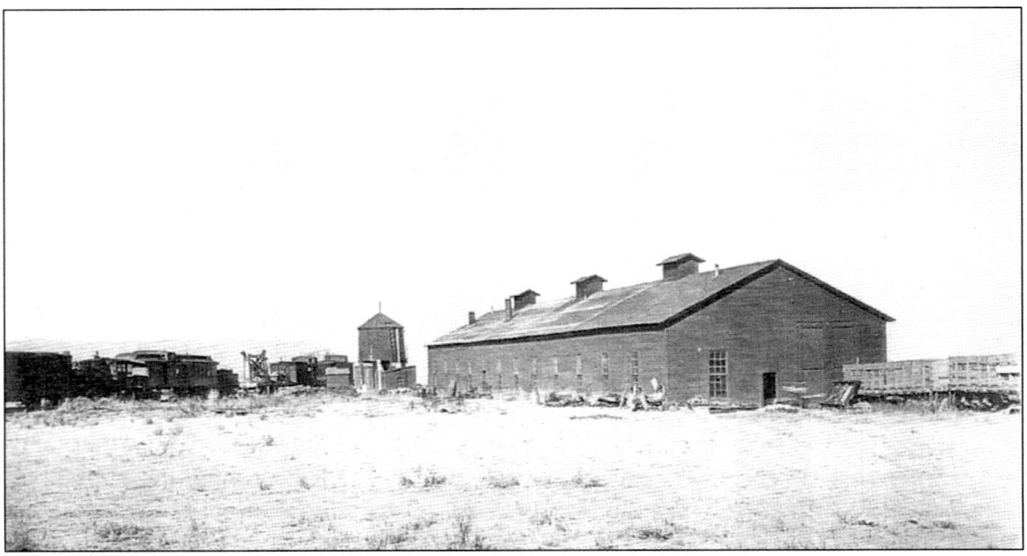

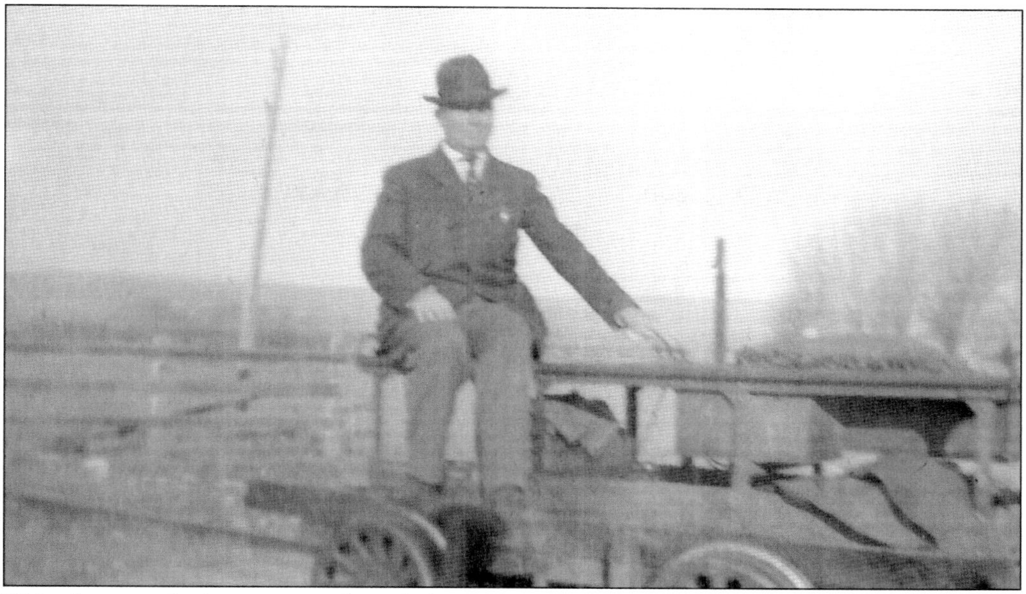

This photograph shows an unidentified man sitting on a Montana, Wyoming, and Southern Railroad handcar. Track maintenance crews and engineers typically used handcars to inspect sections of the railroad and to ferry men and supplies to places in need of repair. (Hogan.)

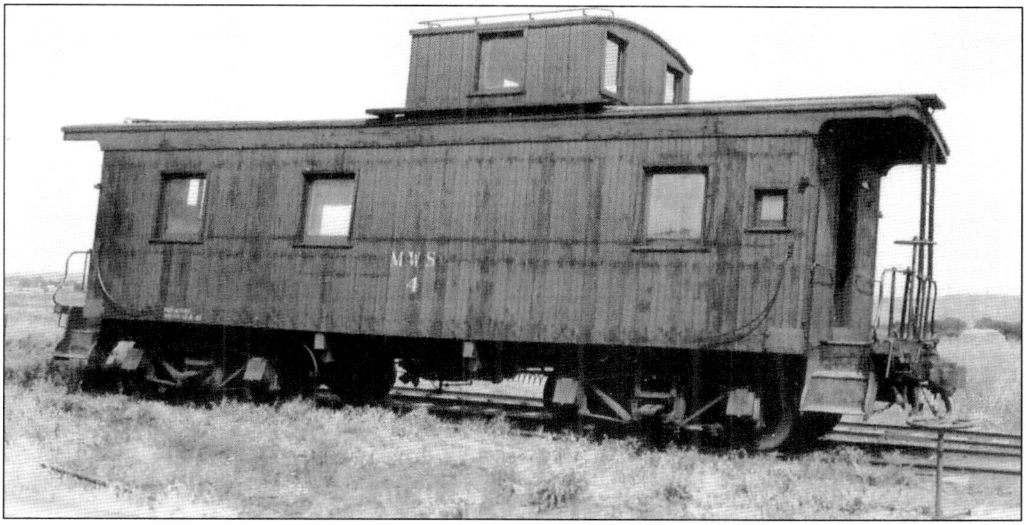

Montana, Wyoming, and Southern Railroad (MW&S) caboose No. 4 sits idle on Clark's Fork Valley tracks. The MW&S primarily hauled coal from the mines in Bear Creek Valley. The company did, however, install a spur track to eastern Belfry to pick up locally grown grain and produce in addition to picking up sugar beets at dumps along its lines. (Wolchesky.)

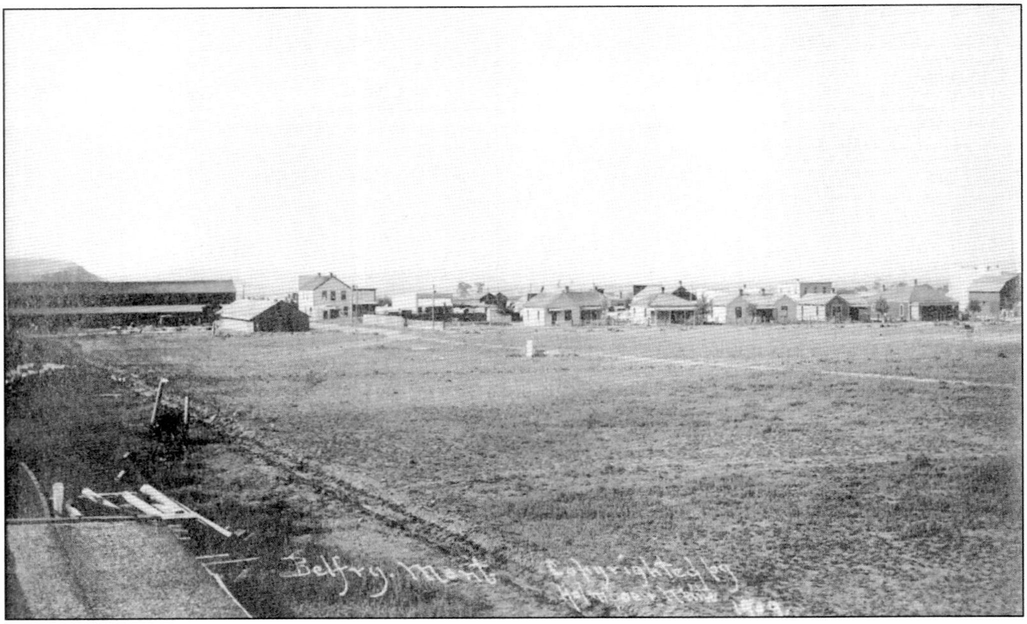

These postcards from 1909 illustrate the extent of Belfry's development since its birth four years earlier. The photograph above looks north up the Clark's Fork Valley and shows the Holland Lumber Yard on the far left and a mostly residential area extending to its right. The backs of some Main Street businesses can be seen in the distance behind these homes. The bottom photograph focuses on a purely residential area of town. A man named Stuart sent this postcard to Grace Fanning in Valley Center, Kansas, and brags of earning "$6.50 last week and $7.35 this week." (Both, K. Hergenrider.)

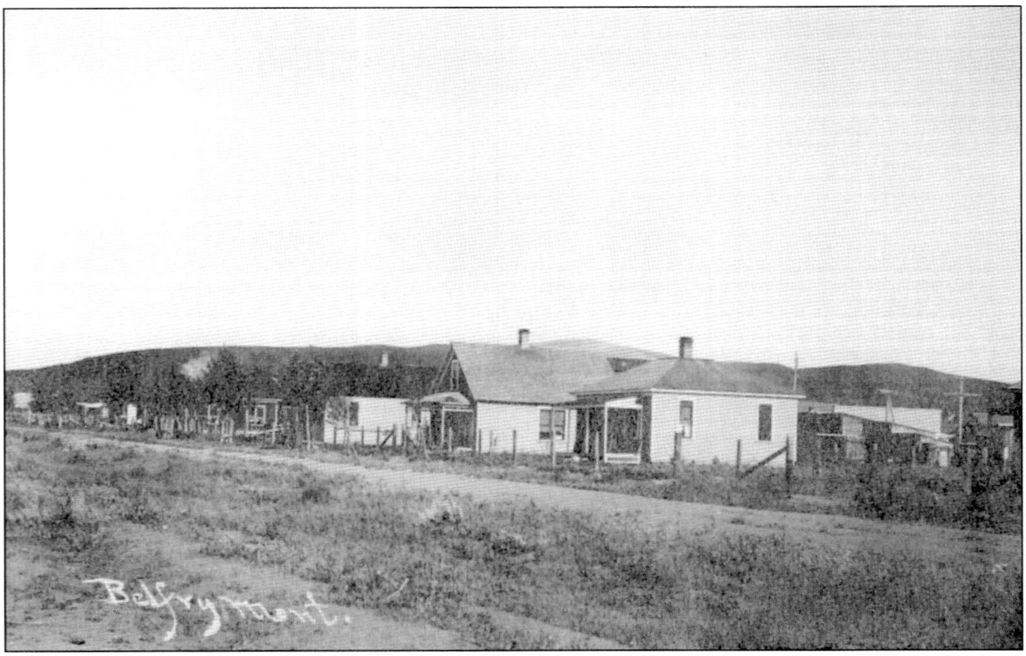

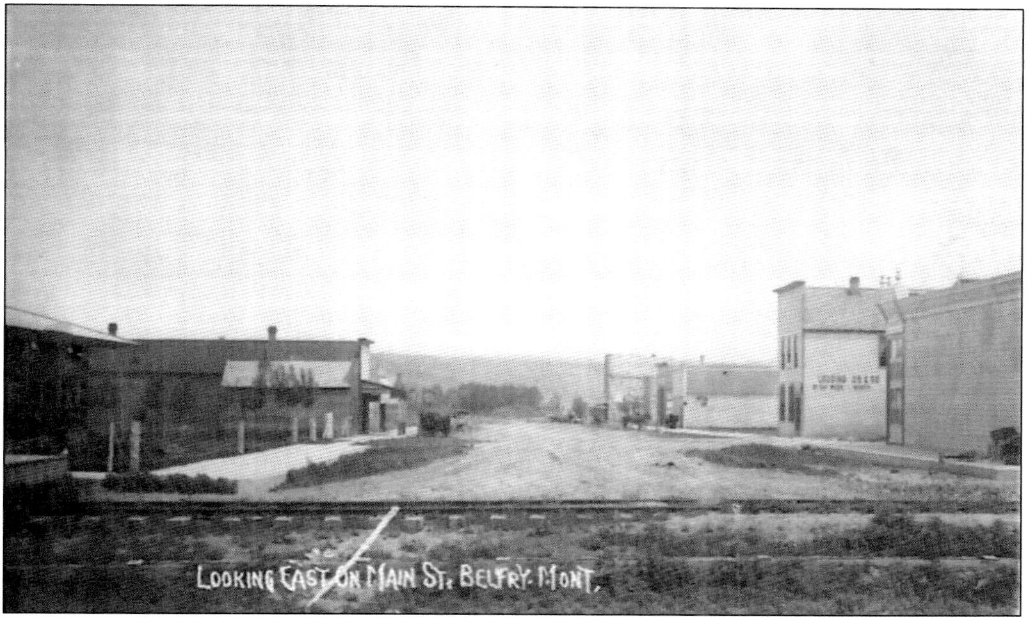

Opposing views of Belfry's Main Street provide an inventory of early day businesses. The 1909 photograph above looks east towards the Pryor Mountains. The tracks of the Montana, Wyoming, and Southern Railroad traverse the foreground with a portion of the depot visible on the immediate left of the photograph. Along the right side of this photograph is the Holland Hardware Store, a boardinghouse advertising rooms for 25¢ and 50¢, the Shamrock Saloon, and a grocery store at the end of the street. The west-looking photograph below shows the grocery store in the left foreground and the porch of the Hancock Hotel on the far right. (Both, Wolchesky.)

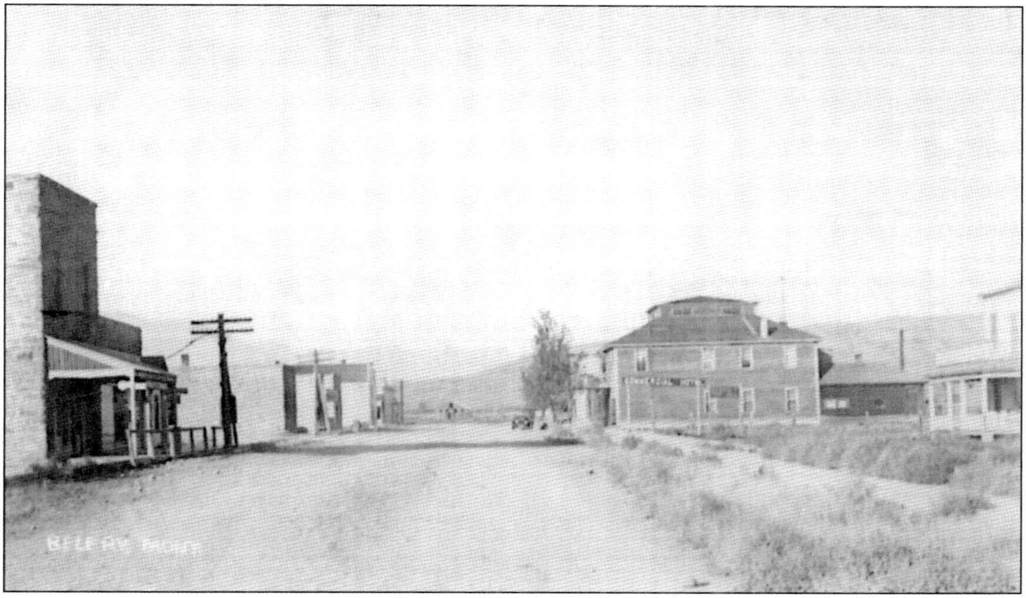

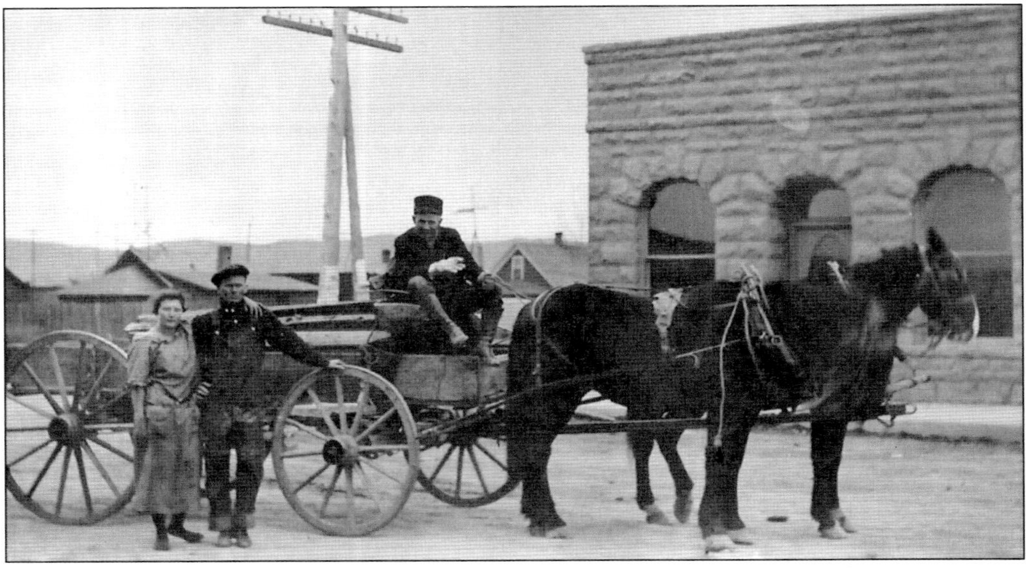

Leon Garrington and his team of horses hauling railroad ties stopped on Belfry's Main Street in front of the Belfry Bank to pose for this 1928 photograph. Standing beside Leon is, from left to right, Bessie Kelsey and Leander Kelsey. Bankers from Red Lodge initially opened the Belfry Bank. (Wolchesky.)

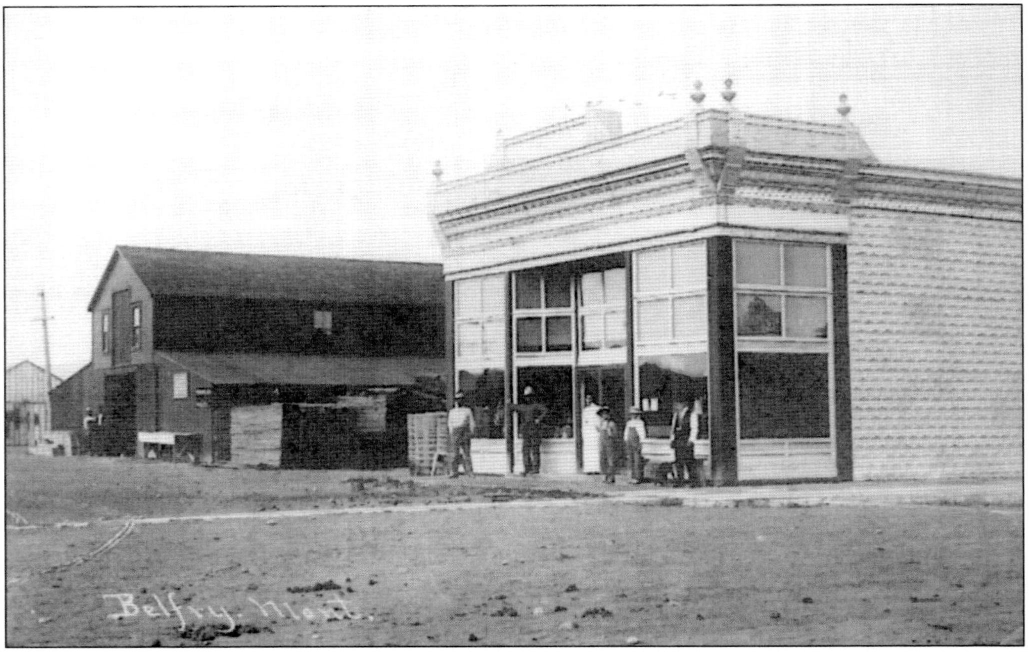

This *c.* 1910 photograph shows Belfry's Holland Hardware Store (foreground) and Holland Lumber Yard (background). Only the Montana, Wyoming, and Southern Railroad machine shop, which could hold four locomotives, outmatched the Holland Lumber Yard building in size. The hardware store's tin siding gives it the appearance of brick construction in this photograph. (Wolchesky.)

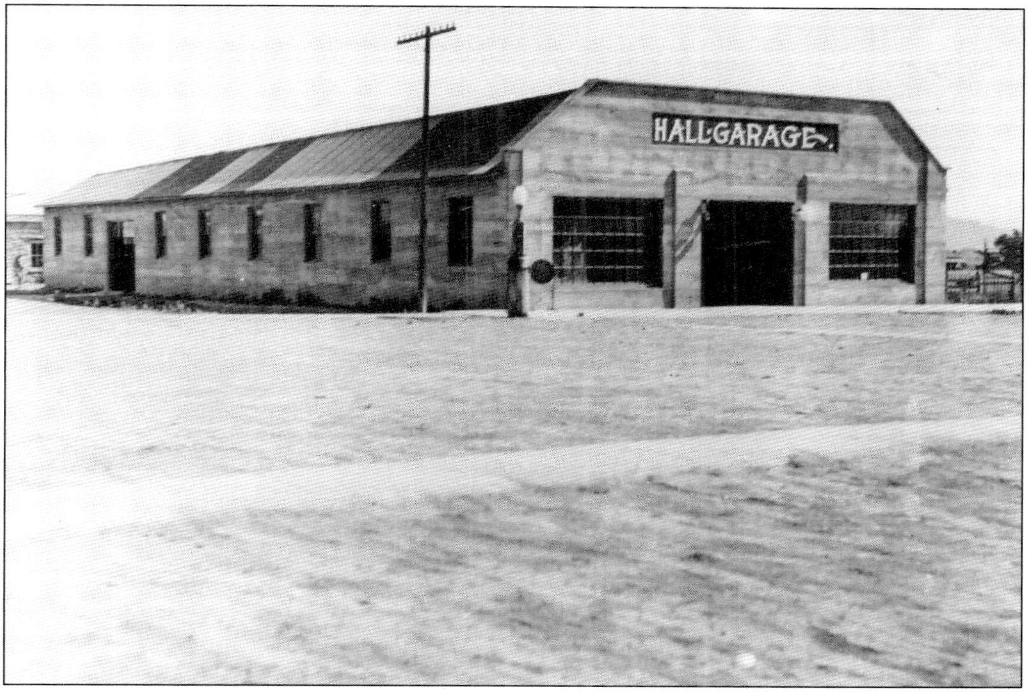

Located next to the Hancock Hotel, the Hall Garage served Belfry motorists from 1920 to 1935. When the Hancock Hotel caught fire and burned to the ground, the blaze set the garage's roof alight, burning everything inside the garage's thick concrete walls. The Hancock hotel proved a boon for the garage before the fire. Hotel patrons paid to park their automobiles in the Hall Garage to keep them out of the weather. In these 1920s photographs, the Hall Garage's sole glass-topped gas pump is visible on the corner (above) and a full slate of automobiles are stabled or await repair inside (below). (Both, Wolchesky.)

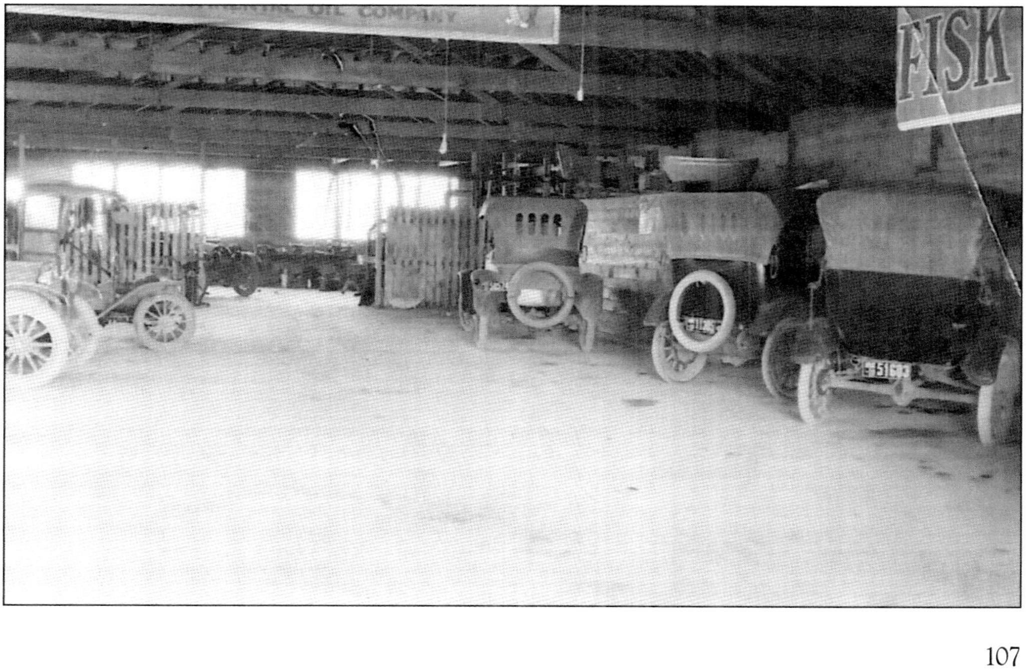

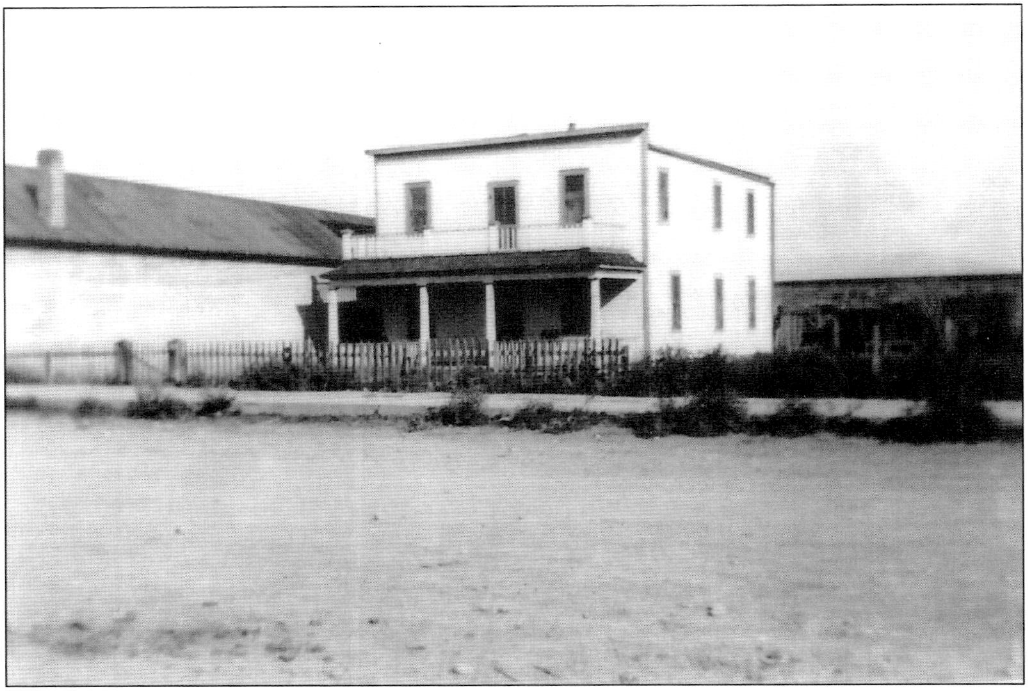

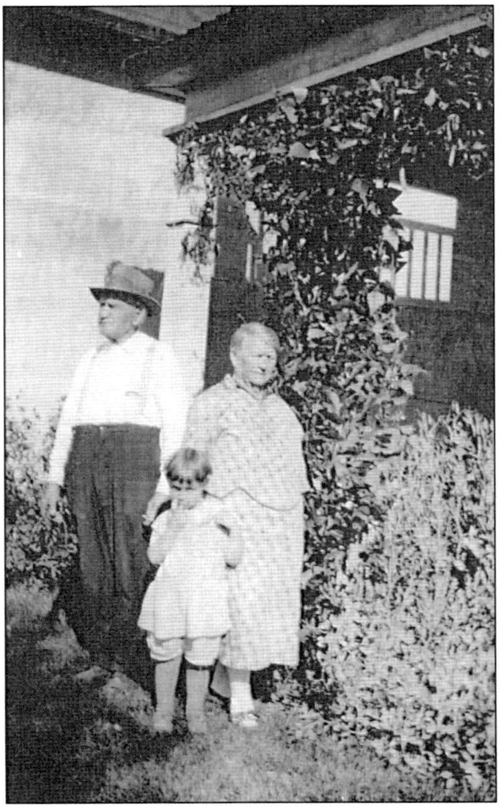

Anna Dayton purchased what would soon be called the Hancock Hotel (above) in the early 1920s from John and Mary Freebury. Anna's 1923 marriage to Owen Hancock finalized the hotel's permanent name. The Hancock Hotel had six guest rooms upstairs with five guest rooms; a lobby; a kitchen; and the hotel's indoor bathroom, with toilet, sink, and bathtub downstairs. Use of the hotel's bathroom by guests and townsfolk came at an additional charge. An outhouse on the hotel's southwest side was also available for free. The Hancock Hotel's well produced unusually soft water for the Belfry area. Townsfolk often borrowed a pail of water to wash their hair. The 1931 photograph at left shows Anna and Owen Hancock and their granddaughter Joise Denney near the hotel's front porch. (Both, Wolchesky.)

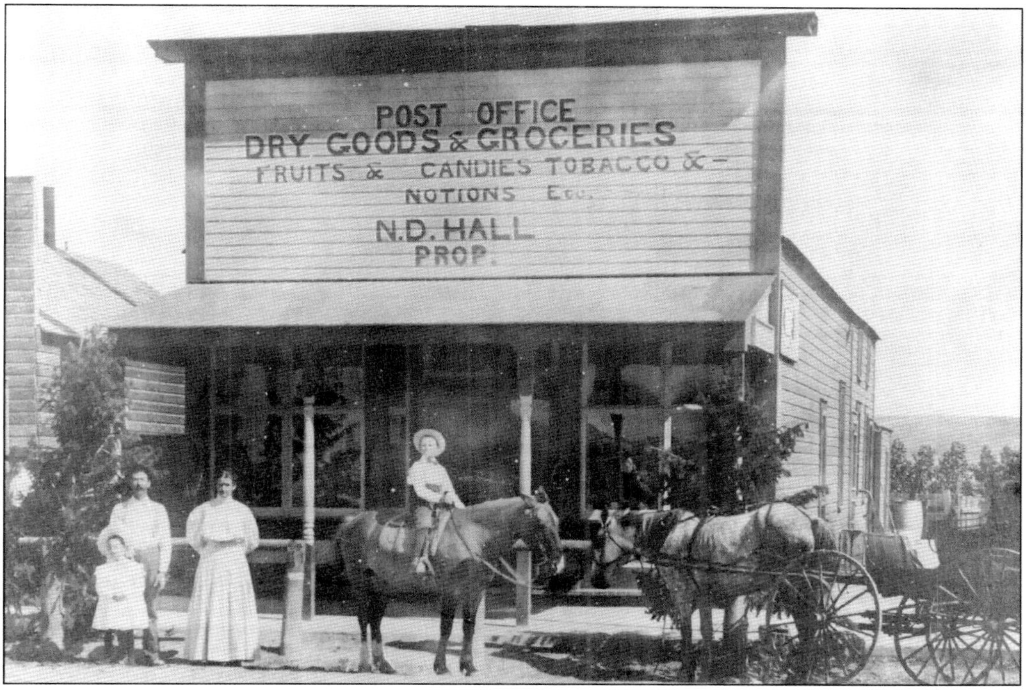

This pre-1910 photograph shows Belfry's first post office. The post office opened in early 1906 with Mary E. Hall as postmistress. It operated out of the dry goods and grocery store owned by Mary and her husband, Newton D. Hall. In the ensuing years, the post office occupied five other locations before the current post office opened in 2000. (Wolchesky.)

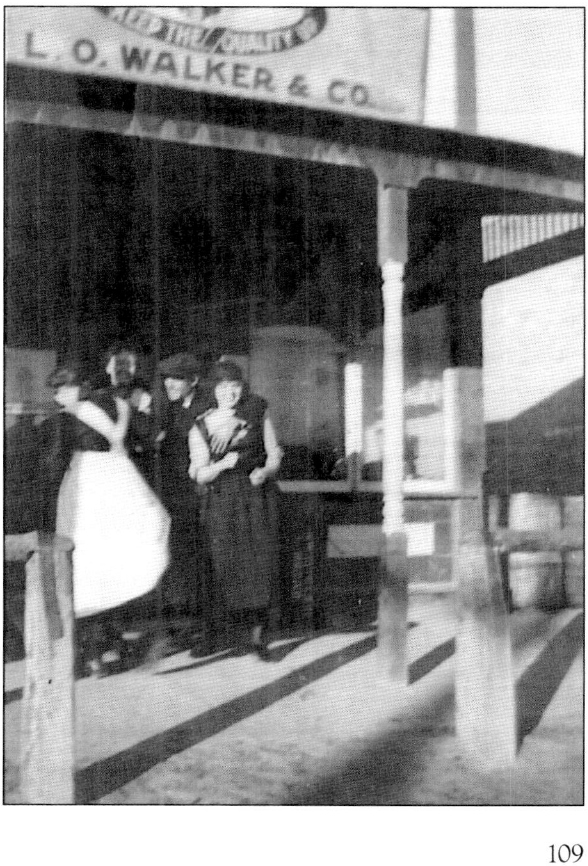

Ben Rarey poses between two women in this early-1920s photograph. The group stands in front of the L. O. Walker and Company Store. The hitching posts in the foreground on either side of this photograph indicate the degree to which people relied on horses for transportation into the 1920s and beyond. (Wolchesky.)

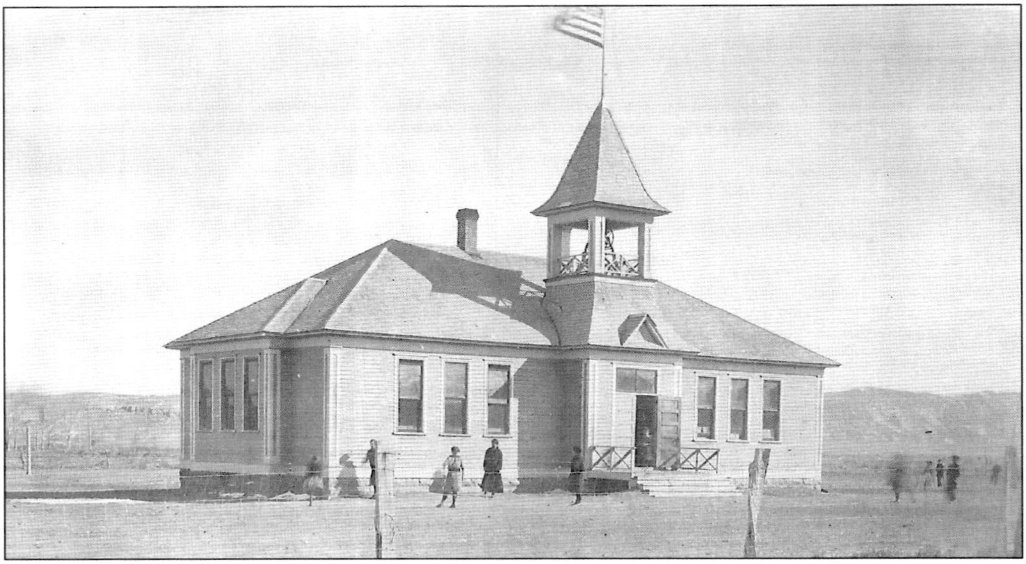

Belfry's first school, named Riverview, resided on Chick Bomie's place south of town. Constructed of logs, and opened in 1897, it served students until 1909 when a new two-room school (above) replaced it. A brick building replaced this school in 1922. (Wolchesky.)

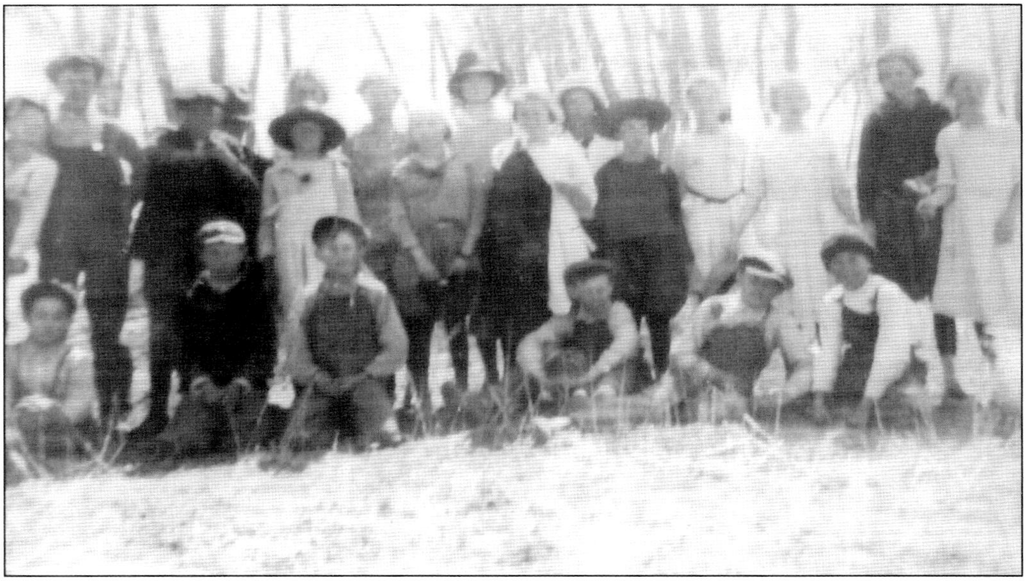

A group of Nora Hogan Ogden's Belfry students pose for a class photograph above. Nora Hogan Ogden served as Carbon County superintendent of schools from 1913 to 1916. After leaving this position, Nora Hogan Ogden taught for a number of years at Belfry. (Hogan.)

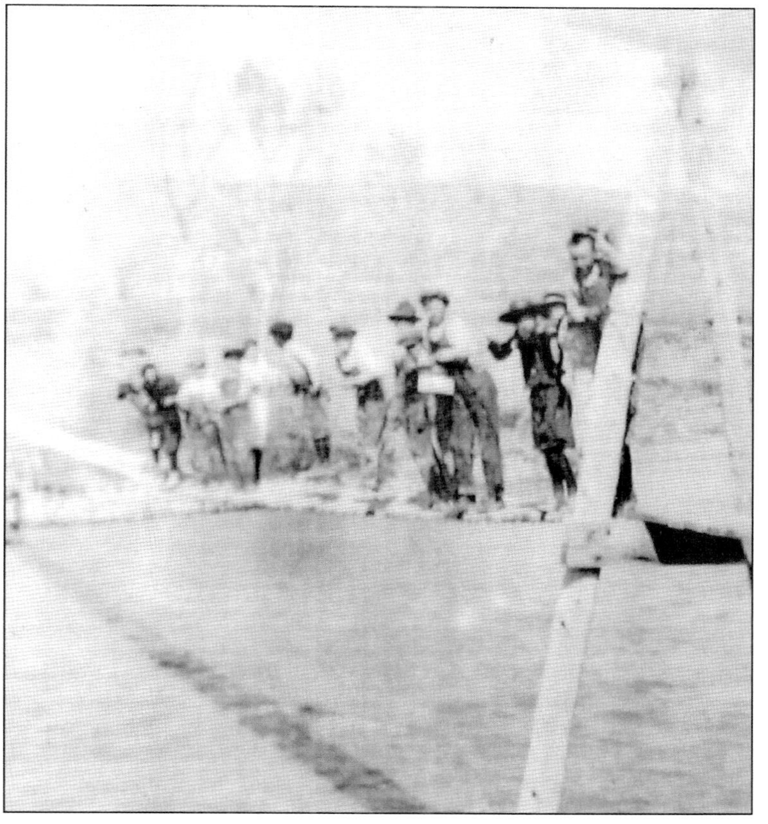

Another group of Nora Hogan Ogden's Belfry schoolchildren crossed a channel of the Clark's Fork River in this c. 1920 photograph. Crossing the Clark's Fork River without getting wet proved to be a constant challenge for every resident of Clark's Fork Valley. (Hogan.)

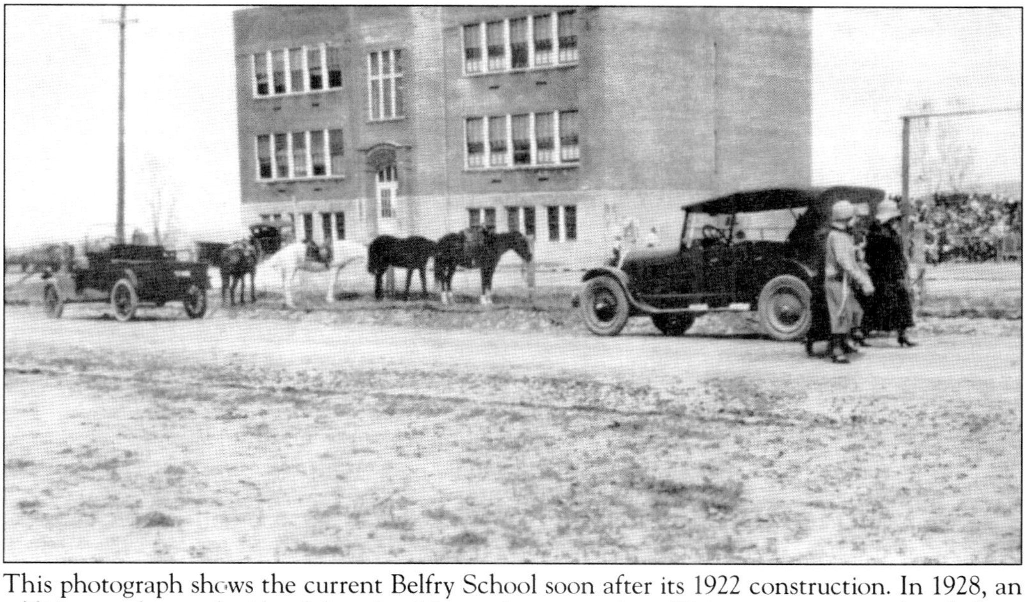

This photograph shows the current Belfry School soon after its 1922 construction. In 1928, an addition to the south side of the school housed a gymnasium. This gymnasium produced three consecutive Montana State Class C basketball championship teams from 1952 to 1954. A 1930s addition added classroom space to the north side of the school. (Wolchesky.)

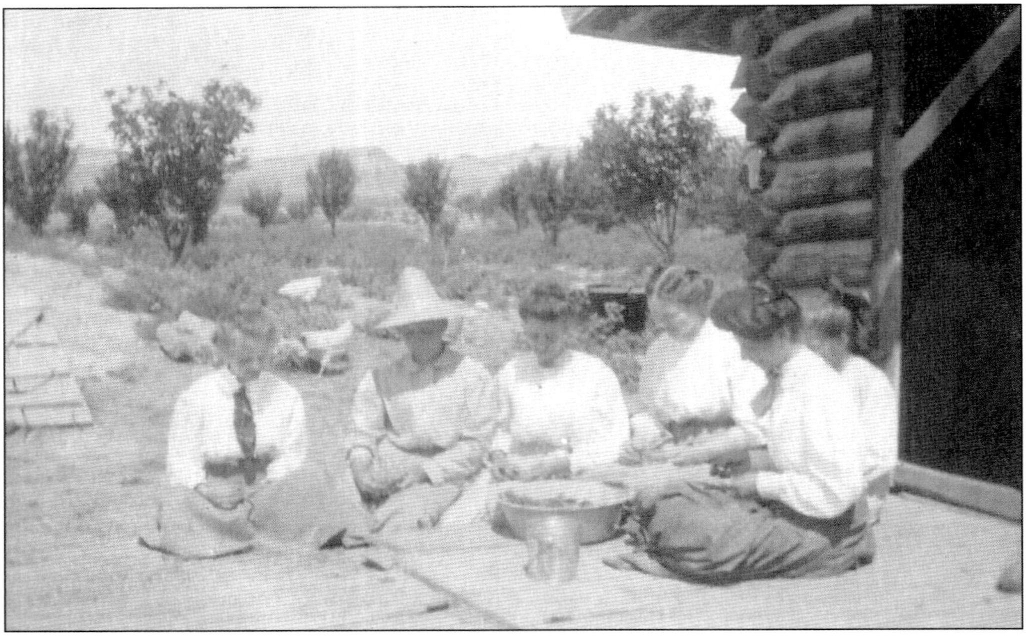

These photographs capture two homesteading families in the Belfry area. In the 1909 photograph above, a group of women at the McLauchlin Ranch prepare green beans for canning. The McLauchlin's apple orchard can be seen in the distance. In 1919, the Johann David Hergenrider Sr. family posed for the photograph below at their home. Included in the photograph are, from left to right, Lydia Hergenrider, Emma Hergenrider, Annie Hergenrider, Johann David Hergenrider Jr., baby Olga Hergenrider, Sophie Dies Hergenrider, Alex Hergenrider, and Johann David Hergenrider Sr. The Hergenriders raised a variety of crops and livestock in the Belfry area over the years (Above, K. Hergenrider; below, CCHS.)

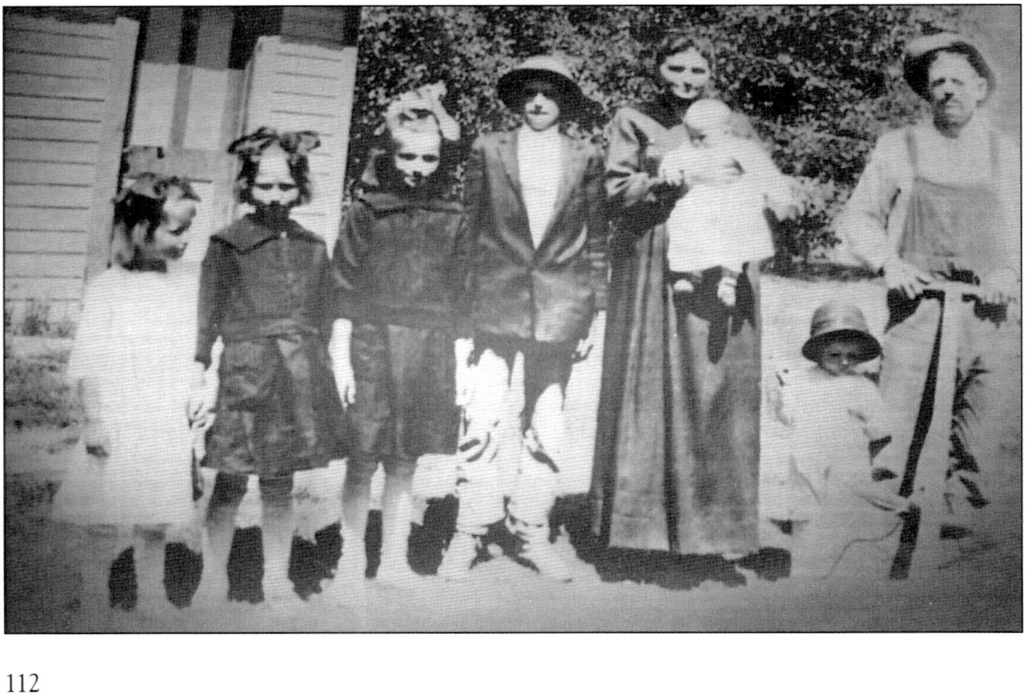

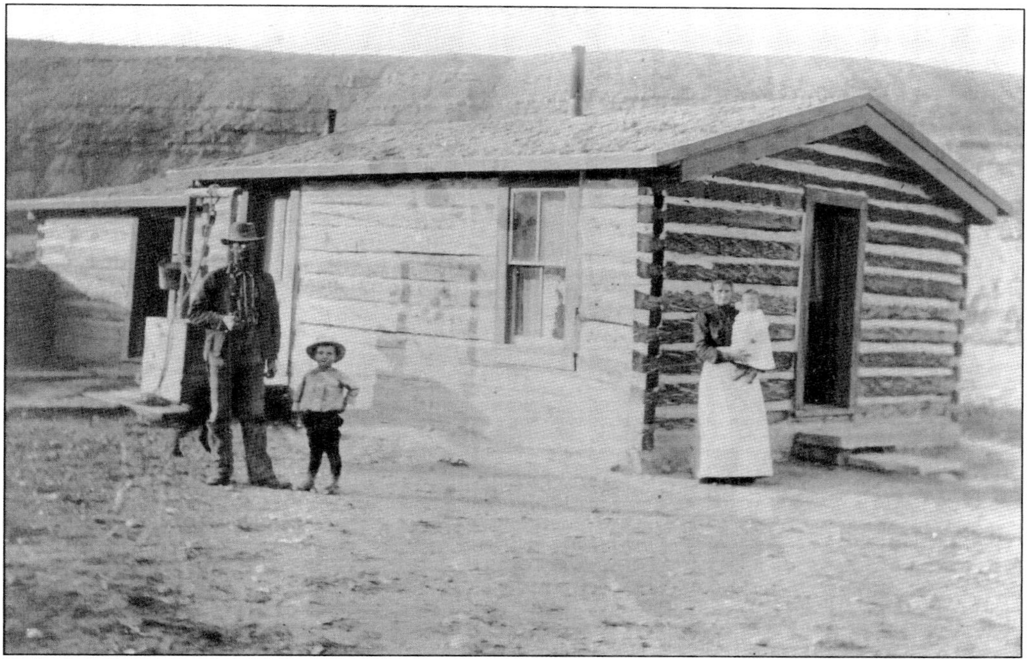

Although the Newton D. and Mary E. Hall family operated a number of businesses in Belfry, these *c.* 1910 photographs show that they homesteaded and produced agricultural crops as well. Above, the Newton family poses in front of their homestead cabin. The family is, from left to right, Newton D. Hall, Roy E. Hall, Mary E. Hall, and baby Laura Pearl Hall. Below, a group of 10 people harvest strawberries from the Halls' fields. A closer examination of this photograph shows that 4 of the 10 pickers are eating the strawberries rather than collecting them. The woman to the far right is Mary E. Hall. (Both, Wolchesky.)

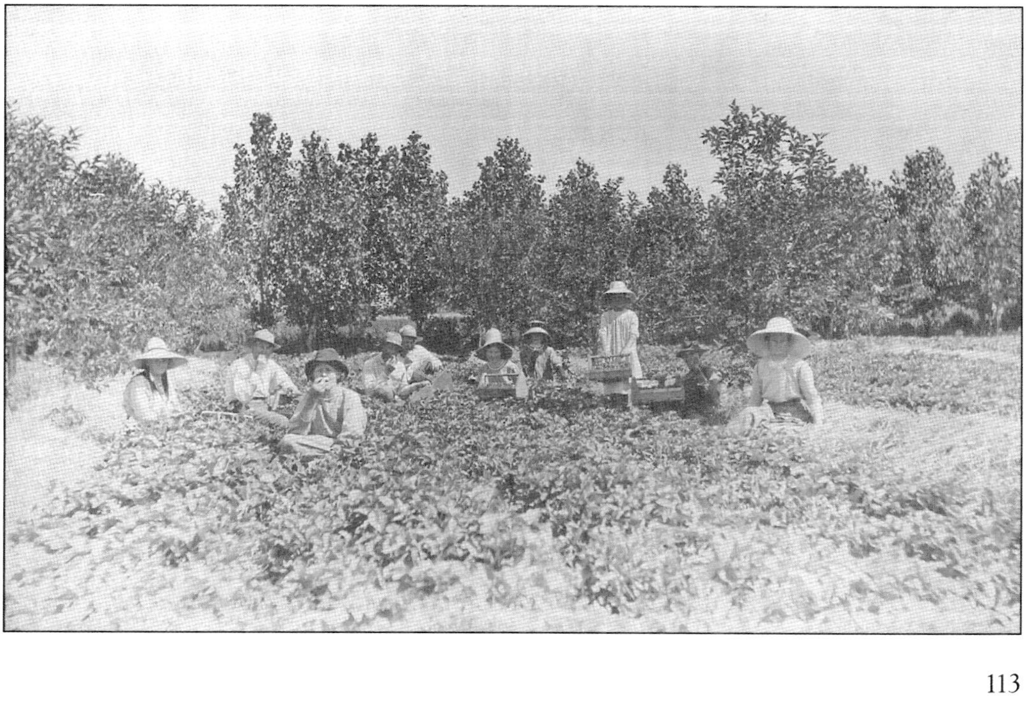

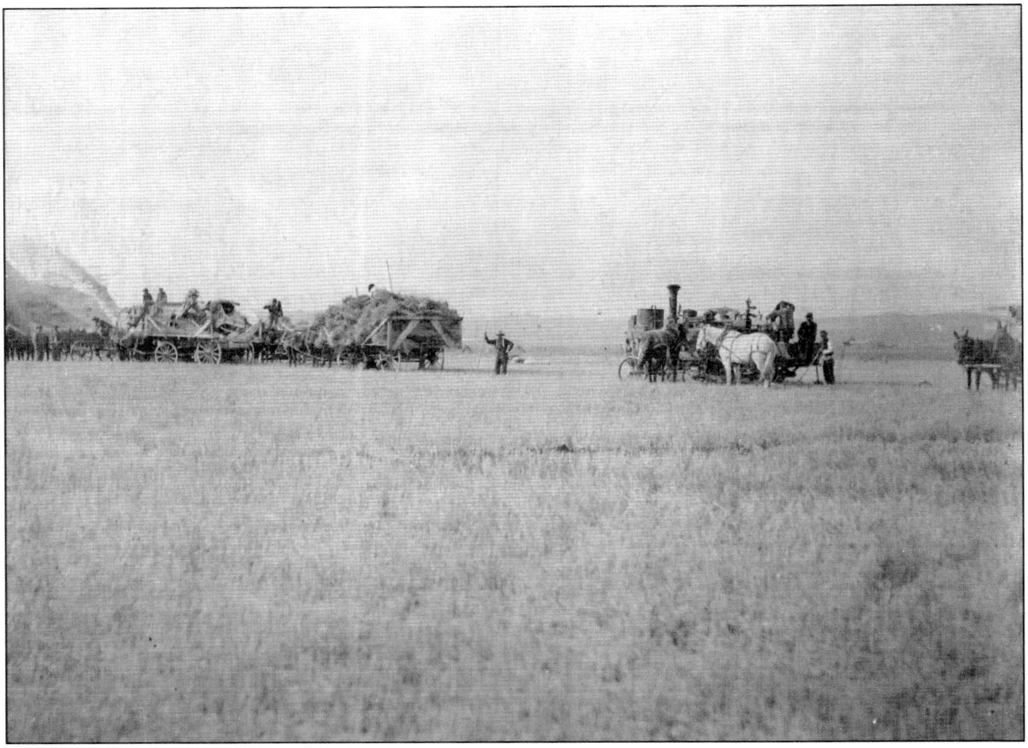

In addition to fruit crops, sheep and cattle herds, and sugar beets, farmers in the southern end of Clark's Fork Valley raised grain crops. Each autumn, harvesting the grain required a large-scale effort on the part of these farmers. The photograph above shows a threshing crew using a steam-powered threshing machine to assist them with the yearly harvest. Always unpredictable, autumn weather in Clark's Fork Valley could include an early snowstorm that made bringing the threshing machine out of the fields a more arduous task than normal (below). (Both, CCHS.)

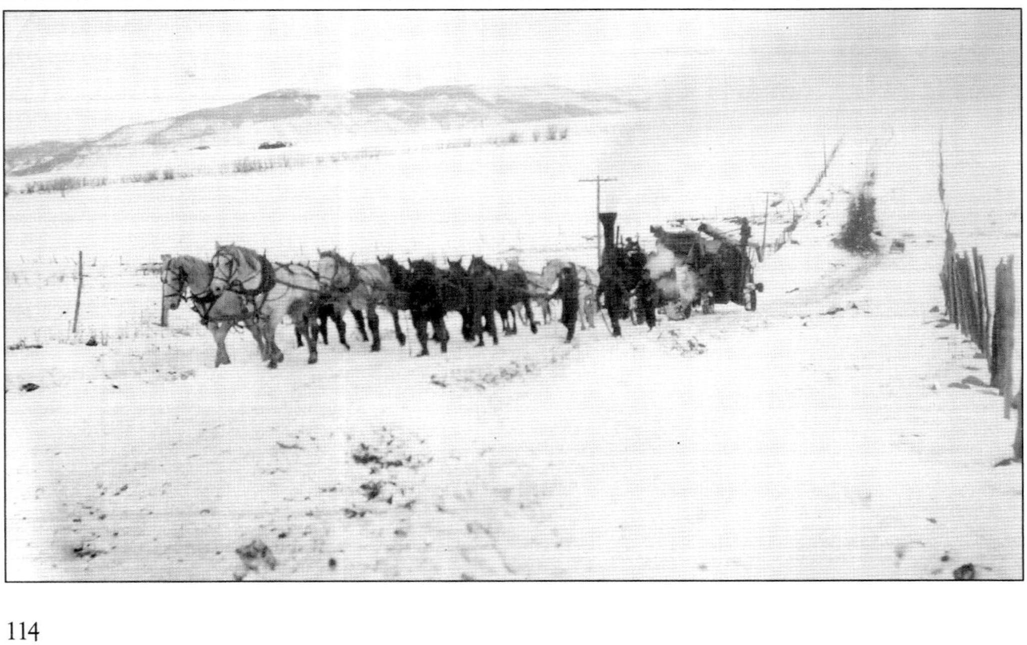

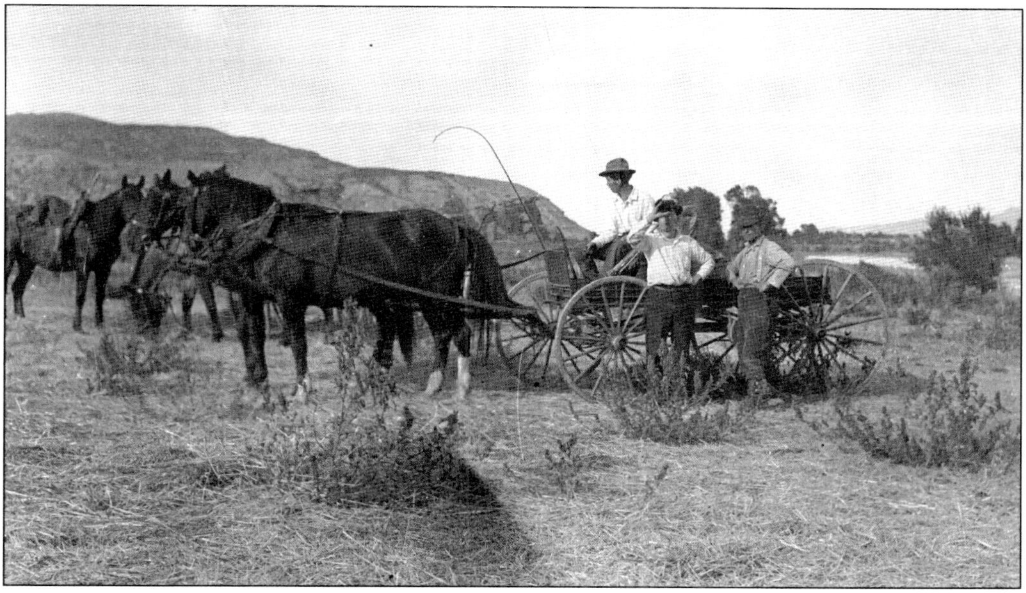

Early Carbon Countv residents fished the Clark's Fork River primarily as a source of food with sport being an added benefit. Pan-fried trout in the summer and smoked whitefish during the winter provided a welcome change to the normal fare. Fishing the river drew valley residents and citizens from ne.ghboring towns, such as Bearcreek, Washoe, and Red Lodge alike. The photograph above shows a group of Red Lodge fisherman preparing to make the 15-mile trek back to town after a day of fishing near Belfry. Below, pair of boys fishes the Clark's Fork River near the McLauchlin Ranch. (Above, CCHS; below, K. Hergenrider.)

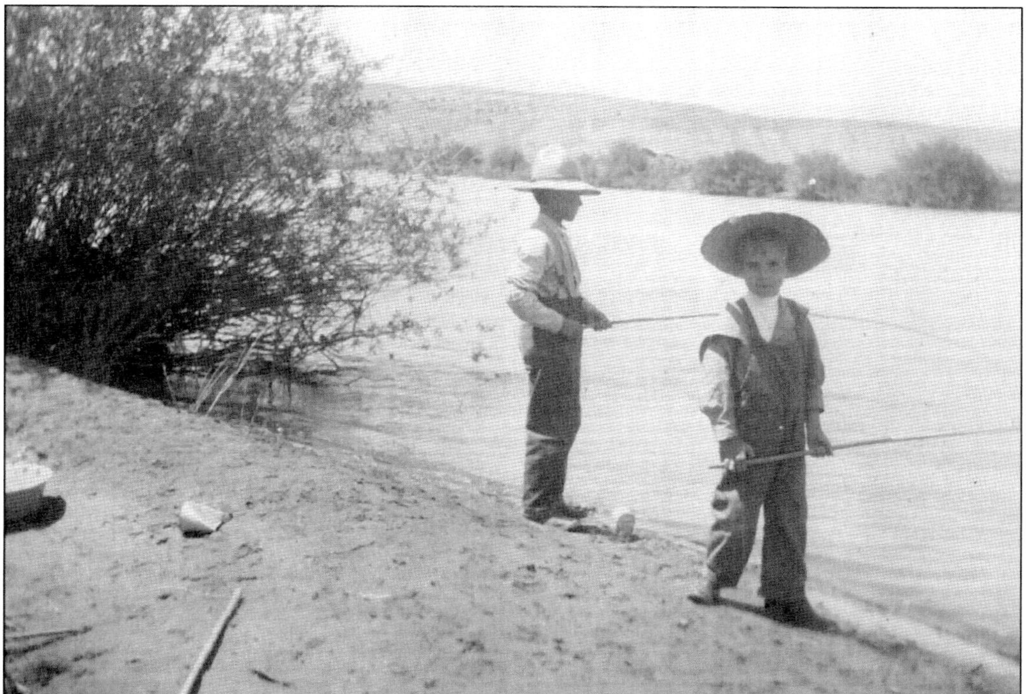

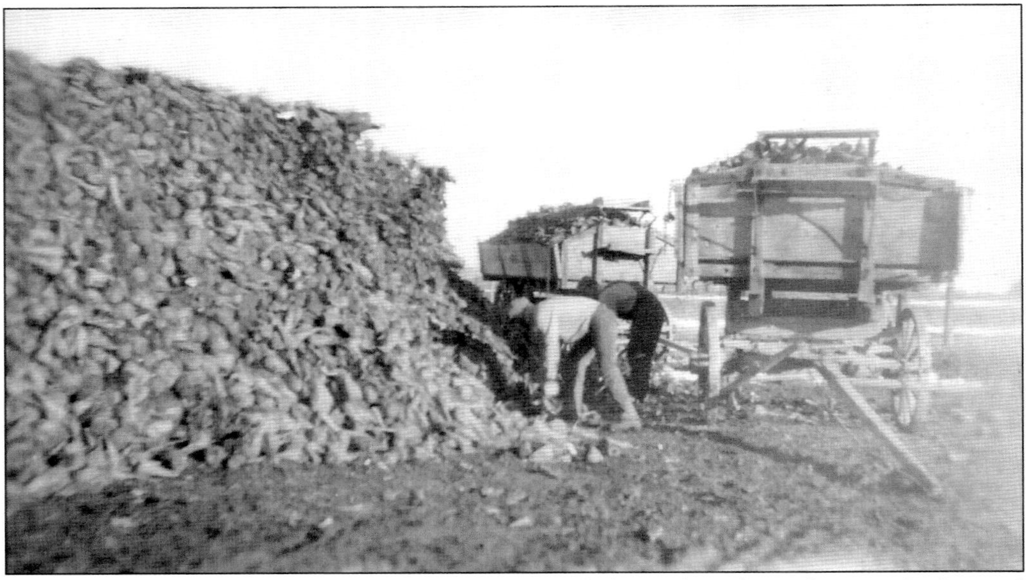

The Montana, Wyoming, and Southern Railroad installed sugar beet dumps between Bridger and Belfry to collect the products of naturally fertile land and man-made irrigation. This early-1910s photograph shows workers at the Golden beet dump located about halfway between Bridger and Belfry. (Wolchesky.)

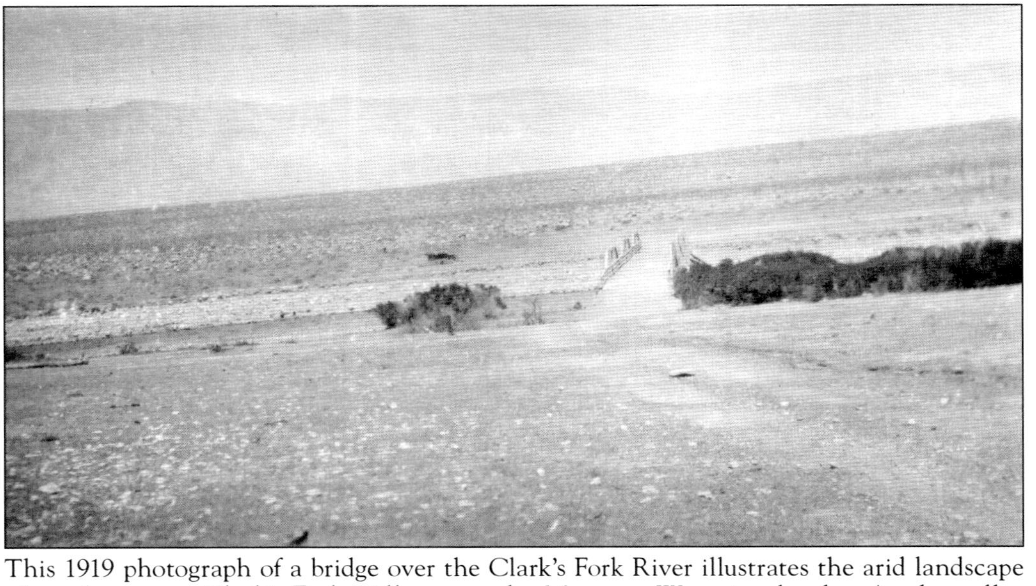

This 1919 photograph of a bridge over the Clark's Fork River illustrates the arid landscape of southernmost Clark's Fork Valley near the Montana-Wyoming border. As the valley approaches the Beartooth Mountains, the soil and climate become much less hospitable to agriculture. (Ferster.)

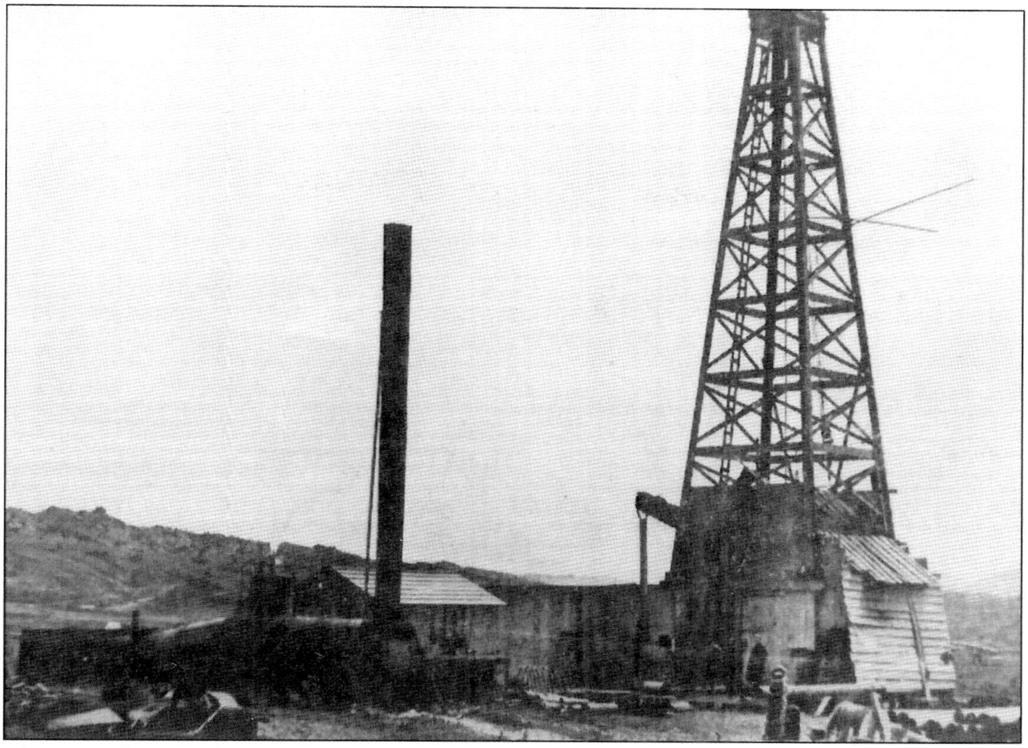

This 1916 photograph shows a derrick on the Mountain States Oil Company claim in the Silver Tip district of Elk Basin. Ten such derricks operated in Carbon County's section of Elk Basin during 1916 and produced 45,000 barrels of petroleum from wells approximately 1,500 feet deep. (CCHS.)

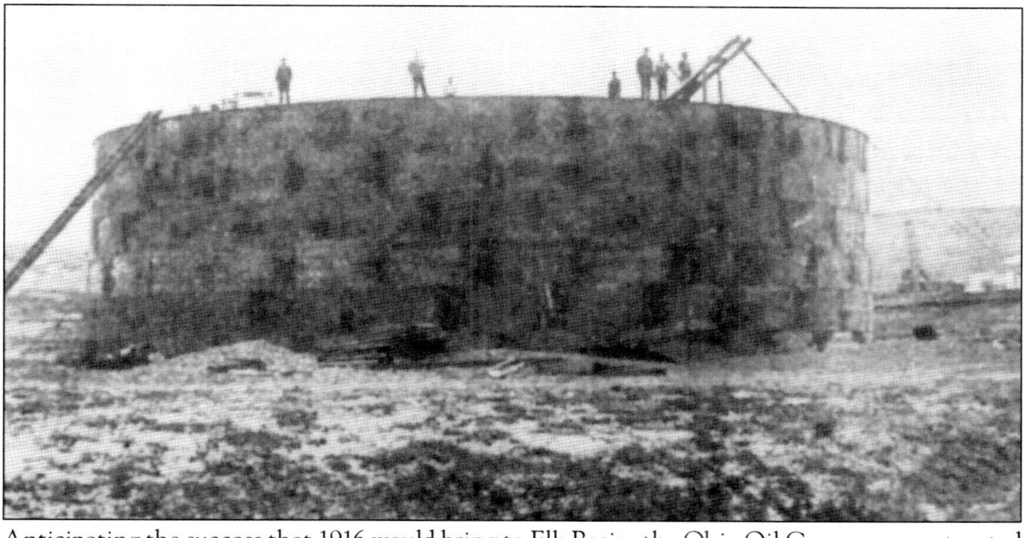

Anticipating the success that 1916 would bring to Elk Basin, the Ohio Oil Company constructed a 55,000-barrel holding tank (above) in June 1916 in southern Carbon County. By 1917, an oil line from the Montana and Wyoming sides of Elk Basin carried as much as 1,000 barrels of oil a day to holding tanks in Frannie, Wyoming, where the Chicago, Burlington, and Quincy Railroad transported it. (CCHS.)

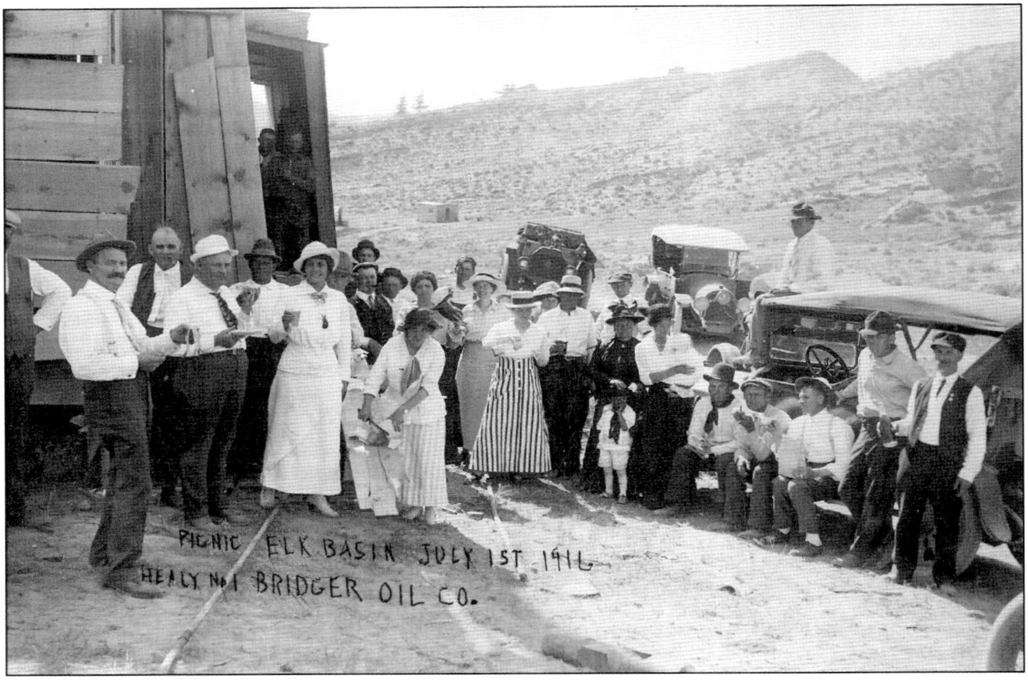

The Healy Derrick No. 1 on the Bridger Oil Company's claim in Elk Basin became the site for this pre–Fourth of July celebration in 1916. Eventually, claims by smaller oil companies like the Bridger Oil Company and Mountain States Oil Company consolidated under the much larger Ohio Oil Company. (CCHS.)

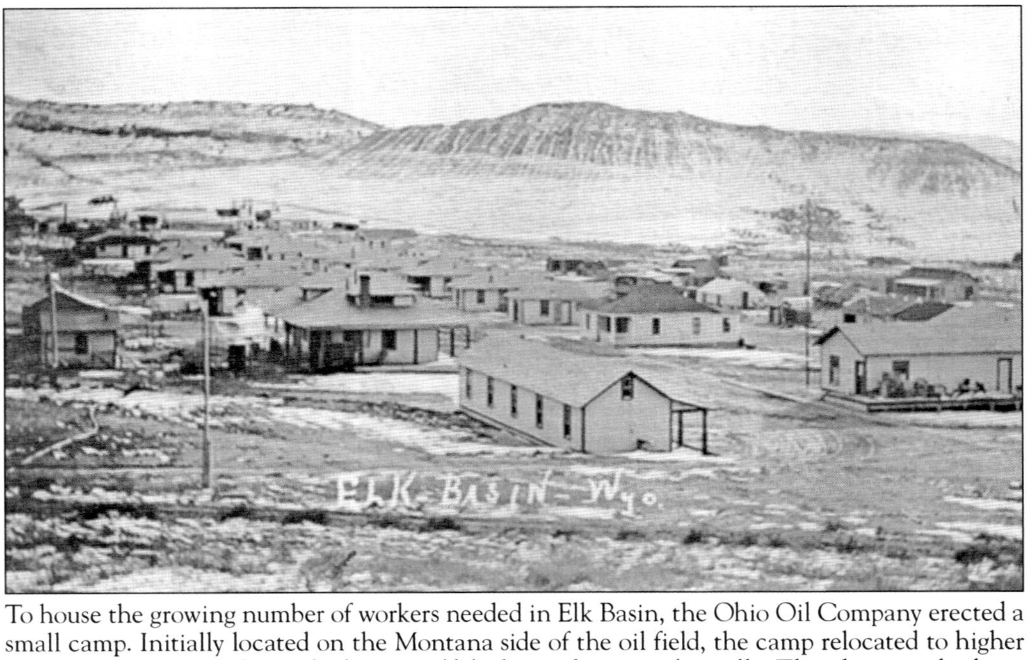

To house the growing number of workers needed in Elk Basin, the Ohio Oil Company erected a small camp. Initially located on the Montana side of the oil field, the camp relocated to higher ground in Wyoming due to hydrogen sulfide fumes from nearby wells. The photograph above shows the second camp as it looked in the 1920s. (K. Hergenrider.)

Eight

Bowler, Warren, and Southeastern Carbon County

Southeastern Carbon County is a wild and barren place dotted with abandoned town sites, schools, post offices, and homestead ranches. It begins as flat, dry, sagebrush country along the section of U.S. Highway 310 that turns southeast at Bridger and stops following the Clark's Fork River, transitions to the arid foothills of the Pryor Mountains, and finally encompasses the Pryor Mountains east to the Big Horn County border. Two small towns grew up along U.S. Highway 310 between Bridger and the Montana-Wyoming border. Ten miles from Bridger at the Wade railroad stop, a school and general store operated for a short time. Another 10 miles south, the town of Warren emerged as a shipping point for a limestone quarry in the nearby Pryor Mountains. Warren is still populated, but the original post office, mercantile, and restaurant have long ceased to operate. Five miles northeast of Wade, the village of Bowler emerged in 1892 near the intersection of the Burlington and Missouri River Railroad and Sage Creek. Bowler's name comes from Jack Bowler, one of the first settlers to the area and a former U.S. 7th Cavalry soldier. Bowler housed a school, a mercantile, and a post office serving homesteaders, mostly sheep ranchers, in the Sage Creek area. The scarcity of water in this area led to many legal actions concerning water rights both within the county and between the states of Montana and Wyoming. The scarcity of water combined with the Great Depression doomed Bowler and most of its neighboring ranches to extinction by the late 1930s. Farther east along the Big Horn River, a number of ranches, post offices, and settlements arose from prospectors hoping to cash in on the Big Horn Canyon gold placer mines. Among these settlements was Dryhead, established in 1919 and named after dried buffalo skulls from a nearby buffalo jump; Hillsboro/Cedarvale, which later became a dude ranch; and Barry's Landing, a point along the Big Horn River where dude ranchers from nearby Lovell, Wyoming, disembarked from the Big Horn River.

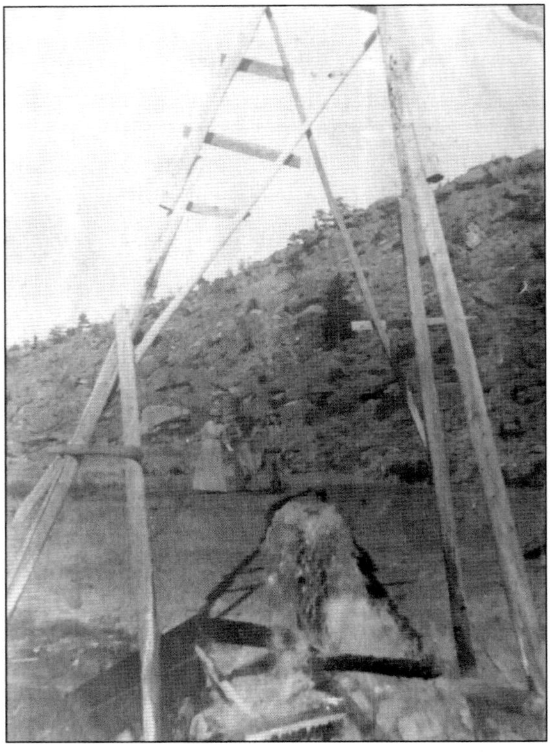

These photographs illustrate two artesian well water fountains between Bridger and Bowler. The water pressure associated with artesian wells results when a well is drilled into the lower end of a non-horizontal aquifer. The resulting water pressure from the aquifer's higher elevations could produce water flows of up to 500 gallons per minute. Water wells of any kind diminished as one approached Bowler Flats, where the primary water source became Sage Creek. Sage Creek alone seldom provided enough water to supply every homestead in the area. This resulted in numerous water-rights litigation and homesteaders quitting their land claims. (At left, CCHS; below, K. Hergenrider.)

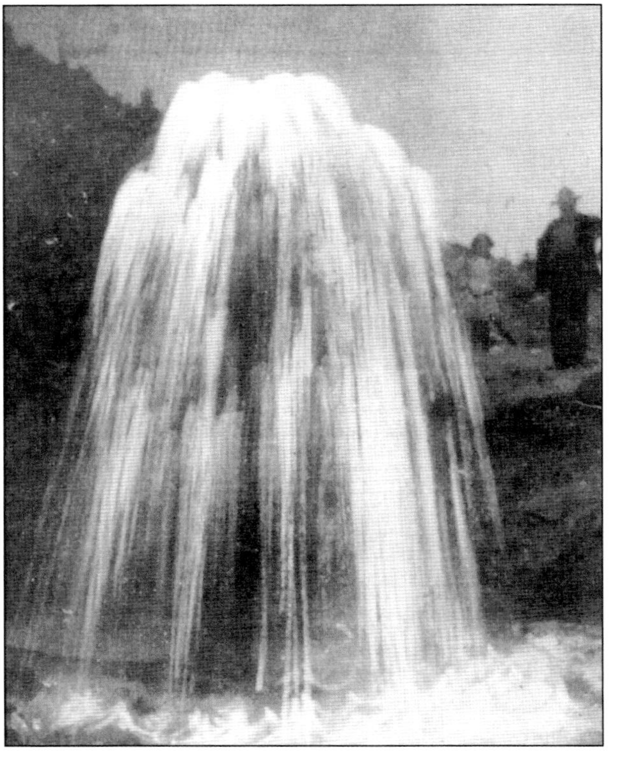

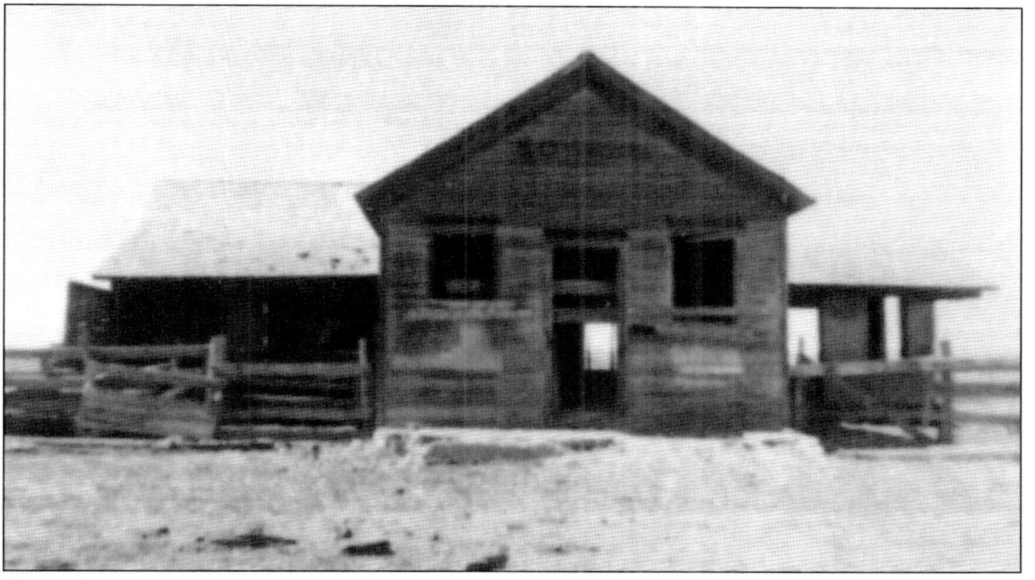

This 1960s photograph shows the remains of the third Bowler Store and Post Office. Bill Miller owned this establishment from the early 1930s until it closed permanently in 1938. Bowler resided in three separate locations. The first location was at Jack Bowler's ranch; the second location was east of Jack Bowler's ranch along the Chicago, Burlington, and Quincy Railroad; and the third (above) near the Bridger Canyon Road. (CCHS.)

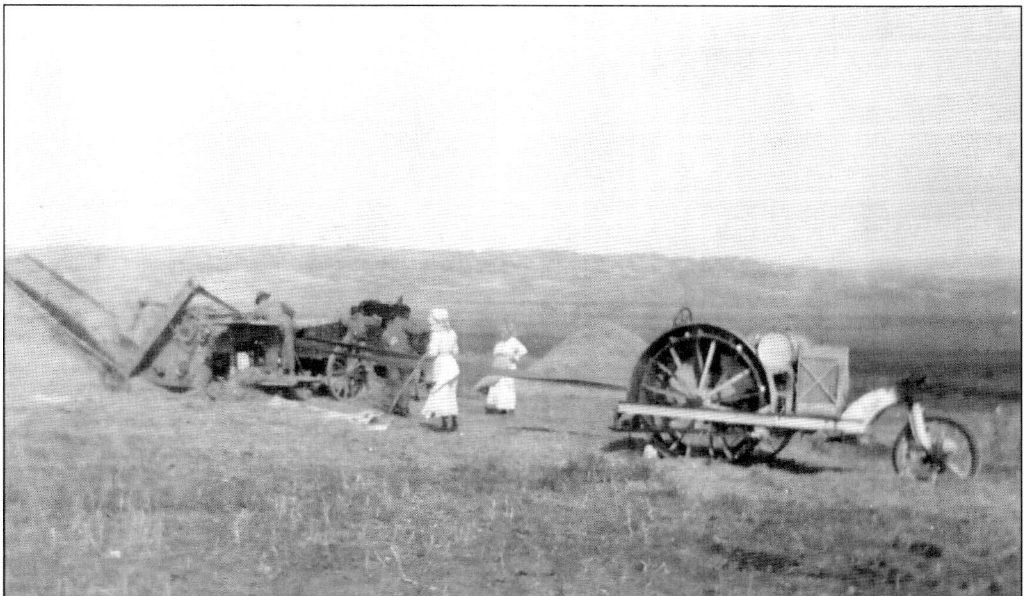

This 1918 photograph shows the Walt Owens family threshing grain on their Bowler Flats homestead. As many as 40 families homesteaded Bowler Flats at the time of this photograph. Low crop yields due to the arid nature of this country, along with the Great Depression, forced many of these homesteaders into bankruptcy in the early 1930s. (CCHS.)

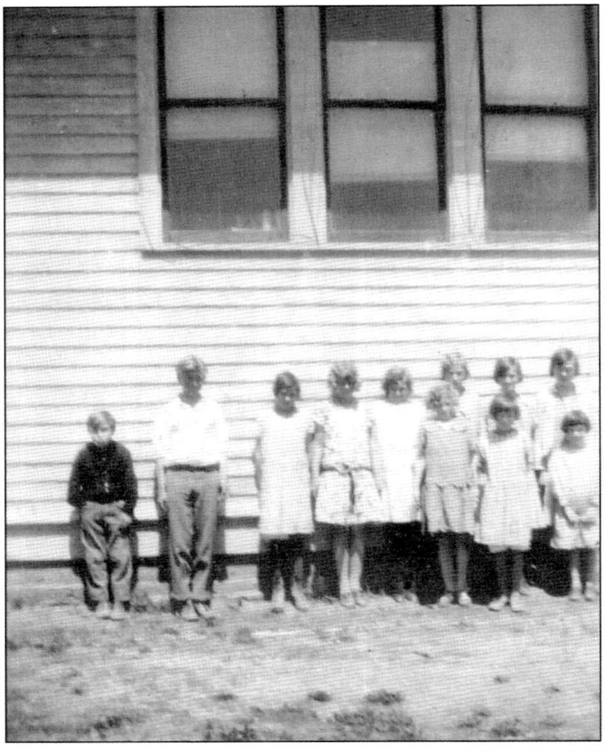

This 1920s photograph shows students standing in front of the Sage Creek School, also called the Bowler School. The school was later moved to Bridger and currently serves as the town's library. Students in this photograph are, from left to right, (first row) Rose Smith, Maude Jones, and Marjory Miller, (second row) Herbert Jones, Einar Indreland, Emma Chestmore, Ronella Smith, Geneva Smith, Eileen Indreland, Margaret Chestmore, and Mary Jones. (Indreland.)

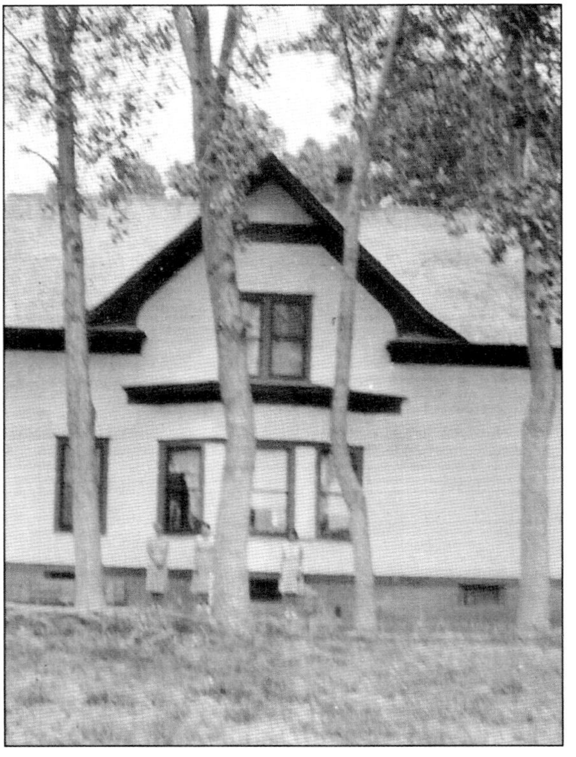

The Sage Creek home of Norwegian immigrants Cornelius and Eli Indreland is shown in this 1920s photograph. Cornelius and Eli also owned land in western Carbon County on Lower Red Lodge Creek. The Indreland family permanently relocated to Lower Red Lodge Creek in the 1930s. (Indreland.)

Two Bowler area girls prepare for a summer swim in Sage Creek in this early-1920s photograph. On the left is Marjory Miller and on the right is Sigrid Indreland. Marjory Miller's parents ran the third Bowler store. Sigrid Indreland's parents raised sheep on Sage Creek. She later married Bridger's Mike Kapor. (Indreland.)

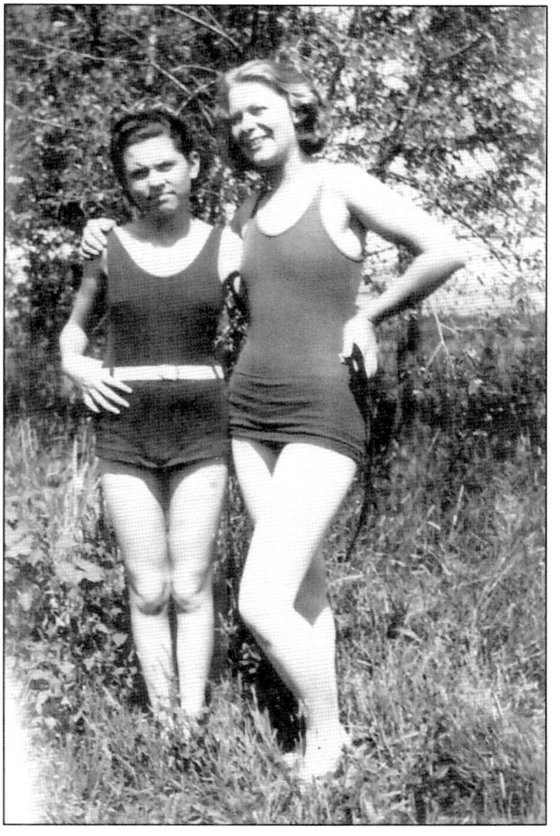

This 1913 photograph of eastern Carbon County's Crooked Creek School shows one teacher with only six students in attendance. Pictured among these seven people are Maude Legg, Ray Teeples, Lee Teeples, Roy Teeples, Mae Teeples, and Edwin Morris. The small class size is indicative of the remoteness of the Crooked Creek homesteads. (CCHS.)

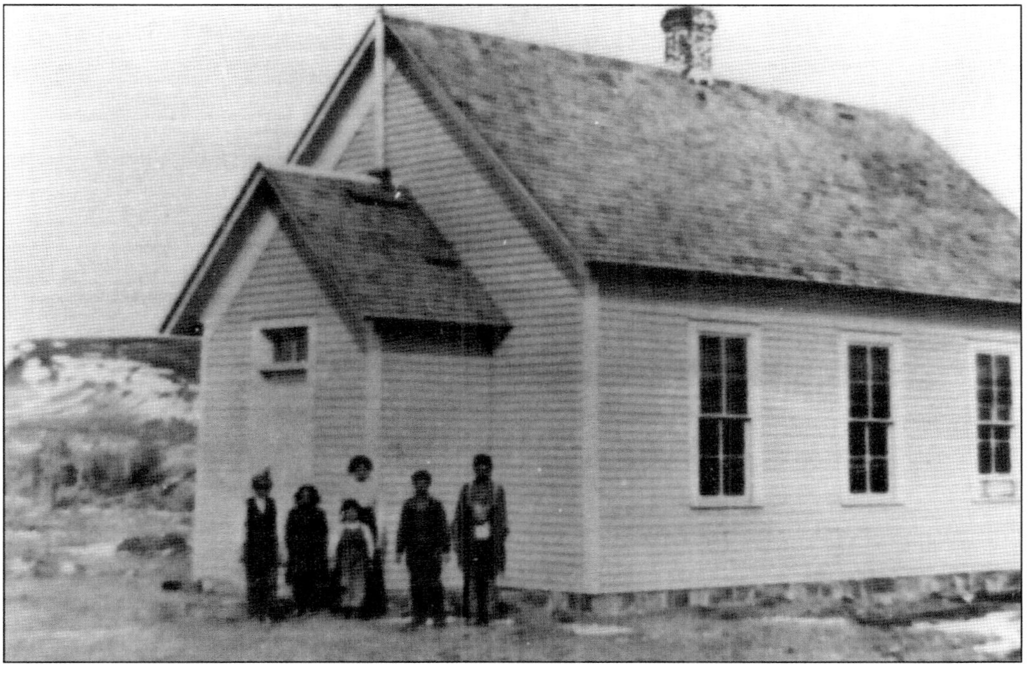

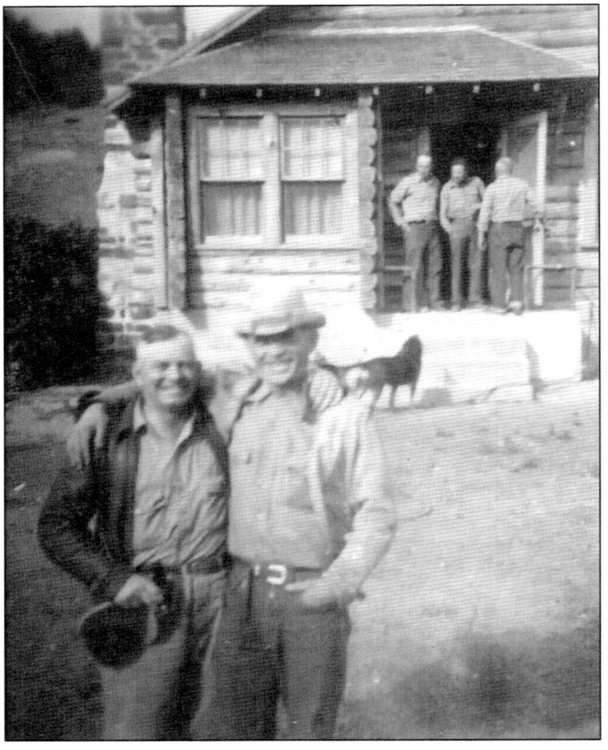

A group of eastern Carbon County cattlemen gathered for these photographs in front of Tom Lazar's cabin high in the Pryor Mountains on Sage Creek. The only man identified in these photographs is Mike Kapor (below, far right) of Bridger. The Larzar cabin illustrates the architecture of most homesteads at higher elevations in the Pryor Mountains. Local limestone provided foundations and fireplaces, while abundant timber provided the necessary lumber. The Pryor Mountains housed several lumber mills in the early 20th century and provided the raw material for lumber mills in Belfry, Bridger, and Fromberg. (Both, Indreland.)

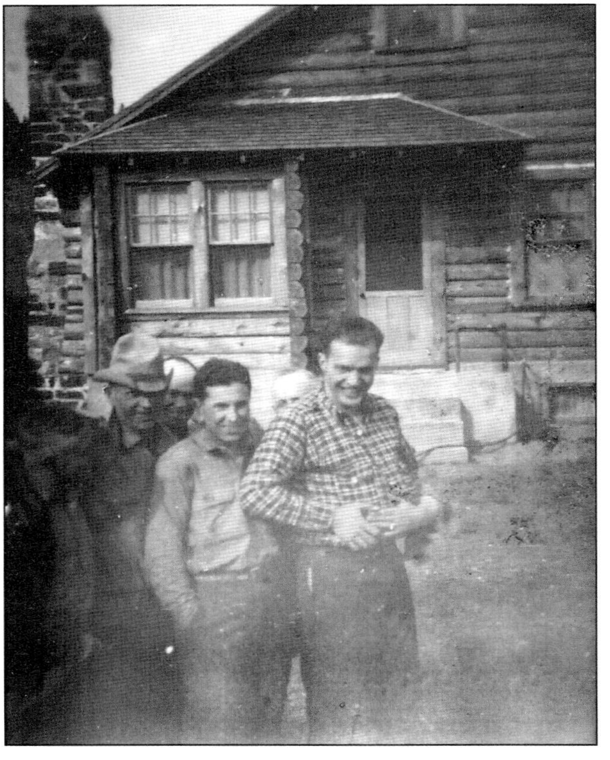

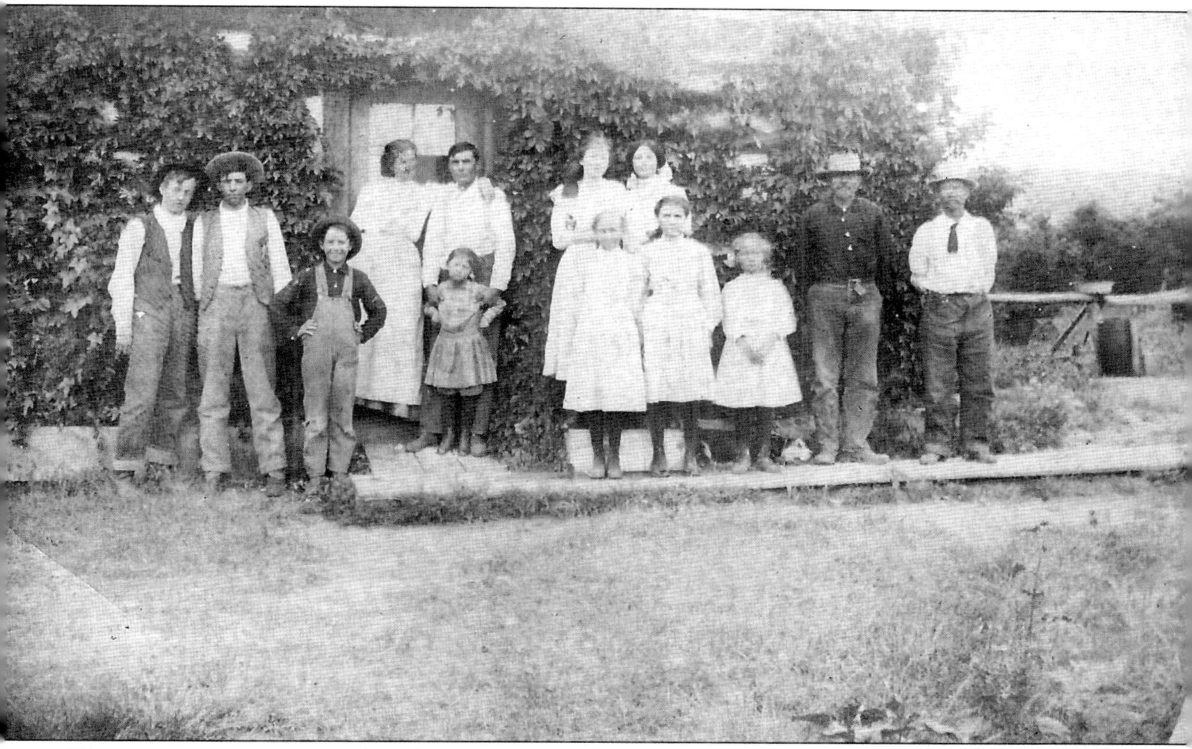

The easternmost section of Carbon County is known as "the Dryhead." This area runs south of the confluence of Dryhead Creek and the Bighorn River on the Crow Reservation. In 1907, Charlie and Emma Phelps homesteaded in the Dryhead area and formed the Lone Wolf Ranch, later called the Dryhead Ranch, shown above in July 1911. In 1915, the Phelps received their land patent for the homestead. The Dryhead Ranch once held the Dryhead School, and the family hosted dude ranchers on occasion. In an early day cattle-rustling case, a posse of Sage Creek ranchers charged Charlie and Emma's son Bud, along with William Sherrin, of attempting to rustle 55 head of C. A. Dana's cattle. The posse came across Phelps and Sherrin in the vicinity of the cattle and assumed they had rustled the herd. A Red Lodge jury acquitted both men of this charge. (CCHS.)

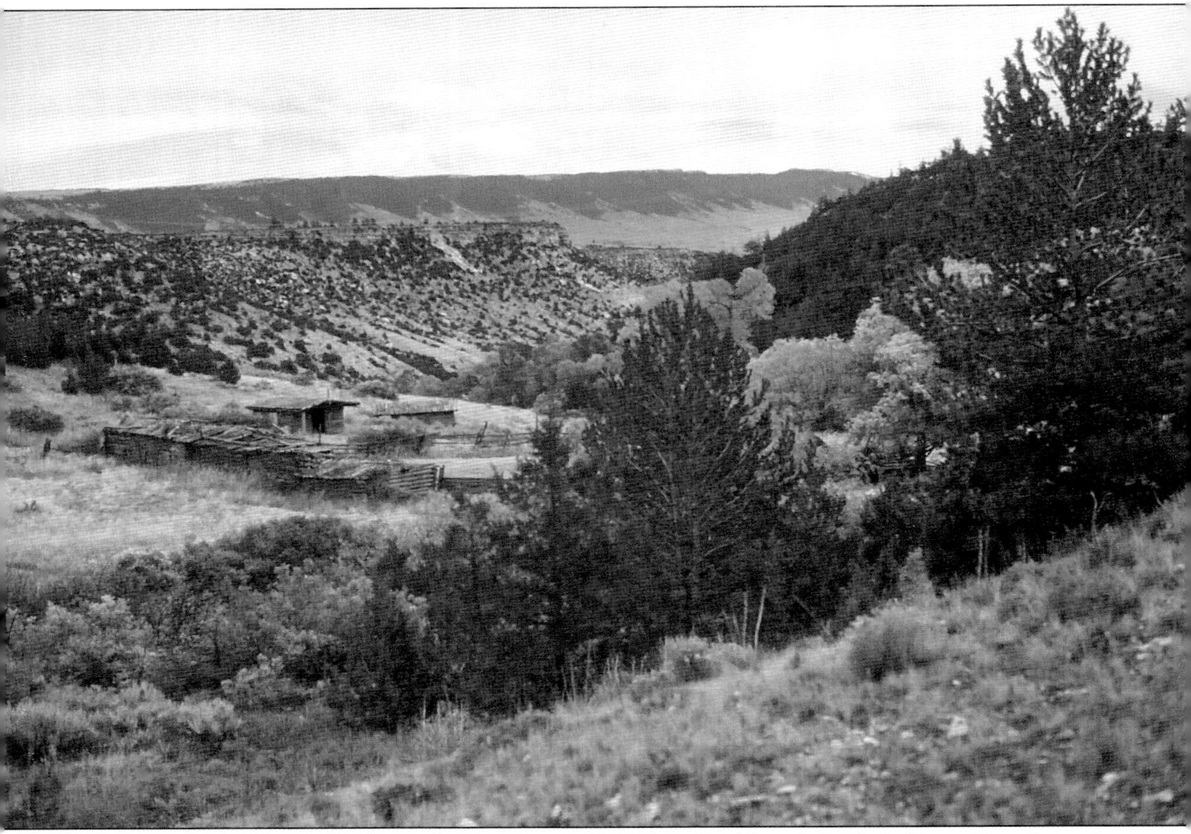

This 1990s photograph shows the remains of Caroline Lockhart's L-Slash-Heart Ranch in the Dryhead area. Lockhart, an early-20th-century journalist and novelist, came to nearby Cody, Wyoming, in 1904 on assignment by the *Philadelphia Bulletin*. With the exception of one year, Lockhart remained in Cody, Wyoming, or summering on her Dryhead ranch until her death in 1962. Caroline Lockhart wrote Western novels in direct competition with Zane Grey. Her most famous novels included *Me-Smith*, *The Man from Bitter Roots*, and *The Fighting Shepherdess*, the latter two of which were made into movies. Caroline Lockhart bought the L-Slash-Heart Ranch in 1926 to raise cattle. Lockhart's cattle venture proved as successful as her novels when, in 1935, her steers topped the Omaha market. The National Park Service now owns the L-Slash-Heart Ranch and it is listed on the National Register of Historic Places. (CCHS.)

Bibliography

Much of the information in this book comes from the files of the Carbon County Historical Society and Museum and the Clark's Fork Valley Museum. Additional and published sources include:

Aarstad, Rich … [et al.]. *Montana Place Names: From Alzada to Zortman*. Helena, MT: Montana Historical Society Press, 2009.

Anderson, Annette. *Bridger Montana: Land of Many Trails*. Bridger, MT: Valley Printing, 2009.

Axline, Jon. *Conveniences Sorely Needed: Montana's Historic Highway Bridges 1860–1956*. Helena, MT: Montana Historical Society Press, 2005.

———. "Something of a Nuisance Value: The Montana, Wyoming & Southern Railroad, 905–1953." *Montana: The Magazine of Western History*, Winter 1999.

Cheney, Roberta Carkeek. *Names on the Faces of Montana: The Story of Montana's Place Names*. Missoula: MT: Mountain Press Publishing Company, 1983.

Clayton, John. *The Cowboy Girl: The Life of Caroline Lockhart*. Lincoln, NE: University of Nebraska Press, 2007.

Fromberg Service Club. *Fromberg: The Fruit Basket of Carbon County*. Fromberg, MT, 1976.

Harvey, David, and the Bureau of Land Management, Billings. *A General Historical Survey of the Pryor Mountains*. Boulder, CO: Western Interstate Commission for Higher Education, 1974.

Kidwell, Art. *In the Shadow of the Beartooth: Clark, Wyoming*. Powell, WY: Desert Moon Press, 2004.

Oliver, Lt. Commdr. George A. (USN Retired). *Joliet: Its Pioneers and Early Days*. Huntsville, AL: Monroe Printing Company, Inc., 1973.

Raymer, Robert George. *Montana: The Land and the People*. Chicago and New York: The Lewis Publishing Company, 1930.

Robbins, Steve. *Voicing the Dead: A Poetic History of Early Day Carbon County, Montana*. Red Lodge, MT: Rocky Fork Press, 2008.

Schwieterman, Joseph P. *When the Railroad Leaves Town: American Communities in the Age of Rail Line Abandonment—Vol. II*. Kirksville, MO: Truman State University Press, 2004.

Trails and Tails Historical Committee. *Trails and Tales South of the Yellowstone*. Billings, MT: Midland Printing and Supply Company, 1983.

Voelz, Bonnie, and Dorothy Spaulding. *My Address Is Heaven: The Bill Linderman Story*. Belfry, MT: Xlibris, 2008.